IN SEARCH OF
BRITISH
HEROES

IN SEARCH OF
BRITISH
HEROES

TONY ROBINSON

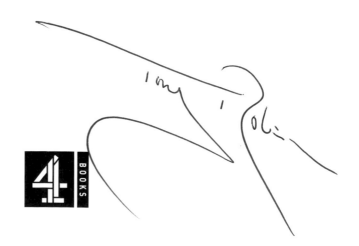

To David Willcock, without whom this book wouldn't have been possible.

First published 2003 by Channel Four Books
an imprint of Pan Macmillan Ltd
Pan Macmillan, 20 New Wharf Road, London N1 9RR
Basingstoke and Oxford
Associated companies throughout the world
www.panmacmillan.com

0 7522 1532 9

1 3 5 7 9 8 6 4 2

A CIP catalogue record for this book is available from the British Library.

Designed and typeset by seagulls
Printed by Butler and Tanner

SPIRE FILMS

This book accompanies the television series *Fact or Fiction*,
made by Spire Films for Channel 4.
Writer and Presenter: Tony Robinson
Executive Producer: David Willcock

CONTENTS

FACT OR FICTION: A SEARCH
FOR BRITISH HEROES, 7

BOUDICA, 14

MACBETH, 52

HAROLD, 94

WILLIAM WALLACE
– 'BRAVEHEART', 136

ROBIN
HOOD, 180

FACT OR FICTION:
A SEARCH FOR BRITISH HEROES

This book is a quest, a search for five British heroes, and in writing it I've managed to unite two separate interests of mine.

First, there's the idea of heroes and the stories we tell about them to explain who and what we are. Since I was a kid, I've been fascinated and inspired by those men and women who seemed to live on another plane, doing great deeds that I could only aspire to. Odysseus, Biggles, Churchill and, once I entered my teens, James Dean and Che Guevara offered me the possibility of inhabiting a world in which I could be stronger, braver, cleverer than I could ever be in the security of my semi-detached home in suburban London, where I earnestly tried to live out my fantasies.

I suspect that every reader will have had a childhood hero or two although, even as adults, how could we fail to be moved by the epic achievements of Ellen Macarthur sailing round the world or Nelson Mandela realizing his dream of a free South Africa? But as we glimpsed those moments of glory, didn't we get a similar feeling to the one we'd had as children when we turned the pages of the adventures of our favourite hero or heroine?

But Mandela is very real to us, while Odysseus isn't. The further we get from a hero, the more that person is smothered by the weight of legend that accrues around them. I wanted to look at some of the storybook heroes of my early life to see what I could learn about them as an adult. I settled for five British heroes who not only fascinated me as characters, but whose stories seemed to me to form part of the fabric of our nation's culture: Boudica (whom I'd grown up with as Boadicea), King Harold, Macbeth, William Wallace (Braveheart) and, finally, the ultimate boyhood hero, Robin Hood.

And the search for them brought into play my second interest: the British landscape. Ten years working with archaeologists have taught me how redolent with human activity every square inch of our island is. Each hillside has been terraced and re-terraced for 2,000 years or more, every valley bears the marks of settlements long since swept away by war, disease and the caprice of nature. Our neighbourhood Boots the Chemist was doubtless built over the foundations of an apothecary, our local Body Shop over a medieval tanner's yard.

So I set out to try and find traces of my heroes in our landscape. But if so many hands had left their prints on it, would it still be possible to pick up an individual trail? Could I, with some degree of certainty, trace the site of Macbeth's death or Boudica's last stand? After wrestling with mutually contradictory academic tomes (all charged with passion and persuasion), chasing countless herrings of varying hues (but mostly red), and tramping around old forgotten corners of Britain from pigsties to municipal car parks, I'm pleased to say the answer is a qualified yes. I'd be a fool to claim absolute certainty, but what I can offer you is, as near as dammit, the real stories of my five heroes.

Except that wasn't really the point of my quest. All five of these individuals can be said, by their lives and, in some cases, by their deaths, to have changed our country forever. By searching out the clues and signs that history has left and by visiting their haunts and homes, I wanted to get a better sense of their true characters, to try and grasp how they would have lived, what they would have seen, and what would have been important to them. Attempting to get into the heads of characters from history is a risky and ambitious task but, using a mixture of fact, legend and imagination, that's what I've tried to do.

I've dealt with the characters chronologically. They lived at some of the most important periods of our history and at times of great change: the Roman occupation, Celtic Scotland in the great age of the Vikings, and the end of the Saxon period before the Normans changed England forever. In Scotland I also looked at the struggle for independence during the high medieval age of chivalry and cruelty. Further south throughout the medieval period tales started to circulate about an inspiring people's champion living as an outlaw in the greenwood. I tracked these stories of Brave Robin from Yorkshire to the Midlands and beyond.

Of course it was hard work, but it was also enormous fun. I've tried to devise a book that will give you an opportunity to share the sense of discovery I so often felt in so many places. Standing in some 1950s housing estate and imagining a crucial battle, or visiting a tiny hamlet that was once a major power centre, becomes an alternative 'virtual' tourism. So as well as being the stories of five heroes and their lives, I hope this book will also be used as a virtual guidebook transporting you in your armchair to unlikely places where, with a touch of imagination, you can still catch echoes of the past. But I'd like to encourage you to make at least some of these journeys in person, so I've included maps and instructions to guide you round the sites.

But whether you choose to make the journey in your Renault Clio or in your head, our first destination is East Anglia.

When the Romans arrived, the tribe they found living in what's now Norfolk were the Iceni. Their leader was Boudica, a woman. To the Romans, who were immensely patriarchal, having a woman in charge would have been sure proof that these were barbarians. They must have thought she'd be a pushover, but they were wrong. When she was provoked to fight she became the focus for British opposition to the Roman occupation and the stuff of every centurion's nightmare. Boudica in her chariot with its revolving blades is the very image of the male fantasy-fear of the emasculating powerful woman. And how fascinating it is to see such legends constantly being re-evoked to suit the needs of the age. When Margaret Thatcher was at the height of her powers the imagery was too good for cartoonists to resist. She was the new Boudica – the dominant woman who drags male politicians along in chains in the wake of her chariot.

The original Boudica must have been turning in her British grave for all the years that she was known as Boadicea. Having fought the hated Romans, she ended up having her name Latinized. I hope she'll appreciate that we've recovered a sense of the pre-Roman culture she lived in and have changed her name back to its original version. The search for her culture and her fight to protect it takes us from Quidenham in Norfolk to Anglesey in Wales, the most sacred centre of ancient Druid religion. Boudica's warpath across Essex and her destruction of the city of London is more than a catalogue of battles. It lights up the whole Iron Age way of life that the Romans found in Britannia and which disappeared under the twin attacks of Roman political organization and the introduction of Christianity.

Nearly a thousand years later and 500 miles north, our next hero also found himself fighting a rearguard action against cultural change. In contrast to Boudica, Macbeth, King of Scots, had a reign that was, by the standards of the time, a triumph. He ruled his people for seventeen years from 1040 to 1057 and, from what we can tell through contemporary sources, both he and his queen, the Lady Gruoch, were popular and successful. 'In his time were fertile seasons' is the highest praise you can offer the ruler of a kingdom whose wealth relies on agriculture.

So why is Shakespeare's Macbeth one of the greatest villains of all time? Obviously Shakespeare was English and there's no love lost between Scottish and English storytellers, but even Scottish historians of the medieval period were giving Macbeth a bad name. With little to go on from historical sources and archaeology, the quest to recover the truth about Macbeth was one of the most intriguing pieces of detective work in the whole project. Here was a character we think we know a lot about because of a work of fiction. Sifting the facts from that semi-historical play takes us through Macbeth's homeland in the Highlands to the traditional place of king-making at Scone. Then we travel to Dunsinane Hill, to Birnam Wood that was supposed to have walked mysteriously to Dunsinane, and finally we set foot

on the holy island of Iona, the traditional burial place for the Scottish kings. Along the road we discover a Celtic way of life that more or less died out with Macbeth as Scotland turned itself into a 'modern' European kingdom of the eleventh century.

At the same time back in England an era was coming to an even more abrupt end.

The Roman occupation was only the first of a series of migrations from the Continent. Saxons, Angles and Jutes all turned up uninvited. By the time of King Alfred in the ninth century they'd been here long enough to believe that they were the true natives of our island and that the Vikings, the latest wave of raiders and immigrants, were the foreigners.

Which makes the life of Harold Godwinson that much more interesting. Harold is often called the last Anglo-Saxon king, the true Englishman contrasting with the foreign Johnnies who came after. But his background is far more complex. He was the product of an Anglo-Danish marriage in the reign of Cnut, the Viking king who ran an empire stretching from Copenhagen to Cornwall.

Harold's great enemy also had Viking connections. Northern France was settled by the Norsemen (the Normans) and William the Conqueror was as much Viking thug as French aristocrat. In 1066 he led his noblemen into Saxon Britain, dismantled the existing aristocracy and completely replaced it with his own.

King Harold has the unfortunate distinction of being one of the most famous losers in history. The date and place of his downfall, 1066 at the Battle of Hastings, are perhaps the best-known facts in English history. The battle, one of the longest and definitely the most significant of the medieval period, is recorded in comic-strip form by the Bayeaux Tapestry. The woven image of the king with the arrow in his eye is as memorable as any war photograph from a later century.

Following in the footsteps of Harold takes us overseas. A king in the eleventh century had to operate on the international stage. Politics in England at this time inevitably involved Norway and France, as well as Rome from where the Pope's influence spread across Europe. Crucially, we cross the Channel to Normandy to try and make some sense of Harold's visit there in 1064. Was it a diplomatic mission that went wrong, a faulty bit of navigation, or a courageous personal mission to maintain the bonds of family that in the end cost Harold his life?

Back in England, we follow Harold as he struggles to keep the remnants of his Saxon kingdom together. There's his vicious fight against the Welsh insurgents in 1063, which left alive, in the words of one historian, 'not one that pisseth against a wall'. We follow his struggles against his own brother Tostig in Northumberland, the battles against the Viking invasion in what is now Yorkshire and, of course, that last stand in the place the Saxons called Senlach: not Hastings at all but a place a few miles inland near modern-day Battle.

Two hundred years later, at the end of the thirteenth century, the peoples of Britain started to form new concepts of nationhood of a kind that we would recognize today, and this caused enormous friction. William Wallace was, above all, a man of the people. Macbeth and his story are remote, mythic and somewhat romantic. It seems right that so much of his story should be set in the Highlands. In contrast, it's just as appropriate that the legend of Braveheart should be set firmly in the heavily populated lands of Central and Lowland Scotland.

The landless son of a minor nobleman, Wallace became, through sheer charisma and military ability, the representative of the realm of Scotland at a time when the traditional aristocracy had no stomach for opposition to King Edward I of England. Wallace can claim to have led the very first People's Liberation Front, and, in that, he was way ahead of his time. Neither the English nor the Scottish nobility liked the idea of an upstart leading a country, and he was rewarded for his patriotism by betrayal and a gruesome death.

Most people know that much already from having watched the movie *Braveheart*, in which a diminutive Australian with an Irish accent plays a medieval Scottish hero who was about six and a half foot tall. Despite minor inaccuracies such as the total omission of a bridge from the Battle of Stirling Bridge, the film does manage to recapture some of the fervour of Wallace's cause with its catchphrase of 'Freedom!' It also rescued Wallace's story from relative obscurity (until recently his history wasn't taught in Scottish schools) and restored him to a rightful place in the pantheon of British heroes.

Two small points particularly attracted me to Braveheart. Historians think his mother was called Joan Crawford (yes, they really do) and one of the earliest histories of him is by a fifteenth-century Scot called John Major (does the name ring a bell?) But I swiftly discovered much more of substance.

The story of the beginning of the Scottish Wars of Independence is tough and nasty. The film of *Braveheart* is in parts quite violent, but nothing can reproduce the systematic cruelty, close-quarter carnage and ethnic-cleansing of the period. It takes a huge leap of the imagination to follow Wallace's bloody trail from his birthplace in Renfrewshire through the battles of Stirling Bridge and Falkirk, to his last journey to London and his execution within sight of Smithfield Market. Many of the most important locations in his story, where once the stakes were so high and the ground so littered with mutilated corpses, have been transformed into havens of twenty-first-century respectability by concrete, brick and tarmac.

A lot of the legendary material about Wallace is very similar to English tales that were currently emerging in England during the Hundred Years War. Wallace was in that way a man for his time. Romances of a nobleman turned outlaw were popular fiction, but Wallace was living the life.

For the most part the ordinary English folk had no investment in the Hundred Years War. It was an aristocratic affair, and all it meant for the man in the field was a change of boss every few years. But even the ploughman and the baker could dream of greatness and,

when they did, there was a ready-made hero for them to model themselves on. His name was Robin Hood.

Never was there a hero whose legend is so well known but whose true story is so obscure. Who was he really? The Earl of Huntingdon? Robin of Loxley? The last loyal Saxon fighting the influence of the Norman invaders? A follower of Richard the Lionheart holding out against the evil regent John and his agent the Sheriff of Nottingham? When exactly did he live, and where?

Robin is the odd one out of our five characters. Books about him are kept in the Religion and Legends part of the bookshop rather than the History section. There are some academics who insist that Robin was never anything but a literary figure. On the other hand there's a clear sense, especially in the earliest stories, that the audience was expected to be familiar with the man whose adventures are being described. But if he actually existed, who was he? The fact that he was an outlaw, and not someone from the social top-drawer, makes it far less likely that details of his real life would have been recorded.

There are so many question marks hanging over Robin Hood that I decided to approach his story in a different way. Piecing together the mosaic that reveals the facts behind the fiction of the real Robin Hood meant using literary criticism, history, and a certain amount of pure detective work.

The resulting picture punctured far more of my preconceptions than any of my other investigations. It also took me to places where I never expected to be either metaphorically or geographically.

There's a well-trodden tourist route around north Nottinghamshire and Sherwood Forest commemorating the exploits and sites associated with Robin, Maid Marian and the various Merry Men. Maps to guide us on this odyssey are readily available from Nottingham's Tourist Board. But I also found myself exploring villages in the forest of Bowland, ruined castles in Shropshire, and a graveyard near Stratford-on-Avon. As a life-long fan of Robin Hood, I was surprised how gritty the true tale turned out to be, involving everything from political rebellion to pure bloody criminality. The archetypal honest-to-God English hero turned out to be as much Ronnie Biggs as Raffles. So different from the saccharine tales of my childhood!

What's fascinating about Robin is not only what he was originally, but what he has become through the constant retelling of his story. This evolution represents a paradigm of the role played by all our British heroes.

This is a book about a journey into history and a quest to retrace the true story of five British people who in one way or another epitomized the clash between the old and the new, the native and the alien. It's also, by extension, about the myths those characters have woven into the nation's story and its character. These great figures are part of the baggage we carry with us into the future. Their reputations have been used to justify many things. By looking at the real people behind those reputations, there's some interesting material to throw into the current debate about what it is to be English or Scottish or British or European. William Wallace is a perfect example of this. How appropriate that the vote on Scottish Devolution took place 700 years to the day after Wallace's victory at Stirling Bridge. When I stood on the spot in Westminster Hall where Wallace was condemned to death, I couldn't help wondering who had the last laugh.

So, whether you're already heading up the A11 to Boudica's home turf, or snuggled in your duvet wondering if you should skip Boudica to find out what happened to Robin, I hope you'll enjoy, as I did, looking into the real lives of these British heroes. For further reference there are plenty of specialized works on the history of both the people and their periods at the end of each chapter. What I hope to do is blow away just a little of the mists of time to reveal the flesh and blood characters behind some of the ghosts that haunt every corner of our country and our culture.

CHAPTER 1
BOUDICA

Tracking down Boudica means following her on the warpath from her homeland in Norfolk, through the City of London, which she destroyed in its infancy, to the most likely site of her last stand just off the A5. Along the way, there's a wealth of archaeological clues to help piece together her life and times in the early days of the Roman occupation of Britain.

When names I've known for decades suddenly change, it drives me mad. I can understand why the people of Sri Lanka and Zimbabwe wanted to reject the colonial name-tags Ceylon and Rhodesia, but it didn't help my 'O' level geography. Marathon bars became Snickers, Jif transformed into the hideous-sounding Cif, and I became intensely irritated. But sometimes there's a valid justification behind a name change, and this chapter is a case in point.

Who's the queen who stood up to the Romans, scything through the mighty legions in her famous chariot with its grisly hubcaps? We've all known the answer since childhood – it's Boadicea. Well, I'm sorry, but it isn't any more.

Over the centuries there have been lots of stabs at her name, including Bonduica, Voadicea, Bunduca and Boodicia. It seems that the best-known variant, Boadicea, is a miscopying of the earliest Roman version in the writings of Tacitus. He named her Boudicca and, in the course of history, some scribe mangled the 'u' and changed a 'c' to an 'e' to make it sound more Latinate, giving us Boadicea.

But the poor woman suffered so much at the hands of the Romans that it's almost criminal to let them determine her name for posterity. She was originally called Boudica (pronounced either Boodicka or Boodeeka), and that's what we'll call her too. Boadicea is

Two symbols of Britain: Thomas Thornycroft's statue of 'Boadicea' in the shadow of Big Ben.

just an imperial conceit which we'll consign to the rubbish bin. Let's hope one day Snickers will go the same way.

Boudica is derived from the Celtic word for 'victory'. She was our first Queen Victoria. The Victorians were only too aware of the parallels, and it's they who brought the early British queen back to prominence. In doing so they not only got her name wrong, they also ensured that the facts of her life were covered by a double layer of mythology.

The first layer was applied by the Romans. The Celts of first-century Northern Europe, of whom the ancient Britons were one part, didn't have a written culture, so they left no record of their version of events. It was the great Roman writer Tacitus who gave us the two earliest accounts of Boudica's life in his *Annals,* and in the biographical history of his father-in-law, *Agricola.* Agricola was in Britain during the Boudican revolt, serving as a junior officer on the staff of Suetonius the Roman governor, so Tacitus had access to an eyewitness. That doesn't mean he was unbiased, of course. His terse account claims to set down just the facts (his abrupt style gives us the word 'taciturn'), but he had his own axe to grind. He personally suffered under the despotic emperor Domitian, and was determined to show that all the ills that had beset the empire had stemmed from the bad behaviour and mal-administration of rulers such as Claudius and Nero. Tacitus was also Roman to the core. To him, Boudica and the ancient Britons were simply barbarians – the Roman catch-all term for bearded foreigners who behaved in strange and un-Roman ways such as letting a woman be the boss. His account is coloured by his belief that, for all their faults, the Romans were heroes, the Roman Empire was generally a Good Thing, and what the barbarians needed more than anything else was its civilizing influence.

The other classical Roman source is Dio Cassius. He was born in Nicaea in modern-day Turkey, in the latter half of the second century. Unfortunately we don't have an original version of his writing. His account comes to us in the form of edited highlights copied out by an eleventh-century monk called Xiphilinus of Trapezus (now there's someone who actually would benefit from a name change). Dio Cassius had obviously read Tacitus and filled out his version with lurid accounts of the weird and barbaric behaviour of Boudica and her horde. Together, he and Tacitus forged the myth of the avenging wild woman.

But much later this Roman myth was taken up and twisted by the Victorians to give us the great British heroine, epitomized by Thomas Thornycroft's famous statue. It was erected in 1902 on the Embankment in London in the shadow of Big Ben and the Houses

of Parliament. The plinth calls her Boadicea. She stands high above the milling throng of tourists, with her daughters at her feet, in her chariot with its famous bladed wheels. She's dressed in the classical garb of a Roman empress rather than the plaids of a first-century Briton. Without reins, and by the sheer force of her personality, she controls two rearing stallions, modelled on horses from Queen Victoria's own stables. The inscription reads: 'Regions Caesar never knew thy posterity shall sway'. She is a patriotic symbol of the queen of England spreading the influence of the British Empire further than the Romans could ever have imagined. She was a key element in the formulation of the figure of Britannia who used to appear on old one-penny pieces.

BOUDICA

Boudica in the style of a very Roman-looking matron with her two distressed gentlewomen daughters. As with all the images of our British legends, this engraving by William Bond is from a much later time. The bulk were done in the seventeenth, eighteenth and nineteenth centuries when people started to take an interest in the past as a key part of their national identity.

It's an absurdly inappropriate metaphor, because Boudica was anti-empire. She was more like the kind of third-world tribal leader who would have organized a rebellion against the sway of Victoria and Britain. And while we're unpicking the myths of Boudica, we may as well start with her most famous trademarks.

DIGGING UP THE TRUE BOUDICA

The one thing we can say with absolute certainty about this 2,000-year-old tribal chief is that she didn't have blades on the wheels of her chariot. Celtic chariots weren't weapons on wheels or ancient armoured tanks. They were lightweight affairs made of wood, leather and wicker, intended as speedy battle taxis, getting warriors to the front line or zooming up to the enemy to deliver a spear, then veering away as quickly as possible. As we'll see, in the one set-piece battle that Boudica did fight, the British lines were so packed that knives on her chariot would have chewed up more of her own side than the enemy.

And pulling these nippy wicker carts weren't great thoroughbred horses or medieval destriers, but small hardy ponies, similar to the ones you still find roaming Dartmoor. They were speedy, but less conducive to myth-making. We know this because of the work archaeologists have done, and their excavations also provide us with another major source for corroborative detail about our heroine.

Our first stop on the Boudica trail, not counting her statue, is a Nissan garage on the Fison Way Industrial Estate in the outskirts of Thetford. Beneath the rows of cars was once a vast temple complex. It was originally thought to be Boudica's palace, but further research has shown that the site wasn't residential but religious. Archaeologists have pieced together what it would have looked liked when it was completed some time in the 50s AD.

As you can see from the diagram opposite, the temple was enormous, measuring 215 metres by 155 metres at the perimeter. The whole area covered 32,000 square metres. Like a series of Russian dolls, there were two ditches and ramparts and no fewer than nine parallel fences leading to a small (but still sizeable) central enclosure. The elaborate defences must have been largely symbolic because a straight corridor lined with upright posts traversed them all from the east. Any invading force would only have had to encounter one grand gateway before entering the central arena, an enclosure bigger than the old Wembley football pitch. The ceremonial nature of the fences and ditches is also underlined by the fact that this central arena itself was almost empty except for a two-storey building left over from a previous enclosure.

Some archaeologists claim that finds of brooches here may have meant it was a meeting place thronged with people who were too tightly packed to notice the loss of jewellery. I think a more convincing argument for this being Boudica's rallying point is a common-sense one. Politics and religion were so intertwined in the Celtic world that this massive

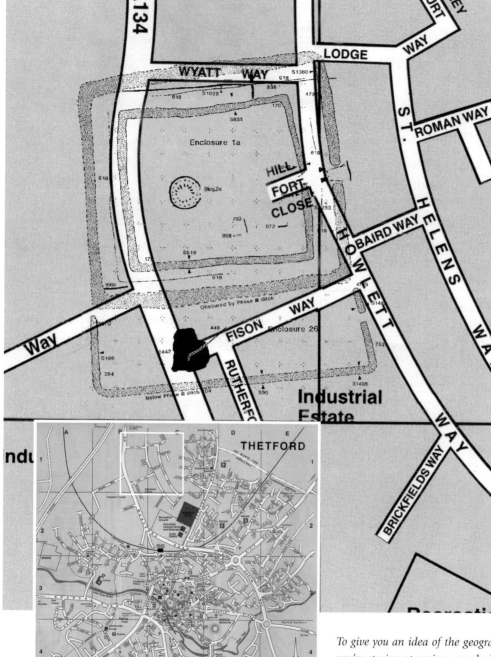

To give you an idea of the geography while you're staring at various car dealerships, I've superimposed the diagram of Boudica's temple complex on to the street plan of Thetford today. The diagram is a simplified version of the archaeological excavation notes. If you go there you'll get a clear sense of the scale of the original.

Thetford was right at the heart of Iceni territory, and was later one of the great capitals of Saxon Britain. Boudica's temple complex is to the north-east of the town centre. The best way of reaching it is to take the A11 bypass and come off at the second roundabout (counting from the south) where the A134, Mundford Road, takes you south towards Thetford centre. There are two entrances to the estate, Wyatt Way (first left) and Fison Way (second left). These two roads are linked by Howlett Way to form a rectangle mimicking the shape of the Iron Age defences. Turn left off Mundford Road at the Ford garage, left again at the Nissan garage on to Howlett Way, and the first left is the tell-tale Hill Fort Close, which reflects the eastern entrance to the temple.

temple complex in Boudica's homeland would have been the natural place for the rebelling tribes to assemble.

If you walk down this little cul-de-sac, you'll be treading roughly the same ground as 100,000 tribespeople did nearly 2,000 years ago as they answered Boudica's summons. Here they filed solemnly through the entranceway and squeezed into the open space of the mysterious arena to witness the Iceni queen launch her famous campaign against the Roman occupying forces.

Dio Cassius gives us the only description we have of her. He says her appearance was terrifying. She was very tall and carried a spear. She had a mass of tawny hair and her voice was harsh and rasping. She wore a cloak fastened with a brooch to a multi-hued tunic (probably plaid, like modern Scottish tartan). She also wore a gold neck ring known as a torc. These chunky pieces of jewellery still turn up on archaeological digs. They were immensely heavy, and it seems likely that they were only worn on ceremonial occasions.

Of course, we can't be sure if this portrait is based on fact or was simply an amalgam of Celtic stereotypes and male fears about women warriors. But like all myths, the fact that she was impressive enough to become such a larger-than-life stereotype in the minds of her enemies is a testament to Boudica's character.

The immediate cause of her insurrection was personal. She had been robbed of her inheritance by the Romans. Their colonial forces had further humiliated her and her tribe by publicly beating her and raping her daughters. Such an insult was enough to justify reprisals by the Iceni, but among the multitudes gathered in Thetford were representatives of other tribes, notably the Trinovantes. Their presence, and the sheer ferocity of what followed, shows there was more at stake than simple reprisal for the terrible acts perpetrated on the tribal chief of the Iceni. The brief campaign that Boudica launched led to four times as many deaths as all the other battles and massacres in this book combined.

To understand the Boudican revolt of AD 60–61, we have to wind back and look at how our island came under the thumb of foreign occupation.

BRITAIN BC

Iron Age Britain was a thickly populated island, but her people wouldn't have seen themselves as 'British'. The country was divided into more than twenty tribal groupings. There were the Caledonii and the Vacomagi in the far north of Scotland, the great tribe of the Brigantes in what is now the north of England, and southern tribes such as the Atrebates and the Dumnonii. In the Midlands there were the Catvellauni, in Essex and south Suffolk the Trinovantes, while the Iceni occupied most of East Anglia.

These tribes shared a common Celtic culture and the religion of Druidism. This cultural heritage extended over the Channel through Gaul and Germany. When European

BOUDICA

Druids wanted training they came over to Britain, the headquarters of this spiritual–political sect.

But there were ethnic divisions between the tribes. Some, like the Iceni, could have traced their roots back to the Celtic invaders who displaced the original nomadic people of Britain around 3500 BC. Others, like the Trinovantes, were far more recent immigrants, so-called Belgic tribes who started arriving in 75 BC from a part of Gaul that the Romans called Gallia Belgica, and were culturally more sophisticated.

The tribes were also riven by border disputes, and whenever the Romans came up against them they played on these tribal divisions. Often their invasion tactics were more an eroding drip than an overwhelming tidal wave.

The first time the British Celts felt the force of the Mediterranean superpower on their soil was a hundred years before Boudica's time, when Julius Caesar arrived in 55 BC. He'd already conquered Gaul, but he made a hash of his first British campaign, losing many of his ships in bad weather, and retreated under strong opposition back to the Continent without crossing the Thames. The next year, 54 BC, he returned with 800 ships. Nobody humiliated Julius Caesar and got away with it.

Significantly, he was invited in by the Trinovantes who wanted his protection against a rival tribe. He moved through southern Britain and received the submission of several tribes including, according to his own account, the Cenimagni, the 'greater Iceni', implying that the Iceni were split into at least two sub-tribes. But then he left again. He'd salvaged his bruised ego, and, besides, he had another rebellion to deal with in recently conquered Gaul. He had neither the willpower nor the manpower to sustain a full-scale occupation of this damp and dingy island.

Britain was considered impossibly remote by the Romans. It was a useful source of tin, and the oysters from the east coast were excellent, but otherwise it was distant and uninviting. Even seventy years later in AD 16 when shipwrecked sailors bound for the German wars were rescued by the Britons, they returned to Rome with hair-raising stories of sea monsters and strange creatures that were half-man and half-animal. You'd have had to be mad to think about conquering such a place.

And he was. The next potential invader was the psychotic despot Caligula. He'd set off from Rome with the intention of conquering new fields for the Empire, but on the beachhead in France, with the cliffs of Britain in sight, he ordered his centurions to fill their helmets with seashells and then declared them the spoils of victory. That's the later version of the story anyway. Historians think it's more than possible that his invasion was cancelled, possibly due to a mutiny by the troops (similar to the rumblings in AD 43 – see below). Collecting seashells was a deliberate humiliation of his timid legions.

THE ROMANS IN BRITAIN

The decisive military campaign was carried out by Caligula's unlikely successor Claudius (Caligula had had most of his potential successors killed). The soldiers instructed to take part in the Claudian campaign complained to their bosses that they were being ordered to carry the battle beyond 'the limits of the known world'. But their concerns were ignored. Unlike Caesar, ninety years before, the Emperor Claudius had good reason for wanting to extend the bounds of the Empire.

Claudius needed some good PR. Nowadays he's thought to have been a good administrator and a competent emperor. He introduced a clean water supply to Rome by building a new aqueduct, the Via Claudia, and provided better stocks of grain for the populace. But in his day, he wasn't considered emperor material. We probably know most about him from Robert Graves's book *I Claudius* and the subsequent TV series starring Derek Jacobi. Claudius was the sort of boy who gets teased at school. Even his own mother called him a 'monstrosity of a human being': he limped, had some sort of disability in his right hand, and slobbered when he was angry. Within a year of becoming emperor he had to deal with an attempted coup that was supported by several members of the Senate. So, as nothing helps an emperor like military success, Claudius resurrected the idea of adding Britain to the imperial collection.

The Roman army invaded in AD 43. The pretext, as before, was internecine strife between British tribal factions.

Caesar's invasion, while only temporary, had established a cultural bridgehead. The tribes were now aware of the Empire beyond the sea. Trading links had been established, and the benefits of having the great military machine as an ally were only too clear, particularly in the south. In AD 40, the tribal leader Cunobelin (Shakespeare's Cymbeline) of the Catuvellauni had died and a power struggle ensued. The leader of the Atrabates appealed to Rome for help against Cunobelin's sons Togodumnus and the famous Caratacus.

The Roman commander Aulus Plautius fought his way through southern Britain, killing Togodumnus and capturing Caratacus (who later escaped to fight another day) in a series of skirmishes probably around the Medway. He then set his sights on the British stronghold of Camulodunum. With most of the fighting done, it was time for Claudius to join the fun of the triumphal parade.

The emperor was a canny politician and ensured that there wouldn't be too much unrest back home by bringing a large retinue of opposition senators and other politicos with him to witness his success. To celebrate his victory, he put on a show of imperial power and splendour designed to underline his credentials to his opponents and cow the natives into submission. Through the settlement of Camulodunum he paraded with his forces. In front of the natives who fought in plaid and woad he marched his heavy infantry,

the Second, the Ninth, the Fourteenth and the Twentieth Legions with their body armour and shields and crested helmets. He also brought with him a unit of his own Praetorian bodyguard. Then there were the cavalry and Claudius's exotic shock troops, a detachment of elephants. Rarely used and unreliable in battle, they were designed to impress. They must have seemed like extra-terrestrials to a population who thought the largest thing alive was an ox. The inscription to his victory records that Claudius received the ritual submission of eleven British kings.

Claudius declared Camulodunum, just north of the existing Trinovantian headquarters, the capital of his new conquered country. It was the first real city in Britain – today's Colchester – and was laid out in true Roman fashion with straight streets, shops and urban facilities. It's thought to have been built on the site of the original Roman military encampment which then gradually became a civilian settlement. Later it acquired the official status of a *colonia*, a place where Roman legionaries could retire after their sixteen-year period of service in the army. As a means of cultural evangelism this was a tried and tested way of bringing conquered peoples into the fold of the *pax romana*.

The existing town centre is laid out several metres above the Roman settlement, the high street shops reflecting the layout of their ancient equivalents. If you park in Short Cut Road, then walk up the high street with the town hall on your left, you'll see the Roman passion for straight lines opening out in front of you. The shops that once occupied the same land as the Lion Walk Shopping Centre would have stocked wine, olive oil, dates and figs (not just dried but fresh too), herbs and spices like dill, anise and coriander, and other Mediterranean luxuries. Archaeologists have even discovered opium poppies, adding a whole new dimension to the idea of adopting Roman habits. It's probably fair to say you could have bought more exotic goods in Colchester in AD 50 than in AD 1950.

And what did Boudica do about the Roman military occupation and the flagrant cultural imperialism of the new regime?

Nothing.

Like the French of Vichy France, there were many more collaborators in AD 43 than people liked to admit after the event. Going along with the Romans had great benefits, and many of the ancient Britons didn't look to the long term, seeing instead a way to win an advantage over age-old rivals in the tribal system.

Boudica may well not have witnessed Claudius's elephant parade in AD 43. She wasn't tribal chief when he arrived, and a ruler called Antedios offered the submission of the Iceni. But there's no doubt she would have heard about the amazing procession. Most of the southern tribes capitulated and accepted the generous terms that the Romans offered to everyone who submitted quietly to the inevitability of Roman rule. They became client kingdoms, as did the Brigantes in the north under another female ruler, Cartimandua. These Celtic tribal leaders were allowed to hold on to their dignity and enjoy the material benefits

Nowadays pre-Roman Colchester is difficult to locate. The clearest physical signs of it are the system of dykes that were originally used to protect the settlement. They lie on the south-western outskirts of the modern city and are known as The Gosbecks. From the air it's still possible to see the outline of Cunobelin's farmstead in crop marks, but an exploration of the area round the Maldon Road (B1022), Stanway Green and Shrub End is likely to be disappointing. Apart from the largest, Gryme's Dyke, the whole area looks like nothing more than a lot of overgrown ditches.

of Roman life. Corroborative evidence from sites throughout Northern Europe shows that it was standard practice for the ruling class of client kingdoms to adopt Roman ways.

If you want to see what an attractive deal this must have been, take a trip to Fishbourne in Sussex, where the Roman villa of Cogidubnus of the Atrabates has been dug up in all its splendour. To get there, follow directions for Bosham in the chapter on Harold (page 98), and Fishbourne is on the way.

Cogidubnus seized Roman luxury with both hands and, like the pigs in Orwell's *Animal Farm*, it was soon almost impossible to tell the difference between him and a wealthy Roman citizen.

In return for their largesse, the Romans obtained cereal, cattle, gold, silver, iron, slaves, hunting dogs and the best oysters in the Empire from up the coast of East Anglia, and it was the client kingdoms that had to provide them.

To fund their policy of Romanization, or civilization as the Romans saw it, the super-power offered generous sums of money to its new colonial friends. These came both from public sources and individuals. The Roman philosopher Seneca personally invested a small fortune in Britain. Had the British tribes been more financially astute, they would have realized that these lifestyle-aid payments weren't made because Seneca and the Romans were nice people. They wanted something in return. But the Celts were simple people whose economy was based on bartering and trading goods. Gift-giving was a key part of their culture – being generous enhanced the status of the giver. It would have seemed natural for a faraway emperor to distribute his largesse.

But the speculators' money was a slow-burning fuse that would eventually contribute to Boudica's uprising. That, though, was still in the future. For now, instant gold and silver seemed too good to refuse.

From evidence on silver coins we know that, some time after the Romans arrived, King Prasutagus took over as King of the Iceni. Perhaps he was installed by the Romans as a more pliant stooge than the previous ruler, Antedios. His coinage bears the traditional horse design of the Iceni with the abbreviated form of the tribal name ECE, standing for Eceni (which shows how proud the Iceni were – they were the only tribe to put their name on their coins). Some also bear the inscription *subriprasto*, meaning 'under King Prasutagus'. The language shows how the two cultures were beginning to fuse: *sub* – under (Latin), *ri* – king (Celtic), *Prasto* – Prasutagus (Celtic name, Latin ending).

Prasutagus's wife was Boudica. It's only an assumption that she was born an Iceni. She may have been a princess from one of the other tribes, possibly the Trinovantes, who were so quick to support her rebellion.

All the indications are that even if Boudica and Prasutagus adopted the frills of a Roman lifestyle, the bulk of the Iceni were far more wary. As we've seen, they were more conservative than the Southern Belgic tribes, and they seem to have been resistant to social change.

The Iceni were principally horse traders. The emblem of the horse on their coinage (reminiscent in style of the emblematic White Horse on the downs of south Oxfordshire) summed up their life. They bred, traded and rustled from other tribes. Their East Anglian homeland was boggy and difficult to farm. You can see the kind of terrain they'd have lived in at the Suffolk and Norfolk Training Area army ranges near Thetford. It's marshy land that is difficult to negotiate, and today it's where the army exercises its six-wheel-drive amphibious vehicles that are part of the nuclear, chemical and biological warfare unit.

Boudica and Prasutagus probably lived in a modest villa where they drank imported wine and ate the fruits of a warmer climate. Their people inhabited thatched round houses, drank home-brewed beer, and ate grain and root vegetables.

The Iceni were great metal workers, making jewellery like the torcs worn by Boudica, ornamental gear for chariots and horses and, of course, weapons. Like all the other Celtic tribes, they were a warrior culture.

Which leads us to the first signs of unrest against the Roman administration. Not all the British tribes had capitulated as easily as the Trinovantes and the Iceni. There was a stern rearguard action being led by tribes further to the north and east. The ringleader of the resistance was Caratacus, who'd escaped from the clutches of the Romans when they first invaded. The Silures in Wales were particularly violent in their opposition, as were the Druids who, it seems, were helping to orchestrate the British campaign. Their headquarters were at Ynys Mon, the sacred Isle of Anglesey.

BOUDICA

You can visit a typical Iceni settlement. There's one signposted off the A11 near Thetford, but be warned – it's quite a complicated drive through a nexus of tiny roads. A slightly easier-to-find option and just as authentic, although not in Iceni territory, is Butser Ancient Farm, an Iron Age working farm used for archaeological reconstructions. Butser is in Hampshire in the village of Chalton, just off the A3 to the east. Leave at the junction before it becomes the A3(M) and work back on yourself. Well worth it!

Iceni coinage.

THE FIRST REBELLION, AD 47

The Romans drew their first line of defence from the Humber estuary south-west to Exeter along the Fosse Way. Beyond this was bandit country. But, in spite of the soft words and promises to the client kingdoms, the Romans didn't completely trust the tribes on the peaceful side of the border. In AD 47 the Roman governor made the fateful decision to disarm the friendly tribes. Robbing a warrior of his weapons was a terrible disgrace. This repressive policy soured the entente cordiale in one fell swoop.

The Iceni rose in revolt. It didn't last long. Historians tell of a brief fight against the Romans who trapped them in a fort defended by earthworks. This rudimentary castle was no match for the seasoned centurions who marched in and destroyed the rebels.

Prasutagus and Boudica seem to have been unaffected by this rebellion. Either the Romans realized they'd made a mistake and were uncharacteristically merciful, or not all the Iceni were involved. Caesar had referred to the 'Greater Iceni', and there could have been one part of the tribe that rebelled while the collaborating King and Queen maintained the peace among their part of the tribe and held on to the perks. Either way, there's no record of any more unrest for the next twelve years. Prasutagus and Boudica must have put up with a good deal in order to preserve the peace in East Anglia, even though they would have realized by now that their Latin colleagues would dump them like a shot if circumstances demanded it. But the event that was to transform their lives happened 2,000 miles away in Rome.

NERO

In AD 54 Claudius was poisoned by his fourth wife so that her son could become emperor instead. The sixteen-year-old Lucius Domitius Ahenobarbus or, as we know him, Nero, thought of himself as an artist rather than a general. He was an out-and-out pleasure-seeker who was quite willing to let his cronies look after the administration of a two-bit chilly province.

The old administration in Britain was replaced by a new and harsher regime. Nowhere were its effects more deeply felt than in Colchester, the heart of Rome's new project.

The Roman army behaved like any occupying force in alien territory. It maintained discipline by employing a background level of brutality and casual mistreatment of its subjugated people. We know from the New Testament and other sources that this was a widespread phenomenon. Colchester Museum displays graphic evidence of the sort of maltreatment that must have been commonplace. There you can see the skulls of ancient Britons executed by soldiers, which were then stuck on poles to encourage better behaviour in the rest of the population. On one, a deep gash caused by a sword blow is clearly visible, while

No one's sure where the original conflict between the Romans and the Iceni took place. The most likely bet is Stonea Camp, a hill fort that was once located on an island in the Cambridgeshire Fens. At some time, this ancient site has had its defensive ditches filled in, as though spiked by successful legionaries. It is now open to the public, and restoration of some of the ramparts gives you a good idea of its original size and scale. You can find the remains about three miles south-east of the town of March. It is reached off the B1093, which runs between the A141 near Wimblington and the village of Manea. The B1093 is bisected by the B1098 which runs to the nearest train station, Stonea. Look out for the free car park near Stiches Farm which is on the outskirts of the site. The Ordnance Survey reference is sheet 143, ref. 446930.

another bears marks that were caused when a sword pommel or other blunt instrument was smashed into the victim's head.

Roman Colchester was dubbed *Colonia Victricensis* (the Colony of Victory) and was full of ex-army veterans who had helped themselves to native land. The usual allocation was about twelve hectares but, if the area was defined as captive territory (land won by expelling the enemy), soldiers could take as much as they wanted, when they wanted. Three thousand of these veterans set up shop around Colchester, driving natives from their land and then treating the former owners as captives and slaves. The current generation of soldiers in charge of security naturally turned a blind eye to the rule-bending of their former colleagues. They too would one day be on the verge of retirement and looking for a nice little place in the country.

So hungry were the settlers for homes, gardens and land that the original defences of the *colonia* were filled in and built on. Like colonialists everywhere, the Romans were so pleased with their progress that they didn't notice the growing resentment of the people they'd conquered until it was too late.

Colchester provided another focus for the resentment of the native Trinovantes. It was decided that the Roman headquarters should have a brand new temple dedicated to the stuttering Claudius, now declared divine by the people who'd had him assassinated.

The temple was conceived and built on a scale unimaginable to tribes used to single-storey thatched dwellings. It was 20 metres high, and made of stone with a tiled roof. The exterior dimensions were 46 metres by 24 metres. There was an inner room known as a *cella* reached through a pair of bronze doors. Outside this to the front and sides was a colonnade composed of pillars a metre thick. At the bottom of a flight of steps at the front was an entrance area with a series of statues. There's good evidence that there was also an altar there, the original focal point of the new cult of the Emperor. Inside there was intended to be a giant statue of the now deified Claudius.

Colchester Museum has a model of what the temple would have looked like when completed, although Tacitus seems to imply that the building was still unfinished at the time of the Boudican revolt. Not only was it on a scale never seen before in Britain (it was higher than today's Norman castle that stands on the same site), but it also underlined the alien nature of Roman religious practice. Druidism was essentially a nature religion, and most rites took place in sacred groves, not in a massive building in the middle of a city.

Even worse, the Trinovantes were used as slave labour to build it and they were taxed to pay for it. The whole enterprise was like a great Roman boot stamping out the message of the Emperor's power. No wonder even the Roman writer Tacitus called it 'a blatant stronghold of alien rule'.

And amazingly, part of it still exists. If you take a guided tour of Colchester Museum you can see the remains under the ruins of the Norman castle. Its whereabouts were unknown until, in 1920, two archaeologists worked out that the 'vaults' of the castle were really part of this long-lost building. Strictly speaking, they aren't vaults at all, but the arched supports for what was the podium, the platform on which the temple was constructed. In the eighteenth century archaeologists cut a tunnel through the sandy soil to explore these Roman remains. As they excavated sand from under the stony mortar, it started to look as though they were uncovering a vaulted cellar. However, there was never a room here. In order to support the weight of the temple, the Romans had bolstered the foundations by digging holes and trenches lined with timber and pouring in a mixture of stones and mortar. The timber was left in place until the mix had hardened.

Now the sand has been fully excavated from underneath these mortar foundations, giving the impression that this is a cellar with pillars and vaults. It's well worth a visit. You can even make out the marks the supporting timbers left in the pillars and on the ceiling where the mortar oozed round them and set.

Because the vaulted supports were load-bearing, archaeologists could extrapolate an accurate picture of the temple that would have risen from these foundations.

It was the Trinovantes who had to bear the burden of the new temple of Claudius, but around AD 60 the Roman administration introduced a swingeing new policy that impacted all the client kingdoms.

Perhaps word had got round that there was trouble brewing in the north and that investment in Britain might not be such a good thing. Whatever the reason, the investors in Rome decided they wanted their money back. The stoic philosopher Seneca had laid out the fantastically large sum of 40 million sesterces, roughly equivalent to £50 million. The Emperor Claudius also had a big financial stake in Britain, giving enormous sums of money to the various client kingdoms. But the Procurator of Britain, Catus Decianus, a slippery politician favoured by Nero and hated by the British, now declared these sums of money were not gifts at all but loans, and that they were to be repaid immediately. The debt collection would involve force if necessary.

The administration abandoned all pretence of fair government. It was traditional to fleece the provinces. A provincial governorship was a key step on the ladder of Roman political life. The perks of a foreign posting helped to repay the debts a politician had so far incurred through the necessary business of greasing palms. There was never any comeback. Even when lawsuits were taken out in Rome against retired governors by aggrieved colonials, they seldom won their case. But it was all a matter of taste and scale. What went on in Britain was seen as beyond the pale even by staunch supporters of Roman governance. But the spark that ignited the powder keg was an abuse of power directed specifically at the Iceni.

In AD 60 Prasutagus died, leaving his wife Boudica as ruler of the Iceni. The fact that at this time two British tribes were ruled by women (Boudica and Cartimandua of the

Brigantes) indicates how common it may have been for a tribal leader to be female. The Romans, of course, thought this was barbarous, and saw their opportunity to make the most of what seemed to them a weak and feeble leader.

Prasutagus had left a will. He was a natural appeaser, and, in an attempt to protect his wife and children, he left half his property to the Emperor. But this wasn't enough for Catus Decianus. He confiscated all the dead King's property. Tacitus says that the royal household was picked over, first by Roman soldiers and then by Roman slaves. This was the true brutal face of Roman rule. The chiefs of the Iceni were also deprived of their hereditary estates, and the King's relatives were treated like slaves.

Then, in a symbolic act of domination and cruelty, Boudica was taken to a public place and flogged. Her daughters were raped – not the random act of conquering forces, but the sort of deliberate sexual humiliation perpetrated in recent ethnic conflicts. Of course these outrages were deeply personal, but both Boudica and the Romans knew they were symbolic as well. Boudica and her daughters represented the Iceni and the Romans wanted to demonstrate who was boss. In her turn Boudica knew that her humiliation represented the subjugation of the entire tribe. Vengeance was due for all the wrongs done to the Iceni. Boudica went to war.

BOUDICA ON THE WARPATH

Dio Cassius records her making a lengthy rhetorical speech here, but there's no reason to think this is factual. The historian was probably following convention and demonstrating what he took to be his character's position. But he also records that she prayed to the goddess Andraste for victory and released a hare into the multitude to determine by the direction in which it ran whether the campaign would be a success. The hare was a sacred creature, one of the few native mammals in Britain from prehistoric times, unlike the rabbit which was introduced by the Romans. This ritual action attributed to Boudica seems highly plausible.

After receiving a favourable omen, her hordes set off south towards Colchester, the hated seat of Roman power, burning and looting Roman farms as they went. Her 'army' was totally different from the Roman forces, which were divided into centuries and legions, each highly organized. This was a whole people on the move. Along with the warriors, there would have been womenfolk and children, carts carrying granny and household supplies with enough space for the anticipated booty of war. The column of over 100,000 people was a slow-moving juggernaut, gathering supporters as it went. The moment of revenge had come for years of oppression. There would have been anticipation, excitement and a sense of release.

The Iceni and Trinovantes must have been rearming secretly since the rebellion of AD 47. Now before them lay a swathe of largely undefended countryside.

BOUDICA

The Roman Military Governor was Gaius Suetonius Paulinus, known simply as Suetonius. He'd taken the bulk of the active Roman forces on a campaign against the Druid stronghold of Anglesey. They were about as far away from East Anglia as they could get. Even with the benefit of new Roman roads, it would take weeks to move enough forces to defend the 'friendly' territories of the south-east.

Anglesey was more than a glorified shrine and theological college. The Druids wielded great political power and were able to weld the factional interests of the tribes into a unified cultural struggle, so the sacred isle was home to many refugees and diehard resistance fighters.

Tacitus gives us a vivid account of the Roman advance on the Druid stronghold. It has the flavour of an eyewitness record by his father-in-law, Agricola. As they crossed the Menai Straits in shallow-bottomed boats or waded across with their horses, the Romans were frozen by the spectacle of thronging hordes of screaming women with 'dishevelled hair like furies', and Druids raising their eyes to heaven and 'screaming dreadful curses'. It must have been an unnerving vision, and indeed a bizarre one. Druids not only had the role before battle of cursing the enemy, they also danced naked in front of the battle line. Suetonius called his men to order and the discipline of the Romans was restored. They became the ultra-efficient killing machine they were trained to be, and advanced on the Druids. After the initial battle Suetonius went on to garrison the entire island and destroyed the last traces of Druid religion that the Romans found so alien. Tacitus makes this process of conquest seem a matter of days, but it would actually have taken much longer.

Historians have suggested that the entire two-front rebellion was co-ordinated by the Druids. Either the Boudican revolt was intended as a diversionary tactic to relieve pressure on the rebels in the north-east or vice versa. Whether by chance or clever intention, there were few troops available to oppose the advance of the Iceni.

Back in Colchester, the inhabitants were complacent, assuming that the rebel uprising would swiftly die down and all would soon be well. But then a succession of frightening portents appeared that struck terror into the superstitious Romans and heartened the British rebels.

The historians record that a holy effigy toppled from its perch and fell face downwards. It was probably a statue of the Roman version of the Greek goddess Nike, who in those days epitomized, not credible sportswear, but victory. It would have been stationed overlooking the altar of Claudius in front of the temple. Then unexplained shrieks were heard in the theatre and the senate house; a ghostly ruined town was seen in the Thames; the sea turned blood red and shapes like corpses appeared on the seashore at ebb tide.

The inhabitants of the Colony of Victory panicked. As we've seen, archaeology has proved that, in the rush for land, the city's original ditches had been filled in. Tacitus wryly remarks that the inhabitants had been thinking of amenities rather than needs.

Opposite: Boudica encouraging the Britons to defend their country against the Romans.

31

The tombs of Longinus Sdapeze (left) and Facili, both defaced and torn down by Boudica's hordes.

Archaeologists have found the old and rusty weapons hastily brought out of storage by retired veterans who realized they had one more rearguard action to fight. But they were vastly outnumbered.

The citizens appealed to Catus Decianus for reinforcements. He clearly didn't take the situation seriously because he sent only 200 lightly armed soldiers from his base in first-century London to join a small garrison of about 700 stationed at The Gosbecks. Tacitus also refers to fifth-columnists, presumably Trinovantians, who were secretly on the British side and hampered the plans for evacuation and defence. Colchester was wide open. Then Boudica attacked.

THE SACK OF COLCHESTER

BOUDICA

When the Romans occupied a town, they tried to preserve anything they thought might be useful. This attack was of a completely different order. The Iceni were a rural people and had no time for towns. The urban settlement at Colchester was a symbol of everything Roman. The Britons wrought a destruction like Hiroshima. They slaughtered the citizens and razed the city to the ground.

The wooden structures of the shops and dwellings burnt easily and were impossible to defend. The Roman veterans retreated to the only stone building in town, the recently completed temple of Claudius. They locked themselves in the *cella*, presumably hoping to hunker down until the Britons had done their worst and left.

But Boudica's warriors weren't content to leave their slaughter unfinished. Archaeologists have calculated that the *cella* might have held as many as a thousand frightened Romans, not just the toughened soldiers who would have known what to expect, but women and children too. They held out for two days. Tacitus's account has recently been fleshed out with archaeological detail.

The stone building would have been hard to burn down and, with the bronze doors bolted, the only way to get at the occupants would have been to climb 20 metres and dismantle the tile roof. The terrified refugees inside would have been in total blackness. Their oil lamps and candles would have burnt out in the first twelve hours. Pressed close in the darkness, choking on the stench of sweat, faeces and fear, this was no military siege but the desperate vigil of prisoners on death row. They could only wait while patient hatred worked on the roof above, prising the tiles away. Then, with the first chinks of light, hope was extinguished, as the hungry barbarian faces peered down into the gloom at their cornered prey.

The destruction of Colchester was total. Boudica has left her testament written plain for today's archaeologists. The debris left from the rubble of the city is known as 'the Boudican destruction layer'. It's bright red. When the daub from timber-framed houses is burnt, it usually reverts to the clay from which it originally came. But the firestorm of Boudica's attack was so fierce that it cooked the daub in the same way that pottery is fired in a kiln. From the comparative thicknesses of this red layer, archaeologists can tell which way buildings crashed to the ground and where there were open areas such as gardens. In spite of its terrible origins, it's also a superb tool for dating. Everything found beneath it is from before AD 60, everything above is later.

Of course this layer has now been covered by the detritus of two millennia. Boudica's Colchester lies metres below the modern-day city. But in a basement store-room at the George Hotel in Colchester high street, there's a window into the wall which frames the red layer at eye level. It's clearly visible, about 15 centimetres thick.

But the Boudican layer isn't the only surviving evidence of the suddenness and intensity of the blazing inferno, so hot it melted glass. We also have a record of some surprising and, in the circumstances, touching details of the daily lives of the citizens of the *colonia*.

The staple food of the time was grain. Carbonized seeds have been found in seven locations in Roman Colchester. Some in Culver Street had been mixed with barley and had started to sprout – a sign that they had been treated to make beer. There are also other organic finds that would usually have rotted, but have been dried and preserved by the heat of the fire. There are pieces of mattress with the pattern still imprinted on them, some dates and plums found in Lion Walk, and figs, lentils, horsebeans and coriander from a pottery shop, where archaeologists have also found red Samian pottery from Gaul. So hot was the blaze that it fired the red slip to black.

You can see many of these finds at Colchester Museum on your way to the temple vaults. But there are other objects there too that bear testament to the anger of Boudica's avenging Britons. A Roman graveyard just beyond the present West Gate of Colchester was attacked and desecrated. At the museum are two defaced gravestones. One is from the grave of a Roman centurion called Facilis, whose carved nose and face had been brutally smashed in. The other is of a soldier from Sardicia, the modern Bulgarian capital Sophia.

Longinus Sdapeze belonged to the *Ala I Thracum,* the first Thracian cavalry regiment. He chose to be depicted in death on horseback, trampling a cowering figure. To the marauding Britons this clearly looked like a gleeful statement of imperialism, so they hacked off the carved face and threw the gravestone carved side down. It lay there uneroded, until it was discovered nearly 2,000 years later. Incredibly, further excavation also found the fragment of face some way off, and it fits perfectly.

This was no casual act of mutilation. Faces and heads had enormous significance to the Britons. This is demonstrated in a further fascinating discovery. Early last century, a boy went swimming in the River Alde near Saxmundham in Suffolk. To his surprise he found a bronze head on the river bed. He took it home with him, whitewashed it, and stuck it outside his cottage like a garden gnome. By chance it was seen by someone who recognized its importance. Eventually it found its way to the British Museum, which paid five shillings for it.

It was from a huge statue of Claudius. There are jagged edges round the neck where the Iceni hacked off the symbolic head of their enemy. At one time it was thought it might be from the giant statue of Claudius which stood in the temple. But the way the head tilts up suggests that this Claudius was mounted on horseback, leaning back in the stirrups to control his steed, and would have been from a statue elsewhere in the city.

The decapitation of this image had symbolic meaning, because our ancestors, the ancient Celts, were head hunters. Classical writers tell of their barbaric practices with horror. Heads were an offering to the gods of war. Warriors would tie the heads of victims to their horses, and take them home where they were highly prized. Elsewhere in Europe, door lintels and specially carved pillars have been found with niches created specially to display such skulls. They were embalmed in cedar oil, or cleaned out and used as drinking vessels. A find in a cave at Býciskála in Moravia of a skull made into a cup provides vivid testimony to this practice.

Druid religion also placed great emphasis on the sacredness of wells, streams and water. Heads left in streams were an offering to the gods. The real head of Claudius was no longer available, so a symbolic head was offered instead.

THE ROMAN RESPONSE

The first soldiers to react to the sack of Colchester were those of the Ninth Legion Hispana, which had distinguished itself in Spain. It was probably based in Longthorpe near Peterborough. Its commander was called Petilius, and he seems to have been something of a hothead. He assumed the British were just an amorphous murdering rabble. But they weren't. Their troops were brave warriors who knew the terrain better than their enemy. Boudica was ready for him.

Part of her forces staged an ambush in the forests south of what is now Cambridge.

The over-confident column of the Ninth Legion fell into the trap. This was the sort of fighting at which the Britons excelled. They were a warrior culture schooled in the mythology of the hero. They fought man-to-man, with the emphasis on individual prowess. The Romans were usually successful precisely because the individual was ignored in the carefully rehearsed system of group tactics and strategy. Here in the boggy woods of Britain, taken by surprise, with no room to regroup and defend en masse, the Roman force was lost. Their short stabbing swords and shields, so deadly in formation, were little match for the furious barbarian onslaught.

When he saw that the game was up, Petilius fled back to Longthorpe with his cavalry, while his infantry were systematically cut to pieces. Petilius barricaded himself in the Roman camp, adding a new palisade within the outer defences to protect his decimated army from the frightening new force in the land.

This was a proper, military victory. The slaughter in Camulodunum may have salved years of frustration and bitterness, but it was no contest. Now, by defeating the Ninth Legion, Boudica had succeeded in out-manoeuvring a battle-hardened unit and had killed 2,500 crack troops with little loss on her side. The British Celts had proved themselves superb guerrilla fighters. If only they had taken the lesson to heart and continued a tactic of sudden stealth and surprise attacks, they might have avoided eventual disaster.

But for the moment, Boudica and her massive force of jubilant natives were on a roll. There was nothing now between them and the next symbol of Roman so-called civilization: London.

LONDON

In AD 60 London was newer than Milton Keynes is today. It was established around AD 50, and it certainly wasn't the main town in Roman Britain. If you can talk in terms of a capital, Camulodunum was it. First-century London was a purpose-built settlement, with a population of about 30,000. It was developing fast but it was still nothing like as important as it was to become.

It was sited at the high tidal point of the Thames, providing excellent communication links with the Continent and the rest of the country. Goods from abroad were unloaded here and distributed round the whole fledgling colony.

If you feel like splashing out on lunch you can get an aerial view of the site of Roman London. At the top of the five-storey building at 1 Poultry, in what is still called the City of London, there is a restaurant called Le Coq d'Argent, with a magnificent triangular roof garden. If you go to the eastern corner and look down, you are standing directly above the centre of the very first London. Cornhill, which lies below you, and the Bank of England to your left mark the north end of the old city centre. It was no Rome. Two thousand years

ago you would have seen only wattle and daub buildings leading to a forum, complete with market, lying across the present-day Gracechurch Street, which cuts across Cornhill before it becomes Leadenhall. The boundary of this central area to the south was today's Fenchurch Street. But the community stretched far wider. Archaeologists have discovered signs of habitation as far afield as Newgate.

The business of its inhabitants then, as now, was business. These were the merchants and money men of the great Roman enterprise. We tend to think of businessmen and financial people as essentially conservative, but the first-century equivalent of the commodity broker in the City of London was a cultural ambassador at the cutting edge of the imperial onslaught on barbarian culture. Opening up a new market was a mutually beneficial enterprise; it helped to establish the Roman stranglehold on a culture by bringing the benefits of wealth and trade to a province, and in return those willing to set up shop in newly conquered territory stood to get rich quick. This was the sort of enterprise where Seneca's millions could have turned swiftly into billions, providing the situation remained stable.

Clearly there was money to be made in first-century London, but then messengers arrived from East Anglia with news of the disaster that had befallen the greatest town in the land. This time there was no complacency. As soon as Londoners realized that the avenging angel of Colchester was heading their way, their leader sprang into action. The Procurator Catus Decianus, who had helped cause the uprising by his outrageous graft, packed and headed for the safer air of Gaul across the Channel. The climate may have been cold and damp, but Britain was suddenly too hot for him. Those who could afford it and had ready access to sea transport swiftly followed his example. There was no question that the fledgling city was going to be attacked. It wasn't if, but when.

But then the first chink of weakness in Boudica's armour began to show.

From Colchester to London it's sixty-odd miles as the crow flies. Any of the crack Roman regiments stationed in Britain could have made the march in three days, but Boudica's tribal caravanserai dawdled. The atmosphere seems to have been closer to a violent school outing than a military exercise. There is no doubt that an advance on London was intended, but there was little strategic planning beyond the idea of rubbing out more Romans.

A shrewd tactician might have moved on London and then planned a series of ambushes on Suetonius's forces as they moved down from Wales. Instead the alliance of Iceni and Trinovantes ambled through what is now Essex at the speed of a bank holiday traffic jam. Nothing increases confidence like success. Numbers swelled as disaffected members of other tribes signed up for an anti-Roman killing and looting spree. Progress was so slow that, before Boudica had even got close to London, Suetonius had learnt of the sack of Colchester, left Anglesey, hot-footed it down Watling Street (the Roman road that follows the course of today's A5) and arrived in London with a small unit of cavalry.

His assessment of the situation was bleak, brief and workmanlike. It was clear that London couldn't be saved. His main forces were marching steadily southwards, but were nowhere near close enough to protect the city. So he gave the order to abandon it, despite the tears, prayers and entreaties of the Romans who'd made a new life there and the Britons who knew they'd be branded as collaborators. Anyone who's watched news footage of helpless peace-keepers in Bosnia or Kosovo awkwardly shrugging off weeping refugees as they plead for protection can imagine the scene.

Those who could move were invited to follow Suetonius and his small force back up Watling Street and away from the danger area. Others fled across the Thames to the tribes in Sussex who were still Roman-friendly.

The only people not joining the line of refugees were the old, the infirm and those who Tacitus says 'were attached to the place'. Perhaps they thought the reports of the atrocities in Colchester were exaggerated and that they either wouldn't be harmed or would muddle through somehow. Or perhaps they were the first-century equivalents of the brave and stubborn East Enders who hunkered down throughout the Blitz determined not to give in to intimidation, preferring to face the worst rather than leave home.

Boudica's destruction was far more effective than Hitler's bombs. What the Luftwaffe failed to achieve in six months, Boudica did in a few days. It was Colchester all over again. Here too the Boudican destruction layer bears witness to the fact that her firestorm engulfed the city. The layer here isn't as continuous as in Colchester, showing that the fires were started separately and that the houses were more sparsely distributed. Nevertheless, the heat generated by the firestorm has been calculated, through the effect it had on pottery and glass, at 1000°C, comparable to another Second World War tragedy, the firestorm that resulted from the bombing of Dresden.

Again there have been finds among the debris – some Samian ware, a cache of money hidden, though never collected, by the owner. But the very few domestic items found underline the fact that there was a general evacuation and that many people escaped with their lives and possessions.

This seriously calls into question Tacitus's assertion that Boudica's campaign cost 70,000 Roman lives. Estimates of Colchester's population vary, but probably no more than 15,000 perished there. London's population at the time was only 30,000 and many of these would have escaped.

Nevertheless, when you consider the number of likely casualties, it's rather odd that more corpses haven't turned up. There are two explanations. The first is that, once the revolt had been put down, the stunned Romans returned to try to rebuild their lives, and part of this process included cremating or disposing of the charred human remains with proper ceremony and dignity. The second is that many of the victims weren't killed on the spot, but were taken off by the Britons to their sacred groves to be ritually executed.

BOUDICA

A number of ghoulish finds have come to light which until recently were thought to come from this bloody era. After leaving Cornhill, if you go down Walbrook, the pavement you are walking on marks the course of a stream of the same name. Several decapitated skulls have been found in the Walbrook, now part of London's sewerage system, where it empties into the Thames. The immediate explanation seemed to be that these were the heads of Roman Londoners struck off and offered to the ancient British gods as thanksgiving for the destruction of the hated city. Why else would they be found in a stream if they weren't the votive offerings of the Celts?

But recent work on these skulls seems to prove that they weren't victims of Boudica's London holocaust after all. They belong to young men, the very people the historians say were most likely to have escaped with Suetonius. And their skulls don't have jawbones attached. This means that their flesh had decomposed and their jaws had dropped off before they were deposited in the Walbrook. It's unlikely that Boudica's people would have hung around long enough to wait for this kind of decomposition to occur.

Although we don't have tangible proof of Celtic barbarity during the sack of London, Roman historians shocked their readers with hideous tales. One writer says that Boudica's followers took the noblest and most eminent women, strung them up naked, then cut off their breasts and sewed them to their lips so it appeared as if the victims were eating their own flesh. Then they impaled them on sharp skewers which ran the entire length of their bodies. In other times we might have dismissed these stories as the exaggeration of writers intent on demonizing the enemy. English historians writing about the story of Braveheart level similar accusations. We've no way of proving any of these alleged atrocities one way or the other. But after Rwanda and Bosnia they do have the sad ring of truth about them.

The histories say nothing about Boudica's role in these acts of torture and summary execution. But perhaps the sexual injuries inflicted on the women of London weren't just casual humiliations of warfare, but symbolic ritual acts of revenge for the violations suffered by the Iceni tribal chief and her daughters.

Tacitus offers a novel explanation for the behaviour of Boudica's troops. He says their eagerness to cut throats, hang, burn, and crucify was a form of retribution in advance. They knew it was only a matter of time before the Romans took control again and administered their usual raft of savage punishments.

There's nothing to back this up. It seems more likely that, at the time, the Britons thought they could restore their country to the state it had been in before the hated Roman invasion. Crucifixions and the like were probably retribution for injustice and harshness already inflicted. This view is backed up unconsciously by Dio Cassius. He tells us that the atrocities were accompanied by sacrifices, in other words ritual offerings to the gods of war. He says that Boudica made her bloody offerings in the grove of Andate (a misspelling of Andraste, the Celtic goddess of Victory), accompanied by feasting and what he primly called 'wanton acts'. Boudica was enlisting the ancient power of the Celtic gods in her fight against the occupiers.

It's quite likely that somebody of her status would have been regarded as at least semi-divine. It wasn't uncommon for tribal leaders to be shamans. And although female rulers were part of Celtic culture, she may have had a special aura about her. She'd succeeded in getting tribes that had fought each other for hundreds of years to pull together against Rome. The sheer fact that she was able to command an enormous army would have endowed her with almost magical qualities. Her initial appeal to Andraste indicates a sense of oneness with the goddess. To the tribal hordes, Boudica, with her charisma and her enormous success at Colchester and London, was certainly an agent, if not the epitome, of the female goddess of victory.

APPEASING THE GODS

We've already seen how our ancient ancestors practised head-hunting on the warriors they conquered. But the accusations against Boudica and her tribes are even more sinister. We're led again into the area of Celtic culture that the Romans found most distasteful: human sacrifice.

There are two radical wings of opinion on Celtic Druidic religion. The straight-down-the-line classical writer's approach, as recorded in Tacitus, Julius Caesar, Strabo, Lucan and others, reports the practices of Druidic religion in shocked tones. Everything is filtered through a cultural prism of disapproval. In contrast, the modern view is what you might call the hippy-dippy approach, where the Druids are proto-environmentalists happily pottering about in their wooded groves being at one with nature. Here they are no more threatening than the respectable middle-aged men in white who officiate at today's Welsh Eisteddfods.

There's certainly archaeological evidence that human sacrifice did take place, and that it was probably still going on into the first century AD. A corpse known as Lindow Man was found in a Cheshire bog in 1984. The current dating of his death is within fifty years of Boudica. He had been stunned with blows to the head, strangled with a garrotte and then had his throat slit, a 'triple death' that matches mythic stories of the three-fold killing of the sacral king in Irish legends.

The man (known affectionately as Pete Marsh to irreverent archaeologists) was of high social standing (his moustache was trimmed and his fingernails clipped). After his death he was laid down in the bog. A criminal execution seems unlikely. He was naked but his body was painted. He wore an armlet of fox-fur. Before his death he had eaten a special meal of bread baked with a variety of cereal grains. There were also traces of mistletoe in his stomach. This parasitic plant was important to Druidic religion and was thought to have magical properties.

BOUDICA

The conclusion that Lindow Man was a human sacrifice is backed up by other bodies found in bogs. Two women from Windeby in German and Juthe Fen in Denmark offer parallels. Both were laid in a bog while still alive and pinned down with branches so that the bog itself did the killing. The Windeby woman was a young girl who was blindfolded, had half her blonde hair shaved, and wore only an ox-hide collar. The corpse in Denmark was of a fifty-year-old woman who still wore a look of terror when she was dug up two millennia later. She'd been pinned down not only by birch branches but also by wooden crooks hammered through her elbows and knees.

We can only speculate on the significance of these sacrifices to the people who made them. But it does seem probable there was a correlation between the method of death and particular Celtic gods. One writer describes how the great god Esus was placated by human offerings who were stabbed and hung on trees to bleed to death. Drowning victims in a bog would be particularly suitable way of appeasing a water deity, and impaling them on stakes could be a bloody thank-you to Andraste the warrior goddess. But the most famous example of ritual slaughter tailored to the penchants of a specific Celtic god is the so-called 'wicker man', recorded by both Caesar and Strabo, and made infamous by Christopher Lee in the film of the same name.

The wicker man was said to be a great human-shaped structure of interwoven branches, a tangled woody prison into which were put both humans and animals. This whole edifice was set ablaze as a great burnt offering to the thunder god Taranis. The fire appeased him, just as flesh consumed by water or bog pacified the watery spirits.

But however shocking such activities may seem to present-day sensitivities, the Romans failed to see that their own culture was equally barbaric. For example Julius Caesar, one of the first Romans to try to describe Celtic culture, was appalled by its adherence to ritual human sacrifice but nevertheless paid for 320 gladiators to kill each other at a games to celebrate his late father's memory.

ST ALBANS

The Iceni campaign was in danger of stalling. The excited, celebrating tribes needed direction and focus. If Boudica sought divine guidance in the groves outside first-century London her first question must have been 'What do I do now?' And there was only one answer: 'Follow Suetonius back up Watling Street and finish him off!' This is possibly what she attempted to do, but what happened next points to fatal weaknesses in either Boudica's tactics or her command of the situation.

Suetonius was in a very vulnerable position. The Druids were down but not out. There were uprisings elsewhere in the country, notably at Margidunum, north of Nottingham. His own forces were stretched and tired. He didn't have time to summon reinforcements

To follow Boudica's route, take the A5 or Edgware Road towards St Albans, turning on to the A5183 just outside Borehamwood. If you've decided not to dog Boudica's footsteps you can reach St Albans from junction 7 on the M1 onto the M10 or junction 22 on the M25. The M10 takes you right to the A5183, but from the M25 you take the A1081 and then turn left onto the A414, until it joins the A5183.

from Gaul. Instead he sent word to the Second Legion Augusta, the legion founded by the Emperor Augustus, based in modern-day Exeter. But its commander Poenius Postumus turned a deaf ear to Suetonius's request. Was this simply insubordination? Possibly not. There's evidence of a rebellion in Somerset at the time, and Poenius could have been pinned down by other revolting tribes in the south-west.

Boudica's juggernaut started to follow Suetonius but once again it was at a painfully slow speed and with no apparent strategy. Tacitus notes that the Britons were far more interested in plunder and booty than in attacking hard targets such as forts and garrisons. They made for 'where the loot was greatest and the protection weakest'. And so the wagons, already loaded with goodies from Colchester and London, started out for Verulamium, present-day St Albans.

Before they reached the main settlement, the usual patten of destroying outlying farms took place. At Park Street a house was burnt to the ground, leaving its own miniature Boudican destruction layer to describe its fate to later generations. A similar layer was found at Gorhambury to the north-west, in the burnt-out remnants of a lightly fortified farm enclosure containing two rectangular buildings and a round house.

These farms belonged to ordinary British farmers, who just happened to be from the wrong tribe. The crusade against the oppressive Romans was beginning to be diverted into settling old tribal scores.

St Albans was already well established before the Romans arrived. Their town of Verulamium was built around the Iron Age settlement of Verlamion. This had been the headquarters of the Catuvellauni leader Cunobelin (Cymbeline). Tacitus rates it as a *municipiumi*, lower than a colony but more important than a simple settlement. It was certainly sufficiently important for Watling Street to be specifically routed through it. After occupation, the Catuvellauni had needed little encouragement to ape their new masters and were in the process of turning their capital into a recognizably Roman town, complete with masonry buildings and terraced housing with colonnades. Unlike Colchester, there'd been no settlement of veterans, and the inhabitants were largely British.

But the Catuvellauni were the traditional enemies of the Trinovantes; Cunobelin had defeated them some years before. There's evidence that, by the time Boudica's forces arrived, the town had been largely evacuated. As a strategic target it was, therefore, useless. The sack of Verulamium was merely an exercise in ethnic hatred.

Roman historians pass over the destruction of Verulamium, possibly because few Roman citizens were involved. But the archaeological record tells us the now familiar story: shattered Samian ware spilling out of plundered shops, intense burning, the red layer. The destruction wasn't quite as complete as in the other two cities, though. No hoards of money have been found, which may indicate that people got out with their possessions. It also seems as though some of the buildings were torched from the

To get a good idea of Roman St Albans, carry on up the A5183 over the junction with the M10 and, as you continue into the city, follow the Roman helmet signs directing you to Verulamium. This takes you to two related sites situated off the A4147 to the south-west of the city: first, the award-winning Roman Museum and, over the road, an amphitheatre in the grounds of Old Gorehambury House. Modest entrance fees give you an instant guide to the only major city to survive an attack by Boudica.

wrong side, with the wind blowing towards the arsonists, thereby preserving the odd wall and artefact.

THE LAST BATTLE

With the British cause degenerating into a civil war, Suetonius had time to assemble his forces and take the initiative that should have been Boudica's. Pulling together parts of the seasoned Twentieth Legion, the Fourteenth Legion and various local auxiliaries for cavalry, Suetonius assembled a fighting force of around 10,000 troops. Dio Cassius believed they were up against 230,000 Britons, although this must be an exaggerated estimate and may include the camp followers who were such a large part of Boudica's bandwagon. The Roman forces were outnumbered, but it was the best Suetonius could do. He maximized his chances by engineering the sort of confrontation that would best suit his way of fighting: a pitched battle from a strong tactical position.

We now jump from St Albans to the final conflict. But we are faced with a monumental historical hurdle. Once again, none of the people writing the story mentions where it took place.

So many times throughout human history a significant battle has been fought, thousands have been killed, and yet, within a couple of generations, no one knows for sure where it actually happened. Hard facts are replaced by legend and local tradition. Modern academics are left to make up their own theories and argue them to their hearts' content. In this case, let's aggregate academic opinion and apply a dose of both imagination and common sense to the issue.

What information do we have to go on? Tacitus, who has his father-in-law for a source, simply says that Suetonius drew up his battle line in a defile (a narrow valley in hills) with a wood behind him for protection. He had his hardened troops in the middle, lighter-armed auxiliaries and cavalry on the flanks, facing the British who swarmed and spread over the plain in front of him. Dio Cassius adds that Suetonius split his troops into three parts. It's not much to go on. There are umpteen possibilities.

If you're in London, you can visit the most romantically located potential battle site. There's a long tradition, commemorated in names like Battlebridge Road, that Boudica's last stand took place just north of the London she'd just destroyed and that her body lies buried beneath platforms 9 and 10 of King's Cross Station. I don't know whether J. K. Rowling had this in mind when she invented platform 9¾, but I reckon the chances of the Iceni queen lying beneath the track are about the same as finding the Hogwarts Express there. It would mean that, having successfully moved from Colchester through London and on to St Albans, she retreated to London again, effectively running away from Suetonius who then tempted her into pitched battle.

To trace Boudica's final journey, you need to go to Mancetter via Watling Street. Rejoin the A5183 leaving St Albans, and at junction 9 on the M1 cross the roundabout to the A5 again. Follow the A5 faithfully as it parallels the M1 north-west via Dunstable and Milton Keynes; past Daventry, Rugby and Lutterworth, and then on as it branches further west and crosses the M69 north of Coventry. As you pass Hinckley to the right and Nuneaton to the left, you'll see signs for Atherstone. Turn left at the roundabout just as you enter Atherstone, and the road leads you into Mancetter.

Opposite: Mancetter, near Atherstone, the most likely setting for Boudica's last stand. The photos are of Mancetter churchyard where Roman finds were discovered proving the presence of the XIVth Legion, and the railway that bisects the battlefeld itself running parallel with the River Anker. The view is towards the wooded high ground where Suetonius dug in.

It doesn't make sense. It would have gone against the general mood of the British and the warrior nature of the Celts to shy away from a confrontation with the Romans. It's far more likely that Boudica persuaded her plunder-rich intoxicated forces to continue on up Watling Street in Suetonius's wake. Boudica's mistake wasn't caution, but being led into a battle on Suetonius's terms.

So King's Cross may be a dead end by itself, but you can still catch a train from there to what is fast becoming our most likely site for the final reckoning. The station at which to alight is Atherstone, but the place you are heading for is Mancetter or Manduessedum, literally 'the place of chariots'.

While on your journey you can mull over some of the other potential sites. Wheathampstead just to the north of St Albans is one possibility, Epping Forest is another. Even Ali G's beloved Staines is a candidate.

None of these, though, has the simple appeal to common sense that Mancetter offers. The only course open to Boudica was to go after Suetonius. Unless he had somehow doubled back, this would mean heading up Watling Street into the Midlands. Mancetter was a base for the Fourteenth Legion that formed the core of Suetonius's forces. Finds of armour and coinage that back this up have been made around Mancetter churchyard.

The geography certainly fits with the description in the histories of Suetonius's chosen battleground. Mancetter church and village are on an open plain. The rail line and the River Anker both run hard by. This would have been where the British took up their position. Overflowing from Watling Street, their excitement would have known no bounds as they saw the Romans lined up spoiling for a fight. The accounts tell of no discernible battle order. But in their confidence, they arranged their carts and the other paraphernalia they'd brought with them in a great semi-circle behind their lines. Their children and aging relatives would provide an audience as the Romans were finally taught a lesson. This makeshift auditorium was to prove fatal.

Suetonius looked down on them from the hill. He'd moved out on to open ground from the legionary fort located by the church. Behind the village to the south-west the land rises steeply to a ridge marked by narrow valleys. There's still woodland along much of this ridge. If you take the road out of Mancetter towards Oldbury you can park near the brow of the hill and walk over farmland to the left to get a clearer idea of the geography.

Here Suetonius surveyed the heaving mass of painted and plaid-dressed warriors over the crests of his drilled and organized centurions. The British were making a racket, screaming war cries, while their Druids hurled imprecations and curses at the enemy.

Tacitus records pre-battle speeches from both Boudica and Suetonius. There can't possibly have been a witness to any address Boudica made, but the lasting image of the Queen riding up and down her line in a chariot addressing the troops would have been clearly visible from the Roman position. The words Tacitus puts in her mouth are an emotional

appeal to right the wrongs of Roman injustice. She ends with a Braveheart-like call to freedom; 'You will win this battle or perish. That is what I, a woman, plan to do! Let the men live in slavery if they will.'

Suetonius offers no rhetoric, only a practical and bluff address that has the ring of reported speech about it. Perhaps it drilled itself into the memory of the young Agricola, tense before this key contest. Suetonius picked on the one point the Romans simply couldn't understand about the Britons. 'Disregard the clamours and empty threats of the natives,' he said. 'In their ranks, there are more women than fighting men... Just keep in close order. Throw your javelins and then carry on: use shield bosses to fell them, swords to kill them. Don't think of plunder. When you've won you'll have everything.'

It was a tried and tested battle plan, and it worked. As the howling ranks of the Britons advanced in their tens of thousands, the Romans stood firm. As the defile narrowed, the British line had to contract. Soon it would have been the same width as the Romans', only much deeper. Their adversaries waited until they could see the whites of the British eyes. Then they struck.

Each legionary was issued with two *pylae*. These were javelins with long heavy heads tapering to an evil point, the shafts designed to become detached so rendering them unusable if retrieved by the enemy. On the given command, with Boudica's forces a mere 20 or 30 metres away, 7,000 men unleashed both their javelins in quick succession into the crush of unarmoured British bodies. The physical effect was devastating. The tribesmen were so densely packed that the Romans couldn't miss. Almost every one of the 14,000 spearheads would have killed, cut or maimed.

The psychological effect would have been equally staggering. The over-confident British advance faltered. Then the Romans set to work, years of training kicking in as the legions charged in to engage the stunned enemy at close quarters. They moved down the hill in wedge-formation, breaking up the shape of the British line.

This was butchers' work. As General Suetonius had said, don't bother to try and kill the bloke in front of you, just smash him in the face with your metal shield boss and let your mate, standing on your left, do the dirty work with his *gladius*, the short but razor-sharp stabbing sword that had won Rome the known world. Punch and stab, move over the bodies, and punch and stab again. The heavily armoured troops moving steadily down the hill into the diminishing British forces. This was the Roman killing-machine at its most efficient. Even outnumbered ten-to-one there was no contest.

Tacitus's terse description rings more true than Dio Cassius's romantic picture of Celtic chariots running to and fro. This is surely based on generalized stories of Celtic warfare. Suetonius's plan meant there was simply no room for Boudica's chariots to operate efficiently, whether they had knives on their wheels or not.

Hemmed in by their own superior numbers and moving steadily backwards, the

British were helpless. They had no room to practise their agile skills with the sword, darting, thrusting and parrying. Instead the Iceni were herded like the horses they handled back home. Shields and *gladii* guided them remorselessly back towards their own baggage train and the horrified British onlookers.

As the bloody mêlée edged back down on to the flat ground, the Roman cavalry moved round to stop the British flanks regaining shape or means of escape. Inexorably Boudica's thousands were pushed back over the River Anker and into the waiting semi-circle of carts.

Normally, the Roman army didn't deal in mass slaughter. Healthy, defeated colonials had too great a value as slaves to make revenge killing worthwhile. But recent centuries have given us many examples of normally disciplined troops who have become possessed by blood-madness through a mixture of fear, fury and adrenaline. Suetonius's men would have had hours before the battle to contemplate their fate if they lost. Now that their lives were assured, they could take revenge for friends and old comrades in Colchester and London.

The killing didn't stop with the soldiers. The watching women, children, elderly and infirm also fell to the encircling ring of swords. Not even the baggage animals were spared. Tacitus says that 80,000 Britons died. If the figure is correct, this was the greatest number of Britons to die in battle in a single day until the mechanized slaughter of the First World War. Roman casualties totalled 400 dead and the same number injured.

But what happened to Boudica?

Tacitus says she poisoned herself – presumably because she saw the cause was lost. Dio Cassius, writing much later, writes that she sickened and died and was buried with great honours. If she managed to escape the slaughter, this may be true. Historians have pointed out that having already suffered such profound humiliation, she would probably not have allowed herself or her daughters to fall into Roman hands again. But both scenarios are much less plausible than another simple answer: Boudica was one of the pile of nameless corpses left after the Romans' blood-lust abated.

Probably not even the British could tell which of their dead was the great tribal chief of the Iceni. Nevertheless, for centuries there's been intense competition to find her burial place.

Most romantic is the notion that took hold in the seventeenth century that she was laid to rest at Stonehenge. Equally charming in a different way is to think of her lying underneath King's Cross Station, although Liverpool Street with its regular service to East Anglia might be more appropriate. Hampstead Heath, Parliament Hill and Waltham Abbey (which also boasts King Harold's grave) also have their supporters. And there's a promising mound in Quidenham in Boudica's homeland of Norfolk known as The Bubberies. But some archaeologists think that the quest itself is misplaced. Ancient British funeral rites seemed to have involved excarnation: in other words bodies were left outside for the air and the birds until the flesh had disappeared, and then the bones were deposited elsewhere. Maybe there's no burial place to find.

BOUDICA

While you are at Mancetter, it would be well worth travelling a little further south to see the reconstruction of a Roman fort at Lunt just outside Coventry. From Mancetter/Atherstone, head back down the A5 and take the M69 south to Coventry, then take the A46 south following signs first for Birmingham. This is the Coventry ring road. At one big roundabout it merges with the A45. Don't be fazed. Take the A45 for Birmingham and watch out for signs for Warwick. Take the A46 for Warwick and as soon as you've joined it look for the tourist information signs telling you to leave it again. Lunt Roman fort is in the village of Baginton just south of the A45 and east of the A46 south for Warwick.

There were Roman victims too. Were their true military losses understated? Certainly 7,000 reinforcements were brought in from Germany after the revolt, and Poenius Postumus, the man who'd robbed his troops of a chance to share in the glory, committed suicide by stabbing himself.

AFTER BOUDICA

But it was the British in general, and the Iceni in particular, who bore the brunt of the Roman backlash.

The fort at Lunt has been reconstructed on the original site, and is just as it would have looked in AD 61. Following the Boudican uprising, it became a supply base for the systematic campaign of suppression that Suetonius ordered to deal with the unruly Britons, one of many such forts established all over East Anglia. In AD 63 a large *gyras* was constructed. This circular arena for breaking horses seems to have been purpose-built to deal with the livestock taken to punish the Iceni.

Some tribes carried on the fight, but it was a hopeless cause. Tacitus says they were ravaged by fire and sword, but that their worst problem was a famine caused by hyper-optimism. They'd been so sure they were going to throw out the Romans and take their grain, they didn't bother to plant a crop of their own in AD 60. Rubbish, say contemporary historians. No self-respecting Celt would have abandoned the practice of time immemorial. There would never have been enough Roman grain to go round anyway. If there was starvation it was because Suetonius was practising ethnic cleansing by burning crops.

A testament to the Roman campaign against the Iceni is to be found in the many hoards of treasure – mostly coinage – that have been dug up from the period. These are probably the personal fortunes of people on the run from Roman rough justice who never lived to reclaim them. One of the most spectacular of these is from Hockwold-cum-Wilton in Norfolk. It consists of Roman silver wine vessels. They'd been battered into silver scrap metal and were probably destined to become Celtic silverware, but adroit restorers at the British Museum have brought them back to their original condition.

Peace of a kind eventually broke out. Nero appointed a new governor, called Publius Petronius Turpilius, who stopped the war. But peace wasn't necessarily the end of repression. The great new forts at Great Chesterford, Pakenham, Coddenham, Worthing, Horstead and Caistor St Edmund kept the population in check. The tribes were subject to transportation and slavery. The Romans saw to it that the boggy lands of the horse-loving Iceni were drained with the help of slave labour, and used for more 'civilized' agriculture.

Historians have calculated that it would have taken centuries before the Iceni population recovered from the total loss of a generation of menfolk. Meanwhile the tribe slipped into the backwater of history.

The late-Iceni reservation of Caistor is just off the Norwich bypass. You can still see its walls buried beneath the earth accretions of sixteen hundred years. From Norwich, travel from the city centre to the A47 bypass. On the A47 you're looking for the junction with the A140 south. At this junction take the minor road east to Caistor St. Edmund.

Like the North American Plains Indians, the Iceni were given a 'civilized' reservation by the Romans, a new capital at Caistor St Edmund which is also known as Caistor-by-Norwich. The Romans called it *Venta Icenorum*, the Market of the Iceni. There were kilns here supplying pottery to the soldiers and a century later a forum and basilica were built. But the Iceni weren't town dwellers. They didn't want a Romanized lifestyle. They'd never had any use for urban settlements. Caistor remained tiny by Roman standards and half empty.

The ruins are melancholic. Caistor is the last stubborn testament to the spirit of the Iceni who, unlike the southern tribes or the Catuvellauni, were willing to go to their graves believing that their rural Celtic life was worth laying down their lives for.

Could Boudica have prevented the occupation? Might she have succeeded in throwing out the Romans? It's an academic but fascinating question. Her revolt was not as widespread as the shocked Roman annalists might have us believe. The British tribes suffered from tribal rivalries that had been deeply imbedded in their culture for hundreds of years. As in Afghanistan today, a coherent response to the Roman threat was just not possible. The southern tribes were resolutely pro-Roman, and Cartimandua, the other female ruler of the Brigantes in the north, had already handed over the rebel leader Caratacus to the authorities.

But success breeds success and, had Boudica adopted a different strategy and caught Suetonius on the hop with a series of guerrilla raids, there's no doubt that she would have picked up more support. If she'd won the military battle and caused Suetonius to retreat, there is just the outside chance that Rome might have decided not to waste more money on a third invasion of the godforsaken island on the edge of the world. It would have been the second time in a hundred years that a Roman invasion of Britain had failed and the empire might have cut her losses and re-established her border safely on the far side of the Channel.

BOUDICA IN HISTORY

And what of Boudica herself? Like the Iceni and the ruins of Caistor St Edmund, her myth lay dormant. Her history was only preserved, ironically, in the writings of the enemy, perpetuated by the male clerics of a religion inimical to Celtic Druidism and fearful of the power of women.

Her story was resurrected over a thousand years later. Not until the time of Elizabeth I did people begin to remember that another great British woman had once fought foreign invaders. And as we've already seen, her place in history was assured in the Victorian age when she became part of nineteenth-century imperial myth.

Boudica is the perfect example of the strange dichotomy that's grown up over the centuries about powerful women. A woman in charge was the Romans' worst nightmare, a

When Margaret
Thatcher cut a
swathe through
male-dominated
politics, cartoonists
couldn't resist
the parallel.

"A woman leader! Hee, hee, hee, is she serious?"

chaotic upturning of the social order. Later generations have underlined that fear by adding castrating scythes to her chariot. She's a figure who Western society, informed by Latin Church values and later by imperial ideology, finds it difficult to deal with. In order to approach such a woman we've made her a caricature, not a living, breathing woman. She's almost a figure of fun. She's summoned whenever we want to characterize but pillory a threatening woman like Margaret Thatcher.

But the desire to make Boudica something other than human is mistaken. There's no doubt she was charismatic, but even in the skewed Roman accounts she never pretends to be anything more than the bruised and humiliated woman she was. There were no scythes, no magic ingredient, she was simply the leader of an obscure tribe who was thrust into the international limelight. And yet she came close to defeating the most successful fighting machine the world has ever seen.

Two thousand years later we're perhaps the first generation who can begin to look at her achievements with an admiration that isn't tinged with fear and hostility.

But she's not the only victim of history's need to demonize and mythologize extraordinary women. In the next chapter we meet someone who's become the epitome of cold-blooded manipulation: Lady Macbeth.

FURTHER INFORMATION

Tacitus, *The Annals of Imperial Rome* and *Agricola*, available in Penguin Classics: the closest to a first-hand account.

Dio Cassius, *Roman History*: don't buy the books, which will cost a fortune. The Epitome of Book LXII is available in a good translation on the Internet at http://www.ku.edu/history/index/europe/ancient_rome/E/Roman/Texts/Cassius_Dio

Julius Caesar, *Seven Commentaries on the Gallic War* (Oxford University Press, 1996) – Caesar's spin on his own unsuccessful invasion.

Paul R. Sealey, *The Boudican Revolt against Rome* (Shire Archaeology, 1997) a good, brief account of Boudica's revolt with the supporting archaeology.

Antonia Fraser, *The Warrior Queens* (Weidenfeld & Nicolson, 1994 – first published in 1988 as *Boadicea's Chariot)* a brilliant, imaginative telling of Boudica's story, set in the context of other great women in history.

Michael Wood, *In Search of the Dark Ages* (BBC Books, 1981) another good compilation (which also has the story of King Harold).

Stewart Ross, *Down with the Romans* (Evans Brothers Ltd, 1996) a good introduction for children.

Philip Crummy, *City of Victory: the story of Colchester Britain's first Roman Town* (Colchester Archaeological Trust, 1997) not the catchiest title, but a fascinating account of the city with a colourful treatment of the Boudican revolt.

Miranda J. Green, *Exploring the World of the Druids* (Thames & Hudson, 1997) a comprehensive guide to the world of the Druids from prehistoric times to the modern day.

Ordnance Survey maps: I've used the 1:50 000 Landranger series. I'm not including every map you could buy as you could spend a fortune. But you might like to obtain map numbers 144 and 168 East Anglia and Colchester, 166 St Albans and 140 for Mancetter.

You can also track down Boudica's world in several very good museums. The British Museum has hogged a lot of the big finds from the period – coins, Iceni jewellery, the head of Claudius, etc. – but if you're in the area call in at:

Norwich Castle Museum and Art Gallery, with a gallery devoted to Boudica and the Iceni. At Castle Meadow, Norwich NR1 3JU. General enquiries: 01603 493625; recorded information: 01603 493648.

Colchester Museum, Castle Park, Colchester, through which you can also visit the vaults of the Temple of Claudius, but only if you join a guided tour in the museum. Check opening times on 01206 282932.

Lunt Roman Fort, Baginton, Coventry, West Midlands CV1 5RN. Tel: 02476 303567.

Verulamium Roman Museum, St Michael's, St Albans, Hertfordshire AL3 4SW. Tel: 01727 751810.

CHAPTER 2
MACBETH

The sites associated with Macbeth offer a perfect tour of the central Highlands. The distances involved are long, so allow plenty of time, and remember not to try it in winter when roads may be closed.

Shakespeare has given us one of the top villains of all time. Macbeth is up there with Dracula, Faust, Darth Vader and Hannibal Lecter. The only difference is that they're characters out of fiction, but Macbeth was a real human being. He was King of the Scots from AD 1040 to 1057, and his stamping ground was the Scottish Highlands. This comes as a surprise to a lot of people, including many Scots.

It's not easy to get a clear picture of the real Macbeth. There are only seven references to him from his own time, and virtually no archaeological evidence. To make matters worse, succeeding accounts become increasingly embellished and distorted, culminating in Shakespeare's great play. It's clear from the outset that there are fundamental differences between the fictional drama and the real-life narrative. But we shouldn't blame Shakespeare too much for that. He was writing nearly 550 years after Macbeth died. We're still not 400 years from Shakespeare's death, and our historians, with all the benefits of modern scholarship, can say very little about the life of our greatest playwright. So it's hardly surprising that the real Macbeth seemed a little shadowy to Shakespeare.

Shakespeare wrote his play in 1606. He based it on the historical chronicles of Raphael Holinshed, who was writing in 1577. Holinshed in turn used earlier medieval chronicles, and the story of Macbeth changed radically through this series of historical Chinese whispers. In addition Shakespeare had his own axe to grind, and wanted to change the character for his own reasons. Nevertheless, Shakespeare's character is so

imprinted on our brains that it is him we tend to see as we approach the real Macbeth. One simple example makes clear how misguided an approach this is.

Shakespeare doesn't tell us what our Scottish King might have looked like. He only draws the character psychologically. Yet there are literally hundreds of actors who have played the Scottish King, and most of them have ended up looking pretty much the same. They have a dark, brooding intensity, black hair, thunderous eyebrows and sallow skin. They come floating to the surface of the mind as one swirling grainy black-and-white publicity still.

But amazingly, in one of the few fragments from Macbeth's own time, we get a description of what he really looked like, and it paints a very different picture.

The *Prophecy of Berchan* is a poem that was probably recited in the presence of Macbeth himself. It isn't really a prophecy at all in that it was never meant as a Mystic Meg-style prediction. It's an Irish poem that is actually a collection of works by different bards telling the story of various kings. The three stanzas about Macbeth are what is known as a 'praise poem'; they start off by recounting sagas and stories from history, and then flatter the King

The Mounth and Central Highlands showing the extent of Moray in Macbeth's time.

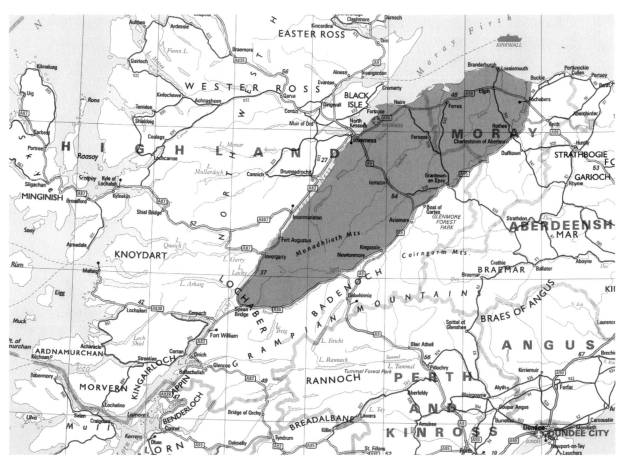

54

Lady Macbeth
(Hilda Britton)
goads her husband
(Matheson Lang) on
to murder most foul.

with events that may well take place during the rest of his reign. Such poems were commissioned by great lords and were sung or recited by bards at feasts in the lord's hall. That's why this one is composed in Middle Irish rather than ecclesiastical Latin. We think it dates from Macbeth's day because the *Prophecy* starts off being quite strong historically, but, when it gets to the time of Macbeth, it peters out and the battles described are unhistorical.

If the poem was recited while Macbeth was sitting in his great hall with his warriors, the future would have had to be a happy-ever-after fantasy. The bard who composed it would have been in the pay of the King and obviously wouldn't have wanted to risk his neck by describing his paymaster in unflattering terms. Nevertheless, his candour confounded all my preconceptions. Macbeth is described as the 'furious red one'. He's also called the 'red king' and 'the red, tall, golden-haired one'. In other words, he was a big chap with a ruddy complexion, and had flowing fair hair. The implication is also that this 'furious' warrior was a man of action with a short fuse, deadly in battle, but perhaps not much given to introspection. In casting terms we're looking at a character more like Gérard Depardieu than Laurence Olivier.

Maybe we shouldn't be surprised to be confronted by a big archetypal Scottish warrior with a ruddy face and temper to match, but Shakespeare's image of the nail-biting political assassin has sunk so deep into our mental landscape that it can be difficult to adjust to new evidence. Nevertheless, that's what we'll try to do. First, though, let's take a look at the opening of Shakespeare's masterpiece.

MACBETH – ACT I

The play begins on a 'blasted heath'. Mist swirls, lightning flashes, the whole place is a haunt of witches who cackle and chant. Into this spooky world come Macbeth and his companion Banquo. They're on their way to Forres to meet King Duncan.

Macbeth has just covered himself in glory, fighting and defeating the King of Norway on behalf of his King. Suddenly, three hideous hags appear and screech a prophecy at him.

All hail, Macbeth! Hail to thee, Thane of Glamis!
All hail, Macbeth! Hail to thee, Thane of Cawdor!
All hail, Macbeth! that shalt be king hereafter!

Macbeth doesn't know what to make of it. He's already Thane of Glamis, but what about these other titles? Just as Banquo is advising him to beware of the prophecy as the work of the devil, a messenger arrives and tells Macbeth that the King has made him the Thane of Cawdor for his bravery. So the second part of the prophecy has come true. Does that mean that the last part might too? It starts to give Macbeth big ideas.

MACBETH

Nobody can deny that it's a barnstorming start to a play, so it will come as no surprise to discover that soon after it was first performed people wanted to see where these events took place.

Macbeth's Hillock, which has been designated the official location of the blasted heath, is actually more of a bump. It's in a little field and isn't accessible to the public unless you ask the farmer. Anyone wanting to make the journey can tiptoe gingerly past grass tussocks, gorse and cowpats, and will be rewarded by a view of a not-very-blasted heath and a lot of traffic on the way to or from Inverness. Notable visitors such as Dr Johnson, James Boswell and the actress Ellen Terry made their way here in the eighteenth and nineteenth centuries to see where Macbeth was confronted by the three ghastly hags. Unfortunately, there's no evidence whatsoever that the hillock has any connection with Macbeth at all.

Macbeth's Hillock is about a quarter of a mile to the North of the A96 at Easter Hardmuir on the road to Forres, which is the road that Macbeth is travelling at the beginning of the play.

This little mound is the tiny tip of a mythological iceberg that the Scots have built up over centuries to celebrate their history, tying any possible castle, field or megalith to Macbeth and other Scottish heroes (as well as bringing in the odd groat).

This mythology was further complicated by Shakespeare who, as far as we know, never visited Scotland in his life, and unintentionally led people up the garden path by ascribing names and titles to people that make no sense. For instance, in the play Macbeth is given the title Thane of Cawdor for services rendered. Cawdor is twenty minutes down the road from Macbeth's Hillock.

Today it's a pretty little village of stone houses with brightly painted doors clustered round a post office and a pub (the Cawdor Arms) and a beautifully preserved fantasy of a medieval castle complete with fairy-tale turrets. But no part of the building dates back to Macbeth's time, and none of the early records associates Macbeth with the settlement. The first recorded Thane of Cawdor crops up in 1295. Shakespeare heard about Cawdor through much later traditions. Nevertheless, once the play had made the village famous, proud residents couldn't resist the lure of going along with the story and including themselves on the burgeoning new tourist trail.

To get to Cawdor, (Macbeth's alleged home) from Macbeth's Hillock (the alleged blasted heath) head back towards Nairn on the A96 and turn off left at Auldearn on to the B9101, which becomes the B9090 after about four miles. Cawdor is another three miles on.

The real Macbeth was a lord in the Forres area, but he was never Thane of either Glamis or Cawdor. A thane (thegn) was a local minor bureaucrat, administering an estate for the king. It was the most common rank in Scotland at the time. Macbeth was the Mormaer of Moray, a much more important title. Mormaers were earls of a province. They held their lands by right and inheritance. They were part of the kingship group, a sort of extended royal family from which the king himself was chosen.

Eleventh-century Scotland was divided into several different mormaerships (see the map on page 156), but none was more powerful than that of Moray. To give you some idea of how Macbeth would have been seen, it's worth noting that the Irish chroniclers, who didn't have a direct equivalent of a mormaer, refer to the Mormaer of Moray as 'the King of Scots' or 'the King of Moray'. So making Macbeth Thane of Cawdor was about as flattering as calling a cabinet minister a local councillor.

But how did he arrive at his exalted position?

MACBETH'S BOYHOOD

We don't know for sure when Macbeth was born, but it was about a millennium ago, some time around 1005. He was the son of Findlaech Mac Ruaridh (Finlay Mac Rory), the Mormaer of Moray. (In the play, Shakespeare follows Holinshed in calling Macbeth's father 'Sinel'. Finel is a rough transliteration of Findlaech and the 'S' crept in because of a confusion with the old-fashioned 'f's in ancient manufcripts.) His mother isn't mentioned in the earliest manuscripts, but it seems likely that she was a relative of Malcolm II, the King of Scots.

It's assumed that he was born in his homeland of Moray. As we've seen, those with money and power had a more peripatetic life in early medieval times, and it's likely he would have spent his early years moving between the great halls of his home territory.

The modern district of Moray is a rough triangle, with the valley of the Findhorn to the west and the Spey to the east. It's the mountains, forests and rivers of this ancient area that would have been Macbeth's childhood haunts.

Medieval Moray was much bigger. At one stage it stretched from the west coast of Scotland all the way to the east coast. The Mormaer of Moray was, in effect, the ruler of a mini-kingdom north of the Mounth (the traditional word taken from the Gaelic that historians still use for the Grampian mountains).

These mountains provided natural protection for Moray, but they didn't guarantee stability. As you can see from the map, eleventh-century Britain was divided into several of these mini-kingdoms under the overlordship of the King of England and the King of Scotland. The boundaries were fluid and subject to abrupt change due to various alliances, advantageous marriages, political manoeuvrings and so on.

In general, the Kings of the Scots were happy to let the Mormaers of Moray go their own way. The main threat to their power wasn't from Moray but from the power blocs of Cumbria and Northumbria, which controlled much of what's now Strathclyde and lowland Scotland. The men of Moray still swore allegiance to the King of Scots. He could call on them in times of crisis to come and fight. But most of all he relied on them to be the northern buffer against another powerful and successful political force, the Orkney Vikings, who controlled much of Caithness as well as Shetland and Orkney.

Being Mormaer of Moray wasn't a job for the faint-hearted. In the lists written by contemporary monks in which the mormaers appear, a sinister little phrase keeps cropping up at the end of their time in office: *A suis occisus est*. It means 'killed by his own people', that is, members of his own family. In 1020, Macbeth's father, Findlaech, fell prey to this occu-

To get an almost aerial view of Macbeth's territory of Moray, visit Spynie Palace, by taking the A941 north out of Elgin. Spynie Palace is an Historic Scotland site that's open to the public and is clearly signposted after three miles. Climb the tower there and – on a clear day – you'll get a 360 degree view of the area.

pational hazard. Macbeth's cousins, Malcolm and Gillacomgain, assassinated him and assumed the mormaership for themselves (Malcolm held the office until 1029 and then Gillacomgain took over).

Such 'cousin killings' were the result of the Celtic system of inheritance. Instead of primogeniture – direct inheritance by blood through the eldest son – the Scots employed a sort of zigzag path through the family line. This was known as tanistry.

TANISTRY

Tanistry is essentially inheritance through nomination within the wider family group. There was no automatic contender for a position within the upper echelons of nobility. Instead, an aristocrat would nominate a tanaise, a successor, usually a cousin or someone from outside his immediate family, in the hope that, when his own sons came to maturity, they would be eligible for titles in return.

As we will see when Macbeth seized the throne, this ancient system of inheritance could create a great deal of confusion about who should actually inherit after the death of a ruler. Nominating a tanaise didn't guarantee that they would be given the throne if there was another, stronger contender who could take it by force.

In the Celtic system's favour, it meant that, in an age when strong leadership by an active warlord was essential, the succession was passed from adult to adult rather than leaving infants in charge. It also avoided the infanticide that direct inheritance often generated. On the debit side, tanistry led to cousin killing. Up-and-coming warriors with half a claim to a title not only caused trouble by removing other contenders to the throne, but also got impatient and grabbed power by force rather than waiting their turn.

It was also less clear-cut than primogeniture. A look at the line of the Kings of Scots (see the table on page 73) shows how complicated it could be. Inheritance through the first-born has the advantage of clarity, although when there was no heir, dangerous chaos could ensue.

Macbeth would have been in his early teens when his father was killed. His own claim to be mormaer was now a threat to the other candidates, especially to his second cousin, Gillacomgain. So it seems that Macbeth fled Moray and was given shelter in the royal court of Malcolm II. He would have expected to spend time at court anyway. He was part of the wider royal family and Malcolm II may well have been his grandfather through his mother's line. The royal court would have been a political finishing school for any aspiring eleventh-century nobleman.

Macbeth's life at court, in exile from Moray, would have been spent in acquiring the skills necessary for an aristocrat of the time. He would have been trained in fighting and weaponry. Andrew of Wyntoun, writing in about 1420, describes Macbeth going hunting with greyhounds. He would also have had an education in medieval Latin. We know he soon became a political asset to Malcolm II because, in 1031, while he was still in his mid-twenties, we catch a glimpse of him working on Malcolm's behalf on the political stage.

Every child learns about King Cnut who tried to stop the waves advancing up the beach, and it's tempting to think of him as a mythic old dodderer. In fact he was a major figure in eleventh-century politics. He was a Viking who'd removed the Anglo-Saxon monarchy in England and established an empire that encompassed both England and Denmark. (We'll also be running across him in the next chapter as patron of the wily Earl Godwin.) In spite of controlling such a vast swathe of territory, he was always looking to expand his borders. In 1031, he invaded Scotland and received the submission of Malcolm, although the chronicles note that this surrender was soon retracted. Two other 'kings' or rulers of Scotland are named at this momentous political event, Macbeth and a man called Iehmarc, who was probably the Lord of the Isles. Macbeth was clearly Malcolm's emissary and a major player on the Scottish stage even before he became Mormaer of Moray the following year.

In 1032, the real Macbeth appears to have committed an act as bloodthirsty as the deeds of his theatrical counterpart. The chronicles report that Gillacomgain, one of the cousins who was responsible for killing Macbeth's father and who had become Mormaer of Moray after his brother's death, was 'burnt to death along with fifty of his men'. At this time in Scotland battles were often little more than skirmishes and the numbers of men involved were quite small. Besieging a castle or fortified hall, shutting up a warlord and his men inside and then torching it was a regular occurrence. Even churches weren't necessarily places of sanctuary. If they were made of wood they could become a handy funeral pyre. While the records don't name Macbeth as the guilty party, he was the beneficiary in two very obvious ways. We know he became Mormaer of Moray after Gillacomgain, and also he married Gillacomgain's widow, the Lady Gruoch, the woman who was later turned by Shakespeare into Lady Macbeth.

To a twenty-first-century eye this seems extremely strange. What would make a woman whose husband had just been roasted alive want to marry the man who ordered the killing? But, as the singer Tina Turner so sagely asks, 'What's love got to do with it?' Gruoch was an eleventh-century woman. In those days marriage was often a matter of political expediency. Sentiment was in short supply.

Gruoch was of the royal blood line herself. Her grandfather was Kenneth III, the King of Scots immediately prior to Malcolm II, so her descendants had a claim to the kingship too. What she needed was a husband who was going to be able to protect her and give her offspring the chance of political success. Macbeth, as someone with an excellent pedigree himself, was just as suitable as Gillacomgain. The fact that Macbeth also adopted her son Lulach as his own shows that there was an implicit deal being struck with the remarriage.

MACBETH

If Gruoch got security in an unstable and violent age, Macbeth benefited too. A marriage to Gruoch was yet another reason for Macbeth to be named as the tanaise when the next King of Scots was selected.

So, by the time Macbeth was in his mid-twenties, the fair-haired young turk had already seen his father slaughtered, had fled in fear of assassination, and had apparently killed a group of fifty warriors in his quest for power.

The battle that Macbeth is involved in at the beginning of the play is against Sueno, the King of Norway. Macbeth meets King Duncan in Forres to receive his reward for valour. In the eighteenth century a monumental Celtic stone that had lain hidden for centuries was discovered at Forres. It depicted a battle and its aftermath. Is it any wonder that people assumed it had been erected to celebrate the victory over Sueno?

The stone was protected for centuries, lying in a field on its side. But it's been standing since 1726 and the face is now severely weathered. Fortunately, it's recently been given its own giant bus shelter to protect it from the elements.

It's a piece of sandstone six metres high. On one side is an intricately carved Celtic cross. On the reverse there is a series of tableaux telling the story of the defeat of an army in battle. Scholarly opinion now dates it a couple of centuries before Macbeth. But it's still known as Sueno's Stone. There are various theories about what battle it depicts. It seems most likely that it shows not Vikings and Scots, but the defeat of the men of Moray by the southern Scots. The point of the stone was to warn the people of Moray against causing trouble (a warning ignored by Macbeth).

While it's another false lead in that it doesn't give a cartoon representation of Macbeth in action, it's valuable in a cultural sense. There are bodies floating under bridges and prisoners of war being summarily beheaded. It depicts the brutality of a culture that would still have existed in Macbeth's time.

In Shakespeare's play we learn nothing about Macbeth's life before he made his bid for the throne. In comparison we know a great deal about his young factual counterpart. Above all, the picture that emerges is of an age where violence and warfare aren't occasional events but a constant fact of life. And it was the lessons learnt from this upbringing that Macbeth brought to his bid for the throne.

To get a good idea of the brutality of Macbeth's age, it's worth taking a trip to see Sueno's Stone. To get there, you push on eastwards from Macbeth's Hillock on the A96, and, as you skirt Forres, you come across one of the most impressive Celtic monuments in Scotland. Heading from Forres to Elgin, you'll glimpse it on your right-hand side just before a roundabout. If you take the third exit here and head back on yourself, Sueno's Stone is in a cul-de-sac on your right where you can park safely.

MACBETH – ACT II

After the battle, Macbeth meets up with Duncan, the epitome of the gracious king. He congratulates Macbeth on his military success but then reveals that he is going to make his own son, Malcolm, king after him which, as far as Macbeth's ambitions are concerned, is a bit of a stumbling block. But he gets a horrifying window of opportunity when the King announces he is coming to stay with the new Thane of Cawdor and his wife.

61

Sueno's Stone and a close up of the battle scene. The second row down shows standing figures by a tent or building. At their feet are heads from decapitated prisoners. The headless corpses are displayed vertically on the left hand side. This photo was taken before the stone was severely weathered.

Macbeth hurries home to make preparations for a desperate murder plot. Egged on by Lady Macbeth, who sneers at him for being lily-livered, he slaughters Duncan in his bed then pins the blame on Duncan's servants, whom he swiftly executes. Sensing danger, Duncan's sons, Malcolm and Donalbaine, flee to England and Macbeth immediately accuses them of being behind the murder. But Macbeth's friends, Macduff and Banquo, aren't quite so sure. They know about the witches' prophecy and suspect that the finger of blame points fairly and squarely at Macbeth, who's already sped off to Scone to be acclaimed king.

Macbeth's early years have no parallel within Shakespeare's story, but we now get echoes of real history in the narrative.

First there's the battle which immediately precedes the play's dramatic opening and which provides the reason for Duncan to make Macbeth the Thane of Cawdor. Shakespeare portrays it as a great defeat for the King of Norway, thanks to the prowess of Macbeth.

In reality the battle was rather different. By 1034 the King of Scots was Malcolm II's grandson Duncan. Malcolm had nominated him in defiance of the tanistric tradition that the throne should go to another side of the family. As we'll see, this caused huge resentment within Scotland. But Duncan had a more immediate problem – the Vikings.

The Scots were fighting a defensive battle against Viking incursion and Macbeth was Duncan's right-hand man protecting the shores of the north. Duncan would have wanted to keep him at arm's length because the people of Moray had a reputation for causing trouble. Nevertheless, he was a useful ally leading the fight against one of the most powerful warlords of the region, Thorfinn the Mighty.

Thorfinn (pronounced Torfin) was Earl of Orkney. On his mother's side he was another grandson of Malcolm II, so Duncan and Macbeth were his cousins. But, as we've seen so many times before, cousins weren't necessarily the best of friends, especially when power, land and money were at stake. Malcolm II had granted Thorfinn the lands of Caithness, possibly to bolster his grandson's position of power in the Orkney Viking pecking order. But when Malcolm died, the Scots tried to reassert control over the Viking-held territory. The resulting skirmishes and final battle echo the story of Shakespeare's Macbeth with one vital difference. The *Orkneyinga Saga*, which records this episode, makes clear that the end result wasn't a victory, but a crushing defeat for the Scots, and in particular for their leader.

And there's a big problem about who this was. The saga refers to the Scottish leader not as Macbeth, but by the mysterious name of Karl Hundason.

The *Orkneyinga Saga* is a collection of the oral traditions of the Viking bards or skalds who composed poems in praise of their lords. They tell the story of the great Viking earls, or jarls, but, in doing so, they incidentally mention many characters from all over the

British Isles and are a valuable historical source. But the bards were remote geographically from the events they relate and so many details are garbled.

The sagas dealing with Thorfinn were composed by Arnor Thordasson, who had Thorfinn as his patron. In an age where so much was transient, to have your own saga was the metrical equivalent of having van Dyck or Gainsborough paint your portrait in all your finery. It was a marker for posterity, to be learnt and repeated throughout the ages. In Thorfinn's case, it worked.

The writer is telling Thorfinn's story, and he isn't too bothered about the accuracy of the peripheral characters, of whom Karl is one. He names all the Scottish kings of the age except Duncan and Macbeth, so it seems probable that Karl is either Duncan or Macbeth or some sort of amalgam of the two. There are telling arguments for and against both candidates. The writer states that Karl became King after Malcolm, which seems to favour Malcolm's son Duncan, but then again the saga confuses Findlaech, Macbeth's father, with an earl called Hundi. This would make Hundi's son (that is, Hundeson), Macbeth. But, if this is the case, why did Karl Hundeson change his name to Macbeth? Later in this chapter I'll try to provide a plausible answer.

For the moment, given that it's highly unlikely that Duncan would have got into a fight in the north without enlisting the services of Macbeth as his general, I'm going to dismiss Duncan's claim and that of the mysterious Karl, and assume that it was Macbeth who led the fight against Thorfinn.

According to the saga, these are the events that led to his defeat. In order to try and regain control of the very north of Scotland, the Scots appointed a man called Muddan as Earl of Caithness. Thorfinn, who saw Caithness as his own, refused to pay tribute. Muddan marched into Caithness with a warband to exact payment and promptly retreated again when faced down by a horde of Thorfinn's Vikings.

In retribution for this abortive move, Thorfinn secured not only Caithness but also Ross and Sutherland, in other words all of the very top bit of Scotland north of Inverness. He stationed himself in Caithness with five longships (each of these would have contained about seventy to ninety warriors, which gives some sense of the scale of these battles), but then sailed back towards his headquarters at Deerness in Orkney, just as Macbeth was sailing north with eleven ships of his own. His fleet passed so close to Thorfinn that his men could see the sails of the Viking ships.

The Scots took the Vikings by surprise and launched an attack at sea. In the days before cannon, this was a case of close-quarter action, locking the ships together with grappling irons and swarming on to the strangers' deck in desperate hand-to-hand fighting. With odds of two to one against him (allowing for some heroic exaggeration), Thorfinn urged the Vikings on to a bloody victory. The poet speaks of the bows spilling blood, presumably washed through the gunwales, and of iron stained black with the caked blood of

the Scots. Macbeth himself escaped with his life, although his flagship was lost and he received a ducking in the icy North Sea.

After this, both sides reinforced. Thorfinn's foster-father, Thorkel, was despatched to kill Muddan in Thurso. Macbeth assembled a force from all over Scotland bolstered with troops from Ireland and went to meet the combined forces of Thorfinn and Thorkel at Torfnes, now identified as Tarbat Ness on the north coast of the Moray Firth.

This would have been a much bigger battle, a thousand perhaps on each side. According to the saga, it was less a battle than a rout. Thorfinn in his golden helmet carried the day and then went on to wreak revenge, plundering Scotland as far south as the Forth.

Tarbat Ness today is still pretty remote – or, rather, it's pretty and remote. It's right on the tip of a peninsula stretching out into the North Sea north of the Moray Firth about an hour north of Inverness, but well worth the pretty drive. The road's a coastal route along the Cromarty Firth, which today is studded with oil platforms rather than Viking longships, but there's still a chance that you'll see dolphins playing in the water and seals basking on the mud.

The eleventh century is an archaeological vacuum in Scotland. There's been an enormous amount of work done on the Pictish period up to the ninth century when Scotland was united, and there are plenty of artefacts from a little later in the medieval age. But Macbeth's era has been neglected. Indeed, the Museum of Scotland boasts only one solitary eleventh-century artefact. But at Tarbat Ness, there's been an incidental archaeological find that seems to back up this part of our story. To the south and east of the village chapel there was once a vast Pictish monastery which a team of archaeologists have been investigating and uncovering. The chapel has now been converted into the Tarbat Discovery Centre, so you can see the finds for yourself.

While looking in a trench just to the side of the Discovery Centre car park, the archaeologists discovered evidence that the Pictish buildings had been burnt, possibly some time in the eleventh century. There's no stone engraved with the words 'Thorfinn woz 'ere', but this burning certainly fits with the notion of a succession of Viking reprisal raids around the time of the Battle of Torfnes.

So while Shakespeare's anti-hero won the battle and was rewarded by the doting King Duncan, the real Macbeth seems likely to have been heavily defeated and almost drowned. We can only imagine the reaction of his King.

But just as the Viking sagas portray the battle as bloody, we now come to one of the most horrific episodes in British literature: the subsequent murder of the King.

THE DEATH OF DUNCAN

Shakespeare portrays Duncan as a venerable and beloved ruler. His murder in Macbeth's own house is an affront not only to human decency, but also to the natural order of

For Tarbat Ness, take the A9 from Inverness. Leave the A9 after Ballchraggan and follow signs for Portmahomack. When you get there, you'll find a harbour village in the lee of the North Sea facing north across the Dornoch Firth, and, just out of town, a lighthouse, right on the end of the promontory. This is Tarbat Ness. Tradition holds that the battle of Torfnes took place on the beach within sight of it.

things. Killing such a good and kind king sends the whole world out of kilter: 'The times are out of joint'.

But the historical facts are very different. Duncan was not a good king for Scotland. In an age where military prowess was a prime requirement for a king, Duncan was a bit of a duffer. It would certainly make sense were we to discover that the campaign against Thorfinn had been his idea. It fits with what else we know of his desire for military success and his dismal failure to get it.

For instance, in about 1039 he launched an attack on Durham. Why Durham? The town was too far into Northumbrian territory to be a feasible point for extending the Scottish southern border. It seems fair to assume he wanted to ransack it for the treasures of St Cuthbert, which even today are still on display at the cathedral. He might also have been trying to live up to the reputation of his predecessor – Malcolm II had scored a notable victory over the Northumbrians at Carham in 1018. But Duncan's attack was a disaster. He laid siege to a city which was well defended by the great loop of the River Wear; his supply lines were too stretched and the defenders put him to flight. The *Annals of Ulster* report that his footsoldiers were slaughtered and their heads collected for display on posts in the marketplace.

This fiasco provided Macbeth with the perfect opportunity to revolt against him. In 1040, the unfortunate King Duncan was forced to put on his sword again and head north into Moray. He never returned.

The great dictionary writer Dr Johnson and his pal Boswell, on their Scottish sightseeing tour in 1773, went to Inverness to see the castle where the play's dreadful act of regicide was committed. Boswell in particular rhapsodized over the atmosphere of the castle, spouting Shakespearean quotes about the raven croaking in the battlements. But they weren't only looking at a building of the wrong date, they were also on the wrong site. Even if Macbeth had owned a castle in Inverness, it would have been on the other (north-west) side of the river. There is a local tradition that Macbeth had a castle on Old Castle Hill on the other side of town to the existing castle. But no trace remains of any eleventh-century site anywhere in Inverness. In fact, even the castle that Dr Johnson and his faithful chum visited has gone. In its place today, you can see the neo-gothic buildings of yet another castle built in the nineteenth century on the same site as the eighteenth-century one visited by Johnson and Boswell

But the central issue isn't the location of Macbeth's castle. More important is the question: 'Where did the King's death actually take place?'

In fact Macbeth didn't murder Duncan in his bed – this is a fiction created by Shakespeare. He killed him on the battlefield. He was fatally wounded at Pitgaveny, just a couple of miles from the centre of Elgin.

This comes from an almost contemporary source, the picturesquely named Mael Brigte the Hermit. Mael Brigte is the Irish name of the historian Marianus Scotus. (The

Scotus here means not Scottish but Irish.) He was a pretty well-travelled hermit. We don't know why, but he was thrown out of the monastic centre of Moville in 1056. He went to the Continent and ended up at the monastery of St Martin in Mainz where he wrote his *Chronicon*, a chronicle of world history. He finished it in 1073. It became popular throughout Europe and was used as a source by many later chroniclers.

Mael Brigte states quite categorically that Duncan was killed *a duce suo* (by his warlord), Macbeth, at a place called Bothgafnane – the Hut of the Blacksmith – and a later historian, John of Fordun, adds that Duncan was mortally wounded in a skirmish then carried a couple of miles to Elgin Cathedral to die. Mael Brigte even gives the date, 14 August. Shakespeare, in the great tradition of the classical storytellers, took a completely different story, the murder of King Duff in 966, and grafted it on to the saga of Macbeth and Duncan, to add a bit of spice to the plot.

THE HUT OF THE BLACKSMITH

There's nothing much to see at Bothgafnane today. It's been identified as modern-day Pitgaveny which consists only of a house and grounds (not open to the public) and fields. No sign of a little blacksmith's bothy at the wayside. It needs a leap of the imagination to sense the violent clash of warbands, the breaking of the line of battle, the fatal wounding and the general slaughter of the footsoldiers that would have followed the defeat.

The ruins of Elgin Cathedral are far more haunting, although these are of a later date than Macbeth. In fact there's only a couple of church buildings from the eleventh century in the whole of Scotland. But you do get a sense of the monastic complex that would have stood on the site. In the eleventh century, monasteries such as Elgin were also administrative complexes, the closest thing Scotland had to cities. They were centres of learning and medicine. By carrying the wounded Duncan to Elgin, his men would have been taking him to the best medical help available, as well as getting him the last rites and the blessing of the Church.

But the local tradition that Duncan was buried at Elgin – restoration work in the eighteenth century suddenly revealed a long-hidden tomb – is almost certainly mistaken. After his death, Duncan would have been given the full honours owed to a Scottish monarch of the time. His body would have been transported overland to the West Coast, thence across the sea to the Isle of Mull and then on to Iona, the ancient shrine of St Columba and the burial place of the Kings of Scots and the Lords of the Isles.

So there was nothing clandestine about the killing of Duncan, and Mael Brigte the hermit shows no sign of surprise when he records it. Under the same system of tanistry which had given Macbeth the mormaership of Moray, he was now within his rights to remove the King when his reign became shaky. To understand why the real Macbeth killed Duncan, it's important to remember that Duncan should never have been King at all.

Pitgaveny, which is believed to be Macbeth's Bothgafnane, is just outside Elgin. You'll need a good Ordnance Survey map to find it. You have to head out of Elgin north-east for a mile or so past the woollen mills on minor roads.

MACBETH

If you look at the table of the Kings of Scots on page 73 (not Kings of Scotland at this time – the king was king of his people not of a land mass), you'll see how the kingship zigzags down through the generations from tanaise to tanaise. This had gone on since the time of the great King Kenneth MacAlpine, who had conquered and united all the tribes of Scotland into one entity. But now different ideas were beginning to seep in from the Continent and England. The new modern way was to keep inheritance in the direct family. That's what Malcolm II was doing when he nominated his grandson Duncan to be king in his stead.

In the play, it is Duncan who nominates his son as king, thus thwarting Macbeth's ambitions, but in reality it was the succession of Duncan himself that was the sticking point. Macbeth didn't have the primary claim. The kingship should have gone to the side of the family coming down from Kenneth III.

But what strengthened Macbeth's position was his marriage to Gruoch, who came from the very line of the family that was due the kingship. In the terms of the eleventh century, he had just as good a claim to be king after Malcolm as Duncan.

While the defeated followers of Duncan were bearing his body westwards to Iona, Macbeth was rushing south. Killing the monarch was just the first step. He would only truly be king when the other Scottish nobles acclaimed him at the ancient Stone of Scone.

If you've ever sat in a teashop and wondered whether scone should rhyme with 'gone' or 'moan', here's a further complication. The place where medieval Kings of Scots were made king is pronounced 'Scoon'.

Scone Palace lies a couple of miles north-east of Perth on the River Tay. This is Old Scone, not to be confused with the village of New Scone which was created when a laird decided to shift his estate workers down the road a bit.

The neo-gothic palace is the seat of the Earls of Mansfield. It was built in the early nineteenth century and is worth a visit, but the true historic significance of Scone lies in its grounds. Once you've paid and parked, mount the flight of shallow steps that leads from the car park to the house. At the top, look back towards the car park ticket office and imagine stretching away to your left, diagonally over the car park, a priory church and, surrounding it, noble halls, monastic buildings and hovels. This was Scone, both a royal and ecclesiastical centre. No trace remains of the old complex as the grounds were extensively landscaped when the current palace was built, but an Augustinian priory was founded here in the early twelfth century on the grounds of an earlier community. This was upgraded to abbey status in 1164, but battered by Edward I in 1296 and then finally destroyed by John Knox's followers in the Reformation.

A thousand years ago, when Macbeth arrived, the buildings would have been much simpler, made predominantly of wood rather than stone. Nevertheless, it was one of the most important places in Scotland.

Opposite: The ruins of Elgin Cathedral just down the road from Pitgaveny, where the mortally wounded Duncan was brought to die.

To see where Macbeth was made King at Scone, head out from Perth town centre across the road bridge to the east side of the River Tay. Turn left and proceed north up the A93 for two miles, and the entrance to the palace is on your left.

Now turn right round so that the palace is on your left. Facing you and slightly to your right is Moot Hill, where the ceremony of kingship took place.

We can create a picture of what Macbeth's inauguration would have looked like from later descriptions and paintings. We know that there was no crowning. In Macbeth's time the symbol of kingship was a sword with which to rule and protect his people. A bard would have recited the lineage of the Kings of Scots from the time of Kenneth MacAlpine onwards. But the crucial element of the affair was for the candidate to be acclaimed while seated on the Stone of Destiny.

The coronation stone of Scotland is a 336-pound block of Perthshire sandstone. Legend held that it was the rocky pillow on which Jacob rested his head when he had his dream of the ladder extending to heaven. It was kept at the abbey at Scone for centuries and brought out when kings were inaugurated. The king-to-be would either have sat on it directly or it would have been fitted into some sort of simple throne. Sitting on stone almost certainly had some sort of pre-Christian significance associated with the idea of identifying the king with part of the landscape, connecting the ruler to the earth.

Moot Hill at Scone Palace. The Stone of Destiny was probably placed on top somewhere to the left of the later chapel.

This simple act was so important that when a king died it sometimes led to a race between rival claimants to sit on it first. There's even a theory that Duncan may have only become king himself because he pipped the other contenders to the stone. This has the ring of plausibility in that he was based at nearby Dunkeld and could certainly have got to Scone far quicker than Macbeth or any other candidate. So is it any wonder that with Duncan dead, Macbeth hastened so quickly to Scone?

Sheriffton

Race Course

Scone
Park

Scone Palace

The
Woody

Old Scone

Scone
Wood

A 93

Visitor
Centre

'43

Quarrymill

A 94

2
MACBETH

Moot Hill is a flat-topped rise just two metres high. The installing of the king took place on top of the hill or possibly in front of it, in the midst of his fellow noblemen waiting to declare their allegiance. There's a replica Stone of Destiny chocked up to form a seat to give you an idea of what it might have looked like.

Although Moot Hill may have been artificially created, there's no evidence to support the legend about how it was made. They say that each nobleman brought a bootful of earth from his own territory and swore allegiance to the new king literally on his own turf before adding the earth to an ever growing pile. Thus Moot – or, some say, Boot – Hill was created.

The real Stone of Destiny is no longer at Scone. As befits an object central to the idea of Scottish nationhood, it's kept under lock and key in the capital at Edinburgh Castle. To see it today, you have to take a tour of the castle and visit the Scottish crown jewels or, as they call them, the Honours of Scotland. The Stone of Destiny lies beside a jewelled crown in a secure case, safe from thieves and the English who forcefully borrowed it for 700 years.

As we'll see, in 1296 Edward I of England came to Scone, ransacked the abbey and captured the Stone of Destiny as part of his annexation of Scotland. He took the Stone back to London where it was housed in Westminster Abbey and became part of English and then British coronation rituals. Attempts were made to snatch this symbol of Scottish pride back, particularly by students in the 1950s, who managed to steal it and break it. The Stone was only returned in 1996 as part of the move towards Scottish devolution.

The real Stone of Destiny.

But there's a fascinating twist. All the time the Stone was in the possession of the English, rumours persisted that it wasn't the genuine article. One version of the story says

that the canny monks of Scone hid the real Stone and let Edward 'find' a suitable replica. Another legend has it that Macbeth himself, in a percipient move, took the Stone of Destiny and hid it on Dunsinane Hill.

No hard evidence exists to support either of these stories. If you go to Edinburgh Castle, you'll almost certainly be looking at the piece of rock that supported the ancient Kings of the Scots.

Scone was not only where kings were made, it was also where they ruled. John of Fordun in his work *Chronicle of the Scottish People*, which appeared about 1370 and is the earliest Scottish chroni-

cle, describes Scone as the 'chief seat of the kingdom' of the Pictish and the Scottish kings. He adds that kings used to sit in judgement enthroned on Moot Hill. Justice would have been executed at the nearby Gallows Knowe.

Scone is excellently fitted to be an administrative centre, being situated in the middle of Scotland on the main artery of the Tay. Macbeth was probably not only inaugurated here but used it as one of his main residences throughout his reign. It's unlikely he would have remained in Moray, which was too remote to be used as a base to retain control of the whole country. The *Prophecy of Berchan* supports this theory. The poet, speaking while Macbeth was still alive, predicts that he will die 'in the middle of Scone' after a duel. But this is not what happened. It proves that the poem was composed before Macbeth's death, but it also demonstrates that the poet assumed that the natural place for Macbeth to be was at Scone.

Which brings us on to the reign of King Macbeth, King of Scots from 1040 to 1057.

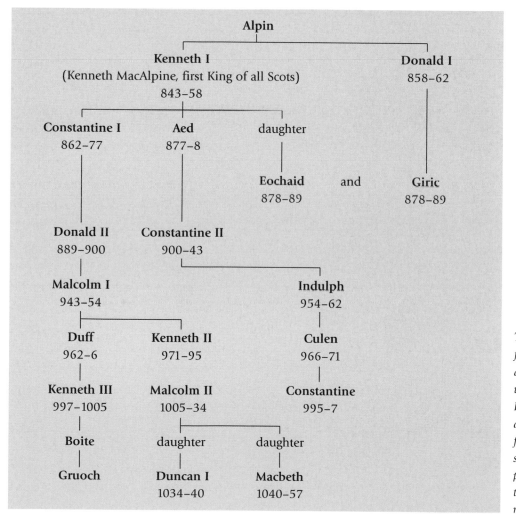

The Scottish Royal family tree. The Kings are marked in bold with their dates. Instead of following down, remember to go from side to side to see how the Kingship passes between the two branches of the royal line.

MACBETH – ACTS III–IV

Macbeth is King, but he's not secure. His friends know too much. He begins a reign of terror.

He has Banquo murdered but Banquo's sons escape. Next, he sends assassins to kill Macduff. But Macduff has left for England – just in time. The assassins kill his wife and children anyway. No one is safe.

In the wake of Duncan's murder the country falls apart amid signs of supernatural disorder. Duncan's horses break out of their stalls and eat each other, day turns to night. And as Scotland comes apart at the seams, so does Macbeth. At a banquet for his nobles, he sees the bloody ghost of Banquo sitting accusingly in his chair. Only he can see the apparition and his nobles are treated to the sight of their brave new King gibbering like a lunatic.

Macbeth can't believe the witches' prophecies have got him into such a fix, so he returns to their dismal haunt to consult them. What he's looking for is reassurance, and they give it to him. They promise him that 'none of woman born shall harm Macbeth' and that he will never be vanquished until Birnam Wood moves to Dunsinane Hill to defeat him. It seems like a watertight guarantee.

Meanwhile, Lady Macbeth, who egged Macbeth on to murder the King, is eaten up with guilt. She sleepwalks while trying to wash the stain of blood from her hands: 'Out damned spot! Out I say!' The crime of Duncan's death consumes her mind until she commits suicide offstage, unnoticed by Macbeth.

Macbeth's reign in the play isn't a pretty picture. The country falls into chaos as he becomes increasingly obsessive, but his tyrannical rule is mercifully short. In reality, Macbeth enjoyed a long reign for his time and a prosperous one. In contrast to Duncan who lasted just under seven years, Macbeth remained on the throne for seventeen. Indeed he was confident enough, ten years after becoming king, to leave Scotland unattended and visit the Continent.

The only hiccup in the early years of his reign occurred five years after he seized the throne, and was the result of Duncan's family attempting a counter-coup. Straight after killing Duncan, Macbeth had tried to hunt down Duncan's two sons Malcolm 'Canmore' (which roughly translates as 'Malcolm big head') and Donald. Malcolm, in line with the new fashion for primogeniture, had been named as heir when Duncan became king. These two young men were likely to be thorns in Macbeth's flesh. But he couldn't find them, so they lived. The chronicler John of Fordun records that they went on the run for two years. Although they got enough help to evade capture, they couldn't muster any counter movement against Macbeth – proof that people were happy enough with the new regime. After two years of hiding in mainland Scotland, they split up and sought support elsewhere. Duncan sailed off to the Western Isles and Malcolm went south to England, first to Cumbria, and later joined up with the Northumbrians led by his uncle, Earl Siward.

2
MACBETH

Dunkeld Abbey,
the power base of
Macbeth's opponents.

Any opposition to Macbeth from within Scotland had to come from elsewhere. Strangely, for a brutal age, Macbeth didn't try to kill or remove other potential sources of rebellion. Possibly he didn't want to push his luck in the early untested days of his reign by alienating the southern power centres, so he didn't move against the man who was his biggest potential threat.

Duncan's father was called Crinan and he was the Abbot of Dunkeld, a hugely important monastic centre. His wasn't just a Church appointment but a key political position. Lay abbots acted like any other political leader of the time. Dunkeld itself was far more than a big religious complex; it was a power centre for Duncan's side of the royal line. In retrospect it was a mistake not to remove Crinan from office.

There's been a religious foundation in the town of some sort for well over a millennium. The cathedral church is still used by the Church of Scotland. It butts straight on to the ruins of former buildings and is set in beautiful grounds sweeping down to the Tay. The earliest ruins date from after Macbeth's time, but there are still patches of eleventh-century stonework incorporated into the intact church. With its picturesque gothic ruins and the distant sounds of hymns wafting across the lawns, it's hard to believe that this place was once the epicentre of political opposition to Macbeth.

In 1045 Crinan led a major rebellion against him. All we know about it is that a battle took place and that Crinan was killed along with 180 fighting men. Given the small numbers usually involved, this shows that Crinan had mounted a sizeable force.

After Crinan's rebellion, there was no serious internal threat for nine years – surely the mark of a good king. Possibly the most significant comment in all the chronicles on Macbeth's reign is a line of Latin poetry inserted into the *Chronicle of Melrose* some time in the early thirteenth century. It says, 'Macbeth was King of Scots for seventeen years, and in his reign there were fruitful seasons.' This was the greatest accolade that could be given to a ruler. The *Prophecy of Berchan* also picks this up, describing Scotland as 'brimful of food from East to West' during Macbeth's reign. This is the very opposite of Shakespeare's play. The times were not 'out of joint'. There was peace, and people had enough to eat. Their two basic needs were being met.

Of course the life of the aristocracy would have been more akin to that of other nobles in royal courts throughout Europe than it was to their people. Enough food in the bellies of the people of Scotland in the eleventh century meant a diet largely based on oats flavoured with herbs. If you lived near water there might be an occasional fish, and meat when it rarely appeared would most often have been stewed to make the most of it. In contrast, Macbeth would have eaten well in his great hall. His place would have been right in the centre. His lords would spread themselves out along two parallel tables, the lower ranks taking the seats furthest away from the fire. They would have dined on roasted meats, and drunk not only mead and ale, but wine. There's evidence of a healthy wine trade from

Bordeaux to northern Scotland at the time, so Macbeth may have been a sophisticated connoisseur rather than an eight-pints-of-heavy man.

We've seen that he was tall, flaxen-haired and red-faced but there's no description of his wife, Gruoch. For more evidence of what they might have looked like, the Bayeaux Tapestry is a good guide. Although there would have been regional variations (for instance, the Scots had used plaid or a two-tone design in their textiles for hundreds of years) the clothes in the tapestry that features in our next chapter, particularly the armour, give a fair idea of how Macbeth would have been kitted out. Scotland was remote and travel was difficult, but there was a good deal of communication with the Continent.

This can be seen quite vividly in an event that occurred in 1052. In England, after a brief period of exile, Earl Godwin of Wessex had returned in triumph to London, and demanded that King Edward the Confessor expel many of the French and Norman nobles that he'd been collecting at his court. Not all of them returned to the Continent. Many fled north to Scotland. We're told that Macbeth greeted them warmly. As we'll see, the Normans actually had Viking roots, so this is hardly a case of Macbeth opening his arms to exotic Continentals. He would have felt quite at home with the Normans, but he also got something out of the deal. It was the Normans who had been responsible for building the first English castles and keeping the Welsh at bay, so their presence would have been a useful asset. It's not clear whether Macbeth used them to rebuild his traditional strongholds, but we do know that these Norman guests gave Macbeth their full military support, eventually fighting with him to the bitter end.

Like Macbeth, his wife the Lady Gruoch, has suffered from her portrayal in Shakespeare's play. We don't know much about her, but she is still one of the most famous women in this period of Scottish history.

For a start, we know her name. And it's significant that she's not called Lady Macbeth. Most women in the early medieval period are depicted simply as adjuncts to their husbands, part of the fixtures and fittings of the court. Fathers and sons are what counted. But Gruoch is named as a queen in her own right, the 'daughter of Boite, Queen of Scots'. It may be that she encouraged her husband in his royal ambitions in the same way as Shakespeare's Lady Macbeth does. She had reason to, given that Malcolm II had assassinated members of her kin to secure Duncan's inheritance. But the only evidence we have implies that Gruoch may have been, not a raving sleepwalker, but a godly and generous patron of the Church.

This reputation for piety also extended to Macbeth. Documents show that they both gave generous religious donations. There are three notes detailing gifts of land made first by Macbeth and then jointly by Macbeth and Gruoch. These include donations to the Culdees (from the Gaelic for 'Clients of God'), an order of monks on St Serf's Island in Loch Leven.

There are two ways to see St Serf's Island nowadays. You can pay for a day's fishing at Kinross on the north of the loch, sail past Loch Leven Castle where Mary Queen of Scots was kept under house arrest, and make for the island at the loch's south-east corner. You're not allowed to land unless accompanied by someone from the RSPB. Besides disturbing the shelduck and oystercatchers, you run the risk of being divebombed by angry gulls. Otherwise, you can get a superb view of the whole loch and St Serf's Island by climbing up to the viewpoint at the top of the hill to the south of the Loch.

Either way, the area's spectacularly beautiful, but bears little trace of the Culdees. Some stone from a later monastic foundation has been made into a shepherd's shelter on the island, but even this is falling down. Apart from a series of humps indicating the outline of the medieval foundation, the eleventh-century structures are invisible. What strikes you most, though, is the sense of isolation. These monks were truly cut off from the world. Thanks to new drainage, the loch is now several feet lower than it was in the eleventh century, leaving far more of the island exposed, but you can still trace the narrow spit of land that would have been above the waterline a millennium ago.

Loch Leven Castle, where Mary Queen of Scots was kept prisoner, overlooks St Serf's Island.

So what does this act of charity say about Macbeth and Gruoch? The ancient texts tell us that the gifts were made with the 'utmost veneration and devotion' and 'from motives

of piety and for the benefit of their prayers'. But were the motives of the royal couple that sincere? It's been suggested that the gift was blood money for the murder of Duncan, a way of buying spiritual assistance to get rid of the damned spot of guilt. But it is more likely that the couple were simply doing the right thing for the time. Many wealthy benefactors donated gifts of land to fund a priest to say masses for their souls. The Macbeths were no more or less generous than other kings. The Culdees of Loch Leven were also given lands by Malcolm II, and by Malcolm III who came after Macbeth. It's like millionaires today funding hospital wings and art galleries. It doesn't necessarily mean that they're good people.

However, there's one other thing we know about Macbeth's reign, and this also suggests that, while he may only have been going along with the accepted pieties of the day, he at least wanted to be seen to be a godfearing king. In 1050 he went on a pilgrimage to Rome.

FROM SCOTLAND TO ROME

In the eleventh century this was a big deal for a king. It involved not only the general hazards of travel, but also the added difficulty of avoiding noblemen hostile to you. In addition it meant taking the risk of leaving your kingdom unattended and open to external threat or internal rebellion. The fact that Macbeth went to Rome at all shows how confident he must have felt about the security of his position. Interestingly, we know that his old sparring partner, Thorfinn, also went to Rome and met the Pope. Did the two cousins travel together as a joint ransom, to ensure that neither got up to any tricks while the other was away?

Macbeth wouldn't have wanted to risk a journey overland through England, because Duncan's son Malcolm had teamed up with his uncle Siward in Northumbria. So his likely route would have been by boat down the east coast, then through northern France down the Rhine Valley and through one of the Alpine passes into Italy, stopping at major shrines and cathedrals along the way. It's a journey of more than 1,800 miles from Perth to Rome. In order to have arrived in Rome by Easter 1050, Macbeth would probably have left home in 1049.

We know about the pilgrimage through our old friend Mael Brigte. Although he was a hermit he had received information from other travellers on the Continent and his account of Macbeth's arrival in Rome seems to be based on such information. The account says that 'The King of Scots, Macbeth, scattered silver like seed to the poor in Rome.'

A show of charity would be expected of a great man arriving in Rome, and the bigger the better. This was not a private act of unseen charity. This was public giving to enhance the reputation and status of the giver. There were no coins in Macbeth's Scotland – the silver would have been cut-up bits of silver plate, distributed as alms. The fact that this giveaway gets reported to a hermit monk writing in Mainz in what is now Germany shows that, as a publicity stunt, it worked.

It could be that Macbeth had a genuine religious motive for making the pilgrimage. It was ten years since he had killed Duncan; he may have been seeking absolution. But there would have been political benefits from his pilgrimage. Macbeth could prove by making a splash in the centre of Western culture that he was no two-bit ruler of a remote kingdom. By travelling to Rome he was helping to put Scotland on the map.

Trying to assess motive at a distance of a thousand years is almost impossible. The fact that a pilgrimage to Rome was useful in raising the profile of both Macbeth and Scotland doesn't automatically mean that the King didn't have personal religious convictions. It's more likely that it was a case of both, rather than either/or. And there's just one more hint that Macbeth had a personal interest in religious faith: his name.

In the eleventh century Macbeth (or *Mac Bheatha* in its Gaelic form) was still an unusual name in Scotland, and the chronicles have many variations on the spelling of it. What makes it striking is its meaning. The '*Mac*' bit means 'son of', as in MacDonald. But *Bheatha* isn't a name at all. *Mac Bheatha* literally means 'Son of Life', a Christian name meaning a righteous man. It could be that Macbeth was actually an adopted name similar to the confirmation names that Catholics still take today. So here we have a convincing and satisfying explanation of the Karl Hundason conundrum. Like Saul of Tarsus becoming Paul on his conversion, the devout Karl retitled himself Macbeth as a sign of religious devotion.

A fantasy on Shakespeare's dark and brooding Macbeth by George Cattermole. Macbeth instructs the murderers with the witches eavesdropping on the sidelines.

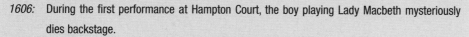

THE MACBETH SUPERSTITION

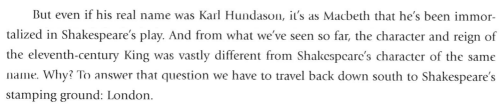

In any play with fight scenes and special effects, things are bound to go wrong occasionally, but here are some of the more famous incidents that have led to the belief that there is a curse on the 'Scottish Play', the name of which is never mentioned in theatres.

1606: During the first performance at Hampton Court, the boy playing Lady Macbeth mysteriously dies backstage.

1849: More than thirty people are killed in a riot outside the theatre where the play is being performed. The riot has been caused by years of animosity between two actors and their rival supporters.

1934: Four actors playing Macbeth fall ill within a week.

1937: Laurence Olivier's *Macbeth*. The theatre's founder dies, the director narrowly escapes death, and Olivier himself is nearly felled by falling scenery.

But even if his real name was Karl Hundason, it's as Macbeth that he's been immortalized in Shakespeare's play. And from what we've seen so far, the character and reign of the eleventh-century King was vastly different from Shakespeare's character of the same name. Why? To answer that question we have to travel back down south to Shakespeare's stamping ground: London.

In 1603 James I of England, who was also James VI of Scotland, had become the bard's special patron. Shakespeare's company became known as 'The King's Men'. This meant they now had more opportunities for performing at court. It was essential for the players to think of ways to flatter their new employer and keep him sweet. Writing *Macbeth* gave Shakespeare the chance to do just that.

The first show was given at a private performance in front of the King at Hampton Court in August 1606. Just nine months previously, on 5 November 1605, London had been shaken by one of the most terrifying political events in James's reign the Gunpowder Plot. After the attempted assassination, James's propaganda experts quickly formulated an official version of what had happened: an evil man had been inspired by the forces of darkness to try and overthrow the rightful king. It was this theme that Shakespeare so artfully exploited. But he did so in a number of ways that were particularly likely to appeal to James.

First of all, the King believed that his family line was descended from Banquo. But Banquo was murdered by Macbeth. So, by vilifying him Shakespeare was blackening the name not only of a man who had killed the rightful king but also of someone who had murdered James's own ancestor. You can imagine a royal cheer going up at the moment in the play when Banquo's son, Fleance, escapes the assassins. 'It's going to be all right,' Shakespeare's plot was saying, 'the Stewart succession is safe!'

James also had two obsessions – the nature of kingship, and witchcraft. He had written treatises on both eight years earlier: *The True Lawe of Free Monarchies* and *Daemonologies*. In *Macbeth* he was presented with a great drama that wrapped up these obsessions in a tidy bundle. Shakespeare portrays a venerable king, Duncan, who is overthrown (thanks to the intervention of the witches), and he paints the mayhem that follows. For aficionados there's even language in the play that hints at the Gunpowder Plot itself, particularly references to undermining and fuses.

HUBBLE BUBBLE

Shakespeare's witches are such a powerful creation that they've helped to form our mental picture of what a witch is. The 'hubble, bubble, toil and trouble' imagery of hags huddled over a cauldron is now part of popular culture. But there's a theory that the most famous scene of all where the witches prepare their satanic brew ('Eye of newt and toe of frog,/Wool of bat and tongue of dog') is actually meant as a sly dig at the Scots.

In England, the Scots were renowned for boiling their food and for combining unappetizing ingredients. The English looked at Scottish cookery much as the French look on traditional British cuisine. The cauldron wasn't a common symbol of witches before Shakespeare, so by creating this image he may have been poking fun at Scottish cooking, having the three hags throw everything bar the kitchen sink into the pot.

The witches who motivate Macbeth's actions and determine the course of the play would have sent a shiver of recognition down the spines of Shakespeare's audiences. Witches were big news. Throughout Europe, witch trials and burnings were all the rage, as people sought to blame mishaps and misfortunes on the devil working in the community. England had been shaken by the publication of *News from Scotland*, a report on the witch trials at North Berwick in 1590–91. It had been alleged that dozens of witches had tried to kill James and his newly married Queen, Anne of

Denmark. It was said that they had raised a storm to swamp the King's ship as he and Anne travelled back from their wedding in Norway. James had personally taken part in the interrogation of some of the accused women. The impression that satanic forces were taking on the most powerful person in the land was reinforced by the demonization of the Catholic gunpowder plotters. Clearly, the devil was trying to get at the divinely appointed monarch whenever he could. Shakespeare underlines the parallel with the North Berwick case by having his witches talk about causing shipwrecks just before they meet Macbeth.

'Cauldron boil and cauldron bubble' – satanic ritual or Shakespeare's version of Delia Smith on an off day?

Back in the eleventh century, the real Macbeth would have been at a loss to understand James's obsession with witches and witchcraft. He might have known the Old Testament injunction 'Thou shalt not suffer a witch to live'. He would also have known about King Saul's visit to the Witch of Endor to get a prophecy about his future (a scene that Shakespeare echoes with Macbeth's consultation). But witches were not seen as a threat. Indeed, the official Church position on witchcraft was far more tolerant than 500 years later. Charlemagne had punished the persecution of witches, and Gregory VII, who became Pope in 1073, specifically forbade the killing of women for supposed crimes such as starting storms and epidemics.

There were undoubtedly relics of folk magic around in eleventh-century Scotland: a bit of cursing here, a fertility charm there, even the odd exorcism. But the policy of the Church in converting the people of Northern Europe to Christianity had always been to be inclusive, to subsume old religions into the new. The Church didn't want to dignify elements of pre-Christian religions by taking them too seriously. As long as people followed Church practice, Celtic clergymen wouldn't enquire too closely into the superstitions of their congregations.

Witchcraft is really a later construct by a Church that created its own monster in order to destroy it. Concern about witches grows in the later Middle Ages. In response to divisions and heresies within its ranks, the Church tried to spread its authority into the minds of individual believers. The Inquisition was empowered to deal with witches. Education and learning had to be controlled and confined to the professional classes. This included medical skills. The long tradition of local women acting as midwives, easing the pain of childbirth (the curse of Eve) with traditional herbal mixtures suddenly seemed threatening.

The publication of *Malleus Maleficarum*, the 'Hammer of the Witches', in 1487, marks the start of serious witch-hunting. In detailing witches' supposed activities like intercourse with the devil and witches' sabbaths it actually increased superstition and fear. The Reformation in the sixteenth century, with its emphasis on the importance of individual faith and an exaggerated belief in the power of the devil, made matters worse. The authorities on both sides of the religious divide sought to tighten control on what people thought. Three million women died throughout Europe in a battle against a largely imagined enemy. This didn't end in England until the last witch trial in 1712 and in Scotland not until ten years later.

The historical Macbeth didn't live in a period when he might have been thought to be in the thrall of dark forces. Indeed, as we have seen, fate seemed to smile on him. The bounty of the land proved the old Celtic lore that a good king brought fertility to the land. He was so confident of his position that he took the best part of a year out to go on pilgrimage. He had a popular and saintly wife. What could possibly go wrong?

MACBETH – ACT V

The play is reaching its climax. Duncan's son Malcolm has returned to Scotland with an English force led by Siward and the trusty Macduff. Shakespeare's tyrant is holed up in his stronghold at Dunsinane, relying on the witches' promise that he won't lose till Birnam Wood comes to Dunsinane or be killed by anyone 'born of woman'. What he doesn't know is that Malcolm has planned a surprise attack on Dunsinane using a primitive form of camouflage.

His soldiers cut down saplings in Birnam Wood and create a moving canopy of trees. Macbeth's startled men report back to him that the wood is moving towards Dunsinane. One prophecy down, one to go.

The attack begins. Macbeth's men are routed but he fights on until he sees Macduff in the thick of battle. They square up. Macbeth shouts his defiance. 'I've got a charmed life,' he says, 'no one born of a woman's going to get me.' Macduff says, 'That's fine. I was born by Caesarean section, not born of woman at all.'

But Macbeth doesn't give up – Shakespeare has him go down fighting. 'Lay on, Macduff,' he screams, 'and damned be him that first cries, "Hold, enough!"' And then he disappears off stage. We don't actually see him die, but Macduff returns with his head and Malcolm goes off to Scone to be acclaimed king.

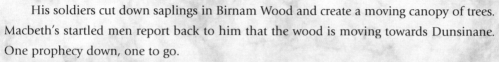

In the early part of his reign, the real Macbeth wasn't sufficiently ruthless or effective in getting rid of possible opposition. Now this mistake came back to haunt him. In 1054 Malcolm Canmore who, fourteen years previously, had escaped Macbeth's grasp, returned with his uncle, the Earl Siward of the Northumbrians. They rode at the head of a large force in order to wrest back control of Scotland.

This wasn't merely altruism on the part of the Northumbrians. They wanted something out of it. The English chronicles record that Siward returned home loaded with Scottish booty, but the English also wanted Malcolm installed to secure a better relationship with the Scots. And this ambition wasn't limited to the Northumbrians. The force that accompanied Malcolm contained southerners. When the final casualties were counted they included personal troops of the English King, Edward the Confessor. Indeed, Malcolm had done service in Edward's court during his exile and, in return for his oath of loyalty, Edward had granted him a manor in Corby, Northampton.

In comparison with the many skirmishes involving four or five hundred people that we have seen before, this was a conflict of a different order. The resulting battle between Macbeth's army and the joint forces of Northumbrians and dissenting Scots was hard fought, and on an impressive scale. Allowing for the usual exaggeration, the body-count was given as 4,500, with two Scots dead for every one of Malcolm's forces. Macbeth's

For Dunsinane, take the A94 through New Scone out of Perth, branch off at Balbeggie on to the B953 and you'll find it on your left after about three miles. Far from being a tourist attraction, the only sign of activity is a quarry eating into the western side of the hill. If you take the road past the quarry towards Collace there's a footpath to the top just where the road turns to the left at a right angle. Then, for the strong of wind and limb, a very stiff walk to the top will reward you not only with a tour of a magnificent Iron Age fort, but a vista that stretches from the Tay Estuary in the south-east, to the distant Grampians in the north.

troops were decimated. He lost all his refugee Norman soldiers. On the English side, Siward's nephew, also called Siward, died, an event that also appears in the play.

The battle took place on 22 July, but none of the early chronicles say where. So it's called the Battle of the Seven Sleepers, after the religious festival on which it happened. It's only in the fifteenth century that the battle is located at Macbeth's stronghold, variously called Dunsin, Dunsian or Dunsinan in the chronicles. This is the Dunsinane of Shakespeare's tragedy. The man who records the event is Andrew of Wyntoun. His *Orygynale Cronykil* is a metrical saga written in rhyming couplets that's led him to be called the 'William MacGonagall of his age'. He was prior of St Serf's on the very Loch Leven endowed by Macbeth and Gruoch, and it was there that he wrote his chronicle. Even though he's writing so long after the event, his work is important because he had access to the great Register of St Andrew's, which is now lost. Wyntoun preserves not only traditions antagonistic to Macbeth and similar to Shakespeare, but also earlier traditions such as the prosperity and justice of Macbeth's reign.

Even though the 2,000-year-old hill fort of Dunsinane, the last redoubt of one of literature's famous characters, is clearly visible today, there are no organized tours to it. There are no signs indicating its whereabouts, no kiosk, no souvenir shops or coffee bars, not even a Macbeth Discovery Centre. In fact, you have to work pretty hard to get there at all.

Archaeology on Dunsinane has been rudimentary: a straight, shallow, grassy trough across the top of the hill belongs to the most systematic exploration of the site – in 1799! Astoundingly, modern archaeologists seem uninterested. What work has been done produced evidence of Iron Age habitation, but nothing from the eleventh century.

Nevertheless, if Macbeth's southern power-base was at low-lying Scone, Dunsinane would have been an ideal retreat in times of crisis. It's unlikely that Macbeth would have chosen to live permanently on the inaccessible height of Dunsinane, but Wyntoun has Macbeth refortifying it. If he'd built up and added to existing defences with the help of Norman engineers, it would have been the ideal command post in time of war. The site's too small for a large force, but Macbeth and his nobles could have holed up there, with the rest of their army camped further down the hill, waiting for Malcolm. The site is close enough to defend Scone, and is virtually impregnable.

Which leads us to the business about Birnam Wood. Wyntoun is also the first to record the tradition of a moving forest. He says that Malcolm sailed right up the Tay to Birnam where he heard the mysterious rumour that Macbeth would be safe until the wood marched on Dunsinane. In response he gets his men to cut down branches as a supernatural tactic of war. Shakespeare, on the other hand, sees Malcolm creating a great screen or shadow for his men to disguise their true numbers, unaware of the witches' predictions.

The most surprising thing about the woods at Birnam is seen most clearly from the top of Dunsinane itself. Whereas Malcolm and the Northumbrians were coming from the south-east, Birnam is to the north-west – the completely opposite direction! So why would Malcolm's forces have marched through it to attack Macbeth? To do so, they'd have needed to have gone in a great loop. The answer lies a mile further up the road from Birnam, at Dunkeld.

In 1045 Dunkeld was, as we've seen, the great centre of opposition to Macbeth. There's no reason to suppose its inhabitants had come over to Macbeth's side in the nine years that followed. So it's likely that Dunkeld would still have been a rallying point for anti-Macbeth forces. When Malcolm and Siward came north, it appears that they split their forces to create a pincer movement. Sailing up the coast from north-east England, one arm of the pincer landed in the Tay Estuary, while the other continued on up the Tay to Dunkeld to rendezvous with Malcolm's Scottish supporters. Then this secondary force wheeled south-west through Birnam Wood to close the trap on Macbeth waiting at Dunsinane. The shock of this brilliant tactic could have been commemorated in the tradition of Birnam Wood joining in the assault on Dunsinane.

According to tradition, when the woods took off for Dunsinane, one tree got left behind. A lot of people think of Scottish forests as pine, but that's only in the most mountainous bits of the Highlands. The original Scottish forests around Perth and southwards

MACBETH

It may not date back as far as Macbeth but the 'tree that remained' in Birnam Wood is venerable enough to be worth a visit. You'll find it on a woodland walk just off the main road through the village of Birnam. (For a more authentic eleventh-century woodland feel, try Kinnoul Woods on the outskirts of Perth.)

A mound of stones at the top of Dunsinane looking east to the King's Seat (the far hill) where one legend says that Macbeth jumped to his death. In the foreground just beyond the pile you can see the dip in the ground marking the entrance to the original hill fort.

were composed of oak, birch and rowan. Birnam Wood today, on the west bank of the Tay, is the most recently planted coniferous forest, but one giant oak remains. Whisper it not but, however massive the trunk, it doesn't date back to anywhere near Macbeth's time.

AFTER DUNSINANE

Macbeth lost the Battle of the Seven Sleepers. But there was one significant name missing from the casualty list: his own. Despite the local tradition that he threw himself to his death from the nearby King's Seat hill, and despite the gory ending to Shakespeare's play, the truth is that Macbeth and his stepson, Lulach, escaped to fight another day. Fleeing northwards, they found their way through the tracks and passes of the Mounth back into Moray, Macbeth's ancestral home.

They held on for another three years, but Macbeth was fatally weakened. His forces had been smashed and Malcolm had been installed as King by Siward at Scone. There were now two kings. Malcolm controlled most of Scotland up to the Mounth, and Macbeth held on to his formidable power base in Moray. But it was only a matter of time before Malcolm took that too.

The end came in 1057. Malcolm had regrouped. He too had suffered losses at the Battle of the Seven Sleepers and this time he didn't have the expert resources of King Edward's men to help him out. But he was biding his time to make not just a decisive, but a symbolic, attack. He made a sudden and fatal assault on Macbeth on 16 August 1057, the Mass of St Mary. It was on precisely the same date that Macbeth had killed Duncan. A seventeen-year vendetta had been repaid.

The final battle was a skirmish compared with the great clash three years before. It took place at Lumphanon in the Strathdon area, not far from the main pass through the Mounth near Ballater. It's not clear whether Malcolm launched a surprise assault and Macbeth tried to cut him off, or whether Malcolm was pursuing him back into Moray after a raid by Macbeth south of the Mounth. Nor do we know exactly where the two sides met. But after the skirmish, the last of Macbeth's followers dragged his body off the battlefield and buried it on a hillside overlooking the settlement.

The road through Glenshee marks the route of Malcolm's march. If you come from the south, it's certainly the most beautiful way to reach Moray. Passing Braemar, Balmoral and Ballater, you turn off just before Kincardine O'Neil for Lumphanon. Approaching the village this way, don't be fooled into thinking that the impressive Peel of Lumphanon on your left is associated with Macbeth. This is another red herring, a thirteenth-century motte and bailey. But we do know that people were present around here as least two centuries earlier than that. One of the few eleventh-century artefacts discovered in Scotland is an axe-head that was found at Lumphanon.

MACBETH

Opposite: The tree that remained. Almost all that's left of the ancient Birnam Wood.

For Macbeth's Cairn, head out of Lumphanon north on the A980. As the road rises out of the village you leave the houses behind. Look out for a steep track flanked by conifers on the right-hand side. Don't go down this yet but stop and get out of your car to find your bearings. Look east across the valley. The track leads down to some farm buildings. This is where you'll have to go to get access to the field that rises up on the other side of the valley. But first, trace a line up this field slightly left from the farm buildings to the same level as you are on the road. You'll see a ring of beech trees. This is Macbeth's Cairn and should match the markings on your Ordnance Survey map.

From most places on the British mainland it would be quicker to get to New York than to Iona. Of course, when St Columba founded his tiny monastery off the west coast of Scotland around AD 563, ease of access wasn't an issue. A monastery was meant to be remote. Today, it requires a good deal of driving, admittedly through spectacular countryside, along the banks of Loch Lomond to Oban, a ferry from Oban to Mull, more driving and a smaller ferry to get to Iona.

The local pub may be named after Macbeth, but tracking down Macbeth's Cairn, the traditional burial place of this King of Scots, is a bit more of a challenge. There are no signposts, and you'll need an Ordnance Survey map to see it marked.

Again, you have to get permission from the farmer to visit the site. Remember your wellies as this is very much a working livestock farm, and prepare for another stiff but rewarding climb. One thing's certain: you'll be entirely alone to soak in the atmosphere. Macbeth's Cairn has a bleak but peaceful air of melancholy: a rubble of reddish rocks covering the body of one of the most famous Kings of Scots.

Perhaps.

But there's another tradition. This says Macbeth's body was disinterred from the cairn and, like Duncan, carried to Iona to be accorded the full honours due to a great Celtic king. People have said that Malcolm wouldn't have allowed this; he was bent on revenge, not honouring his old enemy. But this ignores two things. First, if the same argument had been applied over the preceding centuries, few Scottish kings would have been buried at all. The whole tanaise system rested on a combination of respect for the royal line and recognition that political assassination was part and parcel of the process. Second, there is the sheer scale of Scotland. Malcolm didn't have the resources to prevent a group of supporters moving Macbeth's body. This was particularly true in the winter months immediately after Macbeth's death. Indeed, Malcolm didn't carry on the fight and attempt to conquer the whole of Moray. Lulach, Macbeth's stepson, was proclaimed king for a brief seven months.

But Lulach was only ever king in name. He wouldn't have been able to get south to Scone to become king officially, and Malcolm wasn't going to let another Moray troublemaker spoil his party. He was determined to stamp out Macbeth's line, and seven months later in 1058 he made another raid northwards and killed Lulach at Strathbogie. But Lulach's brief reign in the Highlands would have given him more than enough time to arrange the transportation of Macbeth's corpse from Lumphanon to the shrine of St Columba on Iona.

Iona was one of the great hubs of Celtic civilization. It was here that the Book of Kells, one of the greatest early illuminated manuscripts, was painted and protected until carried to Ireland to preserve it from Viking attack, and it was from here that Columba converted the King of the Picts.

The burial place of the Kings of Scots is in St Oran's cemetery. St Oran's is said to contain the bodies of sixteen kings who reigned up to the end of the eleventh century. After that, Dunfermline Abbey became the official royal cemetery, although Iona continued to be the resting place of the Lords of the Isles. The cemetery is set apart from the main abbey complex. There's a little chapel, built a century after Macbeth, and rows of marked and unmarked graves.

Opposite: Iona, the burial place of the Kings of Scots and the Lords of the Isles.

2
MACBETH

Eilean
Chalbha
Port Chlacha Dubha
Carraig an Daimh
Lagandorain
Ardionra
Dun I
100
Auchabhaich
Port an
Duine
Mhairbh
Port a' Ghoirtein Bhig
51
Fort
Cross
Clachanach
Cladh an
Disart
(rems of)
IONA
Abbey
Mus
Hotel
Eilean Didil
Baile Mor
MacLean's
Cross
Culbuirg
Eilean nan Slat
Nunnery
St Ronan's
Bay
Stac Liath
P
Jetty
Meml
Maol
21
Camas Cuil
an t-Saimh
Shian
Ferry P
Maol Mhàrtuin
Beul-mhòr
Spouti
74
Druim
Aoin
Port M
an Musimul
Port an Fhir-bh
Port na
Port Goirtean
Slugan D
Rubha Beul à Chaolai
Eilean na h-

Sadly, some bright spark in the nineteenth century had the idea of uprooting all the gravestones and putting them into two rows – the 'ridge of the kings' and the 'ridge of the chiefs' – thus ensuring that no one grave could be identified. So, there's no definitive way of proving whether Macbeth lies in the graveyard or not. But it does seem appropriate that he should have ended up at Iona. The Celtic shrine symbolizes perfectly what Macbeth represented: the end of the line of the great Highland kings.

After Duncan the kingship continued to be passed from father to son. Malcolm and his southern Scottish descendants tried to wipe out the last remnants of the Macbeth line, but the people of Moray went on causing trouble until the beginning of the thirteenth century. Malcolm married twice. His first wife was Scottish, but when she died he married Margaret, who was English and the granddaughter of the English King, Edmund Ironside. She had originally arrived at the Scottish court seeking refuge after the Battle of Hastings. She was a pious woman, canonized as St Margaret of Scotland in 1250. But her net contribution to Scotland's history was to make it less Scottish. She instigated reforms within the Scottish Church to try and bring it more into line with Europe, and her children, particularly David I, brought in more and more European innovations and traditions. From the abandonment of tanistry to the introduction of European architecture, coins and material culture, Malcolm and Margaret mark a new start in Scottish culture.

And Macbeth marks the end of an older regime. He was the last king to rule Scotland from the Highlands. And he paid the price when his history came to be written by supporters of the new regime. For them he represented the ever-present threat from the north – the Gaelic-speaking people from the Mounth and beyond – who were different from the southern Scots not only politically but culturally too.

The bias against Macbeth can be seen in the various chronicles. John of Fordun maintains that Macbeth's kingship was illegitimate, and Andrew of Wyntoun puts the knife in, alleging that Macbeth's mother slept with the devil to produce Macbeth. It's also Wyntoun who first records the supernatural elements of the three 'weird sisters'. The stories about Macbeth become embellished by later historians, including Boethius and John Major (more about him in the next chapter), before Holinshed and Shakespeare's play set Macbeth's reputation in stone. But the derogatory process still carries on after Shakespeare, and there is a later book about him, *The Secret History of Macbeth*, in which the King is a lothario and the traditional story becomes a series of bedroom capers.

If Macbeth's reputation suffered because he was the last great Celtic king of Scots, it is perhaps Scotland that was the greater loser. If the curse of the Scottish King has fallen anywhere, it is on the country that finally rejected him and thereby lost out on a whole different future. The oath of loyalty sworn by Malcolm Canmore to Edward II, and the embracing of a pan-European culture by the new political elite, soon came together to spell disaster for Scotland.

But that's with the benefit of historical hindsight. So much can hinge on one life and one death.

Out, out, brief candle!
Life's but a walking shadow, a poor player,
That struts and frets his hour upon the stage,
And then is heard no more…

MACBETH

FURTHER INFORMATION

There's been plenty written on Shakespeare's *Macbeth*. Any edition of the play will have a good introduction, but little has been written on the King himself.

The best single book on Macbeth is *Macbeth: Man and Myth* by Nick Aitchison (Sutton Publishing, 1999).

There's an excellent summary article of what we know about Macbeth's career by Professor Edward Cowan in *Moray Province and People*, ed. W. D. H. Sellar (Scottish Society for Northern Studies, 1993).

Holinshed's Chronicles. You'll get these in any bookshop with a good literature section. I found an old copy of an Everyman book of the chronicles as used in Shakespeare that shows you how William combined stories about different Scottish kings to create his play about Macbeth.

Besides Shakespeare's play, there are many literary treatments of Macbeth's story, the most accessible of which is probably Nigel Tranter's *Macbeth the King* (Coronet Books, 1978).

Ordnance Survey map numbers: The most useful will be map numbers 27 and 28 (Moray), 37 to find Macbeth's Cairn and 53 and 58 for Dunkeld, Perth, and Dunsinane.

As we've seen, compared with Boudica there aren't many physical remains left in museums from eleventh-century Scotland, but you should try and see the real Stone of Destiny in Edinburgh Castle, right in the centre of Edinburgh. Tel: 0131 225 9846.

CHAPTER 3
HAROLD

We take our first foray south of the Thames with the story of King Harold. His homeland was the old Saxon kingdom of Wessex, comprising present-day Hampshire, Dorset and Sussex, and his life began and ended there. But his career took him much further afield, to Hereford and the Welsh border country, to York, which saw his finest hour, and even across the Channel to Normandy where his fate was decided by the man later known as William the Conqueror.

After the death of Macbeth there was a transformation of Scotland's culture and politics, but it happened gradually. In England, though, change occurred with the suddenness and violence of a tidal wave.

And we can pinpoint the start of this change both in time and place. Go to the ruins of Battle Abbey in Sussex. There you'll find a large stone where the High Altar once stood. The altar was deliberately placed to mark the spot where, towards dusk on 14 October 1066, an arrow fired randomly into the air by an unknown archer pierced the eye of King Harold II of England.

That chance shot ended the second-shortest reign of any English king and changed the country forever. Hordes of Normans under the leadership of William the Conqueror took over and removed a whole way of life. The Saxons, who by now had all but forgotten that they too were originally invaders, were completely replaced as the country's rulers. Within a decade, England's language, customs, architecture and politics were transformed.

Harold's death is one of the most vivid images that have come down to us through time. But in a way it's too vivid. His life story was at the mercy of the new regime's propaganda

Opposite: Harold has always held a place in the popular consciousness. This portrait first appeared on a Will's cigarette card in the 1890s.

machine. Consequently, all you ever get to hear about him is that he was the loser at the Battle of Hastings.

But there's a hidden history, a tragic story of scheming, love, intrigue, violence and cold hard cash. This is the real story of the last great Anglo-Saxon king.

HAROLD'S EARLY LIFE

Although Harold was born nearly a thousand years ago, his career has a particular resonance for a modern audience. As with all the best tragic heroes, his rise and fall isn't just a political journey caused by external events and pressures, but a personal odyssey involving his nearest and dearest.

Around 1020, Harold was born into one of the most remarkable families in English history. He could never have dreamt that he would end up as king. His family weren't kings and queens. The Anglo-Saxon royal line traced its roots back to King Alfred the Great, who united the Saxon kingdoms of England in the ninth century, and beyond him to the legendary Cerdic. He in turn was said to be only nine generations away from Woden, the Saxon god of war. It was a venerable dynasty.

By comparison, Harold's family were Johnny-come-latelies, a Saxon version of the American Dream. Harold's second name was Godwinson – he was the son of the great Earl Godwin, who in a culture where social mobility was the exception rather than the rule, had pulled himself up through the ranks through the sheer force of his personality. His rise was so dramatic he inspired legends.

One tradition says that Godwin began life as a *ceorl* (or churl, from which we get our word churlish), the lowest order of Anglo-Saxon freemen. But whatever his original status, he rose from obscurity to become an alderman or earl (the southern equivalent of a Scottish mormaer), under the Saxon King Aethelred, who we now know by the nickname 'The Unready'.

He may have been an arriviste, but Godwin was also a supreme political operator. By wheeling and dealing, he carved out a sizeable empire for himself in Wessex, the old Saxon kingdom that encompassed most of southern England. He became something of a folk hero, famed for his cunning. Like a latter-day Odysseus, tales abounded of his wiliness. One apocryphal story describes how he wangled the manor of Bosham away from its previous owner, the Archbishop of Canterbury.

Opposite: The church at Bosham. The spire was added later, but Harold could well have leant out of the bell-tower windows, watching out for Viking raiders.

One day Godwin and some of his men rushed up to the prelate, catching him unawares. 'My Lord,' Godwin asked as though there'd been some mix up, 'do you give me Bosham?'

'I give you Bosham?' exclaimed the Archbishop. Immediately Godwin and his carefully rehearsed stooges dropped to their knees and grovelled in thanks, making it impossible for the bemused reverend to withdraw the offer without losing face.

You reach Bosham by taking the M27/A27 from either west or east to the western outskirts of Chichester. At the roundabout marking the start of the bypass, take the A259 towards Fishbourne. If you want a sense of how wealthy southern Roman collaborators lived in Boudica's time, stop off at Fishbourne Palace for a while and marvel at the fantastic mosaics. A couple of miles further on turn left for Bosham. When you get to the village there's a T-junction. The left turn takes you along a southern spit of land from where you can get a great view of the village over the water. The right turn (signposted to the church) leads to the village itself.

Bosham on the Sussex coast is a good place to start the Harold trail. The southern earldom of Wessex belonged to Godwin and, in later life, to Harold himself. Although the family led a peripatetic life, the family manor at Bosham would have been one of Harold's more familiar homes. Set inside the protective arms of a natural harbour, Bosham was the home base for the Godwins' private fleet and figures heavily as a place of departure throughout Harold's story.

The beautiful little village is far more of a backwater today than it was in the eleventh century. The sea lies at the end of the main street and laps the very walls of the picturesque cottages in the oldest part of the village. If you arrive at low tide be careful where you park, as it's been known for people to return from a morning's sightseeing to find their vehicle semi-submerged.

Once in the village and parked, make sure you go first to the church, parts of which date back to Harold's day and beyond. King Cnut's daughter is buried here under the chancel arch.

As the most significant building in Saxon Bosham, the church would have had a practical use as well as a religious one. Historians think that the tower, although one storey shorter than today, would have been used as a defensive watchtower against Viking raids. The striking setting offers a view straight down Chichester Harbour to the Solent. And as it's made of stone, it would have been the strongest building to run to for protection if potential invaders were approaching.

The story of how Godwin acquired Bosham isn't just implausible, it also makes him sound like little more than an eleventh-century Del Boy. But although he may have been tricky, he certainly wasn't unprincipled. His integrity saved his family's fortunes and possibly his life.

Since the time of Alfred the Great the Saxons had held off the Vikings, who'd been restricted to the north of England, then called 'the Danelaw'. Gradually the Vikings were pushed back further and further. Then, at the beginning of the eleventh century they returned in force. Aethelred 'The Unready' was a hapless ruler. When he died, the kingship passed briefly to his son Edmund Ironside, before falling to the great Viking invader, King Cnut of Denmark, whom we've met already in the last chapter. Aethelred's other sons fled to Normandy for refuge and his wife tactically married the incoming victor.

Godwin had been a staunch supporter of the Saxon monarchy throughout, and you might have expected him to be purged as part of the old guard. Cnut was a ruthless ruler with a particular penchant for mutilating his enemies by cutting off noses, ears and hands. But Godwin survived precisely because he'd never shown any intention of swapping sides, and had not made overtures to the new king.

The Dane recognized his loyalty to his previous masters. In return, Godwin indicated his willingness to transfer his allegiance to the Viking regime by taking a Danish wife and

giving his eldest sons Scandinavian names: Swegen (Sven), Harold and Tostig (pronounced and sometimes written Tosti).

We know Harold was born during this period of Danish occupation, but we have hardly any other information about his early years. The chroniclers couldn't have had a clue that the young Saxon would become as influential as he did. Besides, with infant mortality a fact of life at all levels of society, there was little point wasting precious ink and parchment on individuals who might disappear before reaching maturity.

So Godwin's sons grew up anonymously. But we know they were educated because the records tell us that Harold's sister had some Latin, and it's certain that her brothers would have been accorded similar privileges. Godwin swiftly became Cnut's right-hand man, and for almost twenty years helped him control the English end of an empire that also encompassed Denmark. But when Cnut died in 1035 shortly before his fortieth birthday, Godwin, usually so astute, miscalculated by supporting the wrong contender for the throne.

The expected successor was Cnut's youngest son, Harthacnut. But, when his father died, Harthacnut was far away in Denmark and the throne was seized by another son, Harold Harefoot, who had the advantage of being in Winchester at that moment, near the royal power centre.

Godwin survived the putsch, although only by the skin of his teeth. So he was desperate to find a way to prove his loyalty to the new and unexpected ruler, and consequently took part in a piece of political skulduggery.

Cnut's widow, Emma, had two Saxon sons by her previous husband, Aethelred the Unready. They were Edward (who would later become the Confessor) and Alfred, and they were both living in exile in Normandy. In the confusion following Cnut's death they made a tentative bid for the throne. Edward sailed to Southampton with a small fleet, intending to make an assault on the royal centre of Winchester. But the locals weren't overly impressed with the proposed return of the Saxon monarchy. He encountered strong opposition along the coast and retreated to the Continent without attempting a landing.

At the same time Alfred landed at Dover, no doubt heading for London. Dover was part of Godwin's domain. To show his loyalty to the new regime, Godwin detained Alfred and his followers and handed him over to Harold Harefoot. Alfred's retinue were cut down in cold blood. Alfred himself was taken to Ely where he was imprisoned, blinded and mutilated. His injuries were so severe and he was so casually treated that he died there from his wounds.

So was Godwin destroying the possibility of the crown returning to the Saxon royal line for his own ends? Not necessarily. He had been put in a very difficult position. A refusal to hand Alfred over would have made him a rebel. And although he wasn't directly responsible for the appalling treatment of the royal prisoner, he clearly shared the blame. If Edward, the surviving brother, ever came to the throne, Godwin would have a lot of explaining to do.

Six years later his worst fears must have been realized. Edward was indeed made the English king after Harold Harefoot and Harthacnut died in quick succession. Godwin swore a solemn oath to clear himself of Alfred's death and gave his new master a magnificent ship with a golden winged dragon at the prow, in an attempt to buy his favour. Nevertheless every time he saw the power-broker from Wessex, Edward must have thought, 'That man killed my brother!'

With Edward, the Anglo-Saxon dynasty was restored. But 'The Confessor', so-called because of his devotion to the Christian faith, was a virtual stranger to his own country. After twenty-six years of Viking rule, he was the new boy, fresh back from Normandy. He needed all the help and experience the surviving Saxon earls could give him if he was going to control England. Godwin may have been instrumental in getting his brother killed, but grudges had to take second place to political expediency. Godwin was particularly vital to Edward's immediate interests. As Earl of Wessex, he controlled the south of England where the royal power bases of London, Winchester and Canterbury where located.

And along with Godwin came his family. He had six sons, all of whom would in time become eligible for office themselves. Harold was the second of these. He'd been in his teens when the young Alfred had been murdered, but now he was twenty and ready to join the family firm.

An anonymous engraving of Harold from the mid-eighteenth century.

A TASTE OF POWER

In about 1043, Edward made Harold Earl of East Anglia. He also gave earldoms to the oldest Godwin brother, Swegen, and Harold's Danish cousin, Beorn. But the greatest family triumph was reserved for their sister, Edith, who in 1045, married the King.

For Godwin it was a political triumph. The offence of his part in the murder of Edward's brother seemed to be forgotten. He was now father-in-law to the King. His family's lands encompassed the greater part of southern England from the Severn to the Wash.

Harold in particular seemed nicely set up. He was in his early twenties and

had already embarked on a successful political career. We can keep track of his progress at this time because, in eleventh-century Britain, land was power, and deeds and documents that refer to his landholdings still exist today.

An earl had responsibility for a large swathe of territory, but didn't own it all. Nevertheless, along with the office, there came ownership of several estates whose income allowed him to do his job. It paid for his professional household troops – the housecarls – that were his private army, and enabled him to protect and police his earldom. It financed the system of officials known as reeves who calculated and collected taxes for him and for the King. It also gave him the sort of lifestyle that became an earl. Earldom didn't come cheap. He would have been expected to entertain the King and his retinue on a regular basis, feasting them in his great hall.

As Harold went about doing his duties, he gained more lands. As a new earl he wanted to win the support of the locals by doing a favour here, spreading a little cash there, offering protection and justice to the people of East Anglia. In return the landowners showed their gratitude by giving him a cut, donating pockets of land to add to his estates. It wasn't corruption, just the way things got done. When Harold moved on to his next post, he kept these lands and so built up his fortune.

To make the young man's happiness complete, he was in love.

The object of his affections was a beautiful young heiress from Norfolk known variously in the chronicles as Edith 'the Rich', Edith 'the fair' or, most romantically, Edith 'Swan-neck'. This was a reference to her smooth white skin, a quality highly prized among aristocratic beauties, as opposed to the sunburnt roughness of women who had to work in the fields.

The relationship may have started out as a tactical alliance. Harold needed to ingratiate himself with the people of East Anglia by making a local match. Edith was a considerable landowner in her own right and may have been looking for a powerful partner to protect her interests. But whatever its beginnings, the affair blossomed into a genuine passion that was to last until Harold died.

Nonetheless Edith was always an unofficial wife. Harold and she had what was known in eleventh-century Britain as a 'Danish marriage': a relationship that had its roots in Viking and pagan custom. In contrast to a Christian marriage blessed by the Church, a Danish marriage could easily be dissolved. As one of the highest-ranking earls in England, Harold had to keep his marriage options open. He knew that later in life he might have to make a political alliance.

As we've seen with Macbeth, love and marriage in the eleventh century didn't necessarily go together like the proverbial carriage and horse. But while Edith was aware that she might have to get divorced if political expediency demanded it, she also knew that her position would be respected even if Harold married someone else in church. Their relationship had a legal standing. Edith's children could expect an inheritance and preferment.

A Danish marriage was neither shameful nor disreputable. Cnut himself had a Danish-style wife before marrying Aethelred's widow, and Harold Harefoot, who was one of the sons from this marriage, later inherited the throne.

Harold Godwinson and Edith Swan-neck were to have six children together. His life as Earl of East Anglia might have been an idyll of domestic bliss if it hadn't been for the black sheep of the Godwin family, Harold's older brother, Swegen.

BIG BROTHER

Swegen is the archetypal aristocratic bad boy. In another age we might have found him fighting bouncers in nightclubs or dealing class A drugs. In the eleventh century, when nobles had a private army at their disposal, the problem child was much more of a problem. Swegen was violent and out for himself. He wasn't a team player in the Godwin family enterprise. Indeed he claimed, without apparent justification, that he wasn't Earl Godwin's son at all, but the illegitimate child of King Cnut. His mother must have been so proud of him!

Trouble started in earnest in 1046 at a time when Wales was split into two kingdoms. Swegen, whose earldom included Herefordshire on the south Wales border, ganged up with Gruffydd, a prince from north Wales, and launched an assault on the southern Welsh kingdom. Alliances and pre-emptive strikes were an accepted way of protecting vulnerable border territory, so this was pretty much par for the course. But what happened as the troops returned triumphantly home was the first of a series of actions that were considered barbarous even in such a violent age.

The chronicles tell in shocked tones how Swegen abducted the Abbess of Leominster, raped her and proceeded to keep her prisoner for a year. It's not clear if this was simply sexual gratification or whether Swegen wanted a similar sort of local marriage to Harold. If he did, his methods outraged a society hardened to most displays of rape and pillage.

It took a year of negotiating and the threat of excommunication to obtain the nun's release. Eventually she was returned to her convent, and Swegen was sentenced to exile. Despite his father's pleadings, Edward and the other earls were adamant that such behaviour couldn't be tolerated. As befits someone who claimed to be descended from the great Anglo-Viking Cnut, Swegen took himself off to Denmark.

But he showed up again like a bad penny in 1049. Predictably, after three years of raising hell, he'd been kicked out of Denmark. His offences aren't specified in the chronicles, but if he'd managed to offend a bunch of Vikings with his bad manners, it must have been something pretty spectacular. Swegen, accompanied by his retinue, sailed back to Britain, cap in hand, to ask Edward's forgiveness. First in line to support his cause was his father, Earl Godwin.

In Swegen's absence Harold had matured. He'd taken command of a ship and had been proving his worth to King Edward as a skilful naval commander by sailing with the fleet that protected England's southern coastline from attack by raiding parties from Flanders.

He was indignant at his prodigal brother's return. When Swegen was exiled his lands had been forfeited and were divided between Harold and his cousin Beorn. Swegen's restoration meant that they'd have to surrender these lands. As a loyal servant of the crown for the last three years, it didn't seem fair to Harold that he should have to lose out for the sake of family unity. Supported by his cousin, he stood up to his father and made it clear he wouldn't give Swegen back his estates.

This division within the Godwin family suited King Edward down to the ground. It gave him the confidence to refuse the exile's request for forgiveness, and he gave Swegen just four days' safe conduct to leave England. But Swegen didn't go. Instead he retreated with his ships to the family manor at Bosham. Godwin, Beorn, Harold and his younger brother Tostig should all have been on standby with the royal fleet at Sandwich in Kent, but they'd been forced by bad weather into Pevensey harbour.

The Godwins were in their ships in the shadow of the old Roman fort waiting for the weather to clear. Who should they see trotting down the quayside but Swegen. He'd ridden along the coast for one last appeal to the family to support his bid for reinstatement.

Harold seems to have held out against his brother, but Swegen was partially successful. For some reason, cousin Beorn changed his mind and agreed to speak to the King on the prodigal's behalf. He and Swegen returned to Bosham on horseback with just three attendants. It was a fatal move.

As soon as he got back to his ships at Bosham, Swegen took Beorn hostage. It was a spectacular breach of trust and it's hard to see how Swegen thought it would help his cause, but he set sail with cousin Beorn trussed up like a turkey. Once at sea something else went wrong – possibly a row between the two cousins over Beorn's treatment – and the affair ended with Swegen killing his cousin and dumping his body in an unmarked grave at Dartmouth.

Once again, he'd gone much too far. The sailors of the royal fleet declared him *nithing*, the Viking term for someone utterly beyond the pale. Six of Swegen's fleet of eight ships deserted him. He was forced to flee to England's enemies in Flanders for support.

Harold went to Dartmouth to recover the body of the murdered Beorn and ensured his cousin a proper burial at Winchester next to King Cnut. He emerged from the episode with his lands intact and his personal reputation enhanced. But he wasn't a free agent. His fortunes still depended on his father.

Incredibly, even after his errant son had raped a nun, murdered his cousin and accused his mother of infidelity, Godwin was still putting pressure on King Edward to allow his return. In 1050 the campaign paid off, and Edward grudgingly allowed Swegen back.

Today Pevensey is little more than a beach and a castle built on the foundations of a Roman fort. There's a roundabout where the eastern end of the A27 meets the A259 coming from nearby Eastbourne. The beach at Pevensey is backed by miles of marshland, which is all that remains of what was once a giant harbour. Nine hundred years ago the sea came inland almost as far as Hailsham, six miles away. The castle once commanded an important strategic position overlooking this inlet. Now it seems washed up by the tide, but it's still worth exploring.

It caused all sorts of tensions. Not so much with Harold. Beorn's death meant that Swegen could be given land from his cousin's earldom without taking away Harold's gains. But there were new figures on the English political stage.

Edward had spent much of his early life in Normandy. Now he began bringing in French and Norman allies to build up his power base and reduce his dependence on the Godwins. He'd given Hereford to his Norman relative Earl Ralph when Swegen was exiled. Swegen's return prompted a bitter land dispute with Ralph. Edward had also imported a new Norman Archbishop of Canterbury, Robert de Jumièges, with an agenda to reform the English Church, thought to be corrupted by its closeness to the secular world. De Jumièges thoroughly disapproved of Swegen's reinstatement.

To make matters worse, Edward had another stick with which to beat the Godwins. His marriage to Harold's sister Edith had been a coup for the Godwins. But she hadn't had a baby, the main raison d'être for a royal wife. Maybe she was barren, but later sources suggest that Edward chose to be celibate either for religious reasons or because he had a revulsion for sex. Nevertheless, if an eleventh-century queen didn't have children, it was her fault. If it hadn't been for the power of the Godwin family, Edward would probably have renounced Edith long before and made another political match with a foreign princess.

But with no royal offspring and Godwin's reckless support for his no-good eldest son, Edward felt confident. At last it was time to do what he must have been planning since he first became king. He was about to set up the man who'd been responsible for his brother's death.

EXILE AND RETURN

It was July 1051. Eustace of Boulogne, Edward's French brother-in-law, had popped over to England on a lightning visit. After holding talks with Edward, he returned to join his ships at Dover in the heart of Earl Godwin's territory.

No one knows what was said between Edward and Eustace, but on the outskirts of Dover Eustace and his bodyguard put on their armour as though expecting trouble. Sure enough, in the inn where they stopped to dine a fight started with the landlord. One of Eustace's bodyguards was killed. A running battle broke out between the locals and the visiting Frenchmen. Twenty locals and nineteen of Eustace's men died in the resulting riot.

This provided Edward with the opportunity to set a trap. He ordered Godwin to harry the people of Dover as punishment. Godwin was faced with the choice of losing the affection and loyalty of his own people by systematically burning, looting and pillaging in his homeland or openly defying the King. He chose rebellion.

In response, Edward called a royal council at Gloucester on 8 September. At issue was not only Godwin's refusal to punish the people of Dover, but also the resurrected accusation of his complicity in the death of Alfred.

HAROLD

Godwin was in trouble. He decided to show up at the council with his forces to try and change the King's mind by making the cost of enforcing the order too high. He summoned his men and rallied Swegen and Harold with their housecarls.

Harold had to get involved out of self-interest, not just family loyalty. If Edward removed Godwin, his sons would surely be next. The three forces rendezvoused at the family manor of Beverstone in Gloucestershire on 1 September. But their show of force didn't sway Edward; it merely hardened his resolve. He persuaded the Earls of Mercia and Northumbria to bring out their troops, portraying Godwin's action as open rebellion. Both sides, though, were unwilling to start a civil war. When a stalemate ensued, the council was postponed until 21 September in London and hostages were exchanged.

In the eleventh century, relatives of warring factions gave hostages to each other to show good faith. They might be kept for years as enforced guests in varying conditions of comfort. At Beverstone, the Godwins offered up Harold's youngest brother Wulfnoth, and Swegen's son, Hakon. It was the last time Harold would see them for thirteen years, and they were to play a vital part in his eventual downfall.

Support for the Godwins swiftly began to vanish. Being on a powerful earl's side was one thing – fighting the lawfully appointed King was another. By the time the Godwins arrived in London for the reconvened parlay, the situation looked bleak. First Edward declared Swegen an outlaw without waiting for the council, then he refused to grant Godwin and Harold safe passage to attend. The King's forces were on the north side of the Thames, Godwin's on the south. With their forces dwindling and no guarantee of safety on the other side of the river, the Godwins didn't dare cross to plead their case.

Edward had won. The most powerful family in England was forced to flee the country. At the beginning of October, Bishop Stigand of Winchester conveyed the king's message. Godwin and his sons were declared outlaws and given five days to leave. Godwin himself sailed from Bosham with most of the family while Harold and a younger brother, Leofwine, left via Bristol for Dublin. To Harold it must have seemed a disastrous end to a promising career.

Edward confiscated their lands and divided them up among the existing earls, their relatives, and his Norman friends and relations. He imposed more Continental bishops on the English Church. And he renounced his childless queen, putting her into the care of a nunnery. After twelve years it seemed he'd got revenge for his brother's death. But he'd hardly had time to celebrate when the Godwins struck back.

Edward had done the unthinkable. He'd removed one of the great barons from the English stage. The other earls now started thinking about the precariousness of their own position. The exiles had taken plenty of cash with them to fit out ships and recruit mercenaries. Tentative overtures to the barons in England received favourable responses.

In June 1052 the Godwin clan returned. While Godwin made sorties along the south coast, Harold sailed from Dublin, entered the Bristol Channel with his fleet, and harried

Beverstone was to prove pivotal for the Godwins. The village is about eight miles south-east of Stroud on the A4135 between Tetbury and Dursley. There's no sign of a Saxon manor, but the castle today is a wonderful mixture of architectural styles with a house nestling in the innards of an older ruin.

the coast of Devon and Somerset. He'd never taken a force into combat on his own account before. His first taste of real action was a skirmish at Porlock on the Somerset coast where he routed a small but significant force, killing more than thirty local nobles.

Then father and son rendezvoused at Dorset before sailing along the coast of Wessex towards London. On the way they picked up support from a population who didn't like the new regime.

The Godwin bandwagon rolled into town ten months after they'd fled in terror. Mooring on the Southwark bank of the Thames, they once again faced Edward's forces on the north bank. (In those days there was no bridge. Emissaries between the two forces had to be rowed across.)

Stigand, the Bishop of Winchester, again acted as go-between. This time the Godwins had the upper hand. Support for Edward was melting away. A truce was called and a council was held the next day.

The Godwins were reinstated. Godwin did the right thing by eleventh-century standards and threw himself at Edward's feet in repentance before taking a solemn oath to clear himself of his 'crimes', but it was still clear who had won. The King was forced into a humiliating climb-down. The Godwins' lands were restored, and Harold's sister returned to the royal marriage bed. As part of the rapprochement, Edward's policy of introducing Norman and French nobles and churchmen was halted. Many of those who had 'come lately into the realm' were unceremoniously booted out.

Some didn't even wait for the verdict. The Norman archbishop, Robert de Jumièges, had packed his bags and fled for his homeland as soon as the council was announced. He took with him Wulfnoth and Hakon, the two young Godwin hostages, maybe to ensure that he got out of the country alive. Others, such as Osborn Pentecost, who was based on the Welsh border, were given a deadline to leave. Most went south, but Osborn was one of a number of engineers who worked on the Norman fortifications, then followed their fortunes north to Scotland to sign up with Macbeth. Along with many of his comrades he died three years later in the battle at Dunsinane.

Stigand the Bishop of Winchester was made Archbishop of Canterbury. He held on to the diocese of Winchester as well, even though this was against Church law. But what must have seemed to Harold like a piffling anomaly by the standards of the time was eventually to be a nail in his coffin.

In 1052 the future looked rosy for Harold. He'd recovered from disaster with his reputation boosted and his military prowess established. Within a year, two other events accelerated his rise to power.

There'd been one significant exception to the general Godwin amnesty. Bad boy Swegen hadn't been allowed back. It seems that one of the terms of the Godwin restoration was that Swegen should first make a pilgrimage of repentance. Never one to do things

by halves, he'd set off barefoot for the Holy Land. He died of cold near Constantinople in September 1052 on the return journey.

Before this news reached England, Godwin himself was dead. The chronicles say that during the Easter festivities of 1053 he keeled over speechless. At sixty, the wily politician had succumbed to a stroke.

Godwin, Earl of Wessex, was buried in Winchester and King Edward named his successor. Harold Godwinson was to assume his father's title and lands. At thirty-one, Harold was the most powerful earl in Britain. He was out from under the stigma of his troublesome brother and the burden of his father's awkward history with Edward. He could now establish his own reputation

EARL OF WESSEX

Harold Godwinson was to spend thirteen years as the Earl of Wessex and the King's right-hand man. His domain extended throughout southern England. The next brother in line, Tostig, was made Earl of Northumberland. It turned England into a giant Godwin sandwich. When two younger brothers, Gyrth and Leofwine, were also given earldoms, the clan became one of the richest families in Europe.

Harold was the eleventh-century equivalent of a multi-millionaire. He'd continued to pick up land throughout his career. The map of England was a patchwork of territory that he owned personally. From the Domesday Book we can get some idea of what he was worth. The taxable value of his lands alone was £5,000 per year. A slave woman had to survive the winter on three pence. It's easy to understand why Harold's personal standard was an armed man embroidered with thread of purest gold!

Harold seems to have been as smooth an operator as his father, and he wasn't above treading on toes to increase his wealth. Like his father, he was accused of appropriating lands from the Church. While it's true that he did end up with disputed lands, the Norman chroniclers who detail these crimes omit to mention that King William was quite happy to take over these properties without restoring them to their original owners.

Harold's estates underpinned a lavish lifestyle. This would have included great feasts and expensive gifts for favourites, but his great passion was hunting, and specifically hawking. Hunting with hawks was a favourite aristocratic sport that required great skill and patience. A peregrine falcon can fly faster than any other bird, and it was this noble creature that would have been a vital part of Harold's retinue as he moved from manor to manor. He would also have kept birds for his guests: small hawks like the hobby for the ladies and, in case the King came to visit, a goshawk, the bird that only royals were allowed to fly. We know that Harold's interest was such that he had a library of books about hawking.

But it wasn't all fun. A good proportion of Harold's income went on his official duties. In 1056 these included travelling abroad. Edward was still childless and Harold went on a mission as far as Germany to try and track down an atheling – a suitable heir – from a missing branch of Edward's family now living in Hungary. Tacked on to this visit, he probably made a pilgrimage to Rome. He was a man of his age and, like Macbeth, followed the standard religious customs for the devout aristocrat.

All English aristocrats had their pet religious projects. King Edward had given the kingship a fixed base for the first time, on the island of Westminster upstream from London. But besides locating his palace there, he lavished money on the monks of Westminster, turning their abbey into one of the most important in the land.

Not to be outdone, Harold poured money into a major building project at the Abbey of Holy Cross at Waltham. His choice was a very personal one. The church contained a miracle-working crucifix, a carving of the Holy Cross. One chronicle records that Harold, who may like his father have been prone to strokes, had an episode of paralysis and was cured by a visit to Waltham and its marvellous cross. He not only paid for the bricks and mortar, but ensured that the abbey acquired high religious status. On his European pilgrimage he'd visited many religious centres, and he persuaded them to part with some of their highly prized religious relics. Bits of the True Cross, saints' bones and the like had their own hierarchy according to their ability to work miracles, and possession of good relics significantly enhanced a church's reputation.

The town of Waltham Abbey in Essex is named after the church that was once its economic hub. Nowadays it's a pretty market town trying to hide behind a sprawling outskirt of industrial units and warehousing. It's very easy to get to, lying just off junction 26 of the M25 on the A121.

Odda's Chapel at Deerhurst. Much smaller scale than later medieval foundations but compared with houses made of thatch and pig dung a major financial investment.

To ensure the various relics were given due dignity, Harold splashed out on the abbey's fixtures and fittings. These included a gold and marble altar, great Gospel books with silver covers, and a chasuble, or priest's ceremonial cloak, made with 8 kilos of gold thread. When the abbey was finally dedicated on 3 May 1060, on the Feast of the Finding of the True Cross, it was a national event. The service was conducted by the Archbishop of York, and the King, Queen and leading nobility were all present.

The abbey lives on as the parish church of Waltham. If the centre of town is busy, there's a park with car parking that you can access from the ring road. This is part of the Lea Valley trail and you follow signs through the park to the abbey. In its heyday in the Middle Ages, the foundation was massive. The stone outline of the medieval abbey can still be seen in the grass. It stretches twice as far as both the existing church and Harold's foundation. Indeed, that original Saxon church was largely cannibalized in the expansion, with just one trace of a wall left in the crypt. And the riches that Harold collected and donated disappeared too. When the monastery vanished with Henry VIII's dissolution, so did the gold and ornaments with which it had been endowed. It is nevertheless an impressive building.

By funding Waltham Abbey, Harold hoped to secure his eternal salvation. It had the added benefit of enhancing his reputation as a great lord of wealth and generosity. But this lavish spending would have counted for nothing among his peers if he hadn't been supremely skilled in his public duties, in particular at defending the realm.

For the first ten years of his earldom Harold built a great reputation as a warrior and politician defending England not from the Vikings to the north or the Normans to the south, but from the Welsh.

THE WELSH CAMPAIGN

One of Edward's reasons for bringing his Norman friends to Britain had been defensive.

Today, Wales and the border country round Hereford are littered with castles, but in the eleventh century they were virtually unknown. The Anglo-Saxons didn't know how to build them. King Alfred the Great had started a tradition of burghs (fortified hill settlements), but there were no purpose-built structures. Over on the Continent, the Normans had come up with the technology of the motte and bailey castle. These were easily defended strongholds that could be thrown up by engineers, and gave a double line of defence. Although small, they provided an ideal base in hostile territory from which a knight and his men could dash out to battle or retreat from an invading force without giving ground.

There are examples of motte and bailey constructions all over the country, but a particularly significant one for our purposes can be found at the village of Eywas (pronounced U-ass) Harold in Herefordshire. The village's name comes from Harold's eventual owner-

HAROLD

If you want a really vivid picture of eleventh-century church building, go to Deerhurst in Gloucestershire. Deerhurst lies a couple of miles south-west of Tewkesbury. In Harold's day it was the location for another religious project. The sponsor here was Odda of Deerhurst. Odda was a Norman interloper, but a man who seems to have been universally popular. His chapel still remains in the village at the end of a dead-end lane past the church. It's a modest timbered barn with few windows, and contrasts starkly with the light and height of the later Norman architectural style. You'll find Deerhurst by taking the M5 to either junction 9 or 10 and then following the A38 until you get to the B4213. Deerhurst is signed from here, as is Odda's Chapel.

ship of the area, but the castle here was built by our old friend Osborn Pentecost who was forced to flee to Macbeth when the Godwins returned.

Compared to other castles, both ruined and restored, with their turrets and towers, moats and crenellations, Osborn's creation is pretty uninspiring. Many locals aren't even aware that there was a castle in the village at all. It's simply known as 'the mound'. However, if you do make the journey up through the village to the tree-covered hillock you get an idea of how impressive these newfangled castles would have been in the eleventh century.

Osborn's castle lies on private land, but the owners are in the process of trying to encourage interest in 'the mound'. The steep tree-lined hill is the inner sanctum of the castle, the bailey. If you stand at its foot, you're in the larger area known as the motte. Both would have been protected by a wooden palisade. Looking out over the countryside as the ground falls away, it begins to feel like a formidable defensive obstacle. In the eleventh century it was sorely needed.

The land south and west of here towards Monmouth was known as Archenfield and was some of the most hotly disputed territory in Britain. Over the course of the eleventh century, it changed hands time and time again. The English earl in charge of Hereford needed to be tough, single-minded and a skilled warrior.

Sadly, in the mid-1050s this was far from the case. Hereford was in the care of Edward's brother-in-law, Earl Ralph of the Vexin, who had survived the purge of Norman nobles. To go with the new technology of castle-building, Ralph had brought some other newfangled ways to Hereford, like fighting with cavalry instead of in the traditional way, on foot. Nevertheless, the Welsh flooded over the border in 1055, overrunning Hereford and burning the minster, and there's a certain glee in the conservative-minded Anglo-Saxon historians' description of the defeat of Ralph's ultra-modern army. Indeed, Ralph became known, although not to his face, as Ralph the Timid.

In response to this Welsh invasion, Edward sent in a national force headed by Harold, whose first moves were not spectacular. Like many good commanders, he was willing to be bold, but hated risk. After chasing the Welsh back over the border, he contented himself with strengthening the defences of Hereford, and opened negotiations with the Welsh leader, Gruffydd ap Llewellyn, who'd succeeded in uniting the two kingdoms of Wales for the first time. This caution shows that Harold was as much a diplomat as a warrior. He was always willing to negotiate to avoid needless bloodshed.

But Harold's other strategy was more controversial. When the Bishop of Hereford died the following year, he encouraged the King to appoint his own personal chaplain, Leofgar, to the vacant see. It was another move to help bolster the area, but it was deeply unpopular and eventually backfired.

Why was this controversial? Well, Leofgar's facial hair was a big problem. He had a fine set of moustaches which he insisted on keeping even as a bishop. A moustache at that

Eywas Harold lies in the Golden Valley of Herefordshire just off the A465 which runs between Hereford and Abergavenny. It's about 45 minutes on from Deerhurst, taking the M50/A40 to Ross-on-Wye and then cross country up the Monnow and Dore Valleys.

time was the mark of a warrior, and though it wasn't unusual for a prelate to go into battle, this was like a vicar turning up to preach a sermon in combat fatigues and camouflage paint.

Pretty soon Harold decided that Leofgar was much too warlike, a conclusion backed up by the disapproving monks who wrote the chronicles. Fortunately for Harold, after less than four months in office, Leofgar died during a rash pre-emptive strike on south Wales using only local forces. Again Harold had to return with a large army to sort out the mess. But the national force was too unwieldy for mountain warfare and soon it became clear to Harold that the only option was a diplomatic solution. He negotiated recognition of Gruffydd as King of All Wales in return for him acknowledging Edward as overlord.

Nevertheless, the ensuing peace with Wales was only temporary. Gruffydd was a constant threat to the border and raided with impunity. He was protected by an alliance with Earl Aelfgar of Mercia in the English Midlands. And when Aelfgar died in 1062, Harold achieved a brilliant and lasting solution to the problem.

Aelfgar had been the head of the other great English family – the rulers of Mercia – and was a natural rival. In the long term his death opened the door to Harold's ambitions, as Aelfgar would have done anything he could to thwart Harold's bid for the crown in 1066. In the short term his demise freed Harold to deal with Gruffydd ap Llewellyn of Wales once and for all.

Harold was now personally responsible for the border with Wales. Ralph the Timid also died in 1057; his earldom was split up and Harold became overlord of Hereford and Gloucester. He now knew that turning up to fight in Wales with a mass of infantry would be pointless. Wales then, like Afghanistan today, was a treacherous landscape unsuitable for heavily armoured troops. Instead Harold decided on a daring cavalry raid to catch Gruffydd before he'd heard the news of the death of his ally, Aelfgar.

Covering 100 miles in a matter of days, he struck Gruffydd's palace in Rhuddlan, near the Welsh coast. Gruffydd escaped at the last minute by sea, but Harold burnt the palace and Gruffydd's ships. It was the first example of Harold's ability to strike swiftly over long distances.

It was an important psychological blow, but Harold followed up with a brilliantly executed campaign to destroy Welsh resistance. He and his younger brother Tostig, the Earl of Northumberland, attacked on two fronts. The year was 1062. In three years the two brothers would be at each other's throats in a fatal family feud, but for the moment the Godwins were acting in perfect unity.

While Tostig moved through the Welsh countryside making lightning raids with light infantry forces, Harold commanded a fleet that struck at different points along the Welsh coast, raiding and harrying. These terror tactics removed the main advantage of the Welsh – their ability to move through difficult terrain.

HAROLD

Gruffydd was forced back into the mountains of Snowdonia. The Godwins' ruthless campaign underlined the Welsh King's inability to defend his own people. As an overlord he was a spent force. The recently united kingdoms of north and south Wales had little sense of what we'd call national identity. In the end the dispirited Welsh finished the job for Harold, sending him Gruffydd's head as a sign of submission.

The battle was won and Harold again opted for peace rather than crushing the Welsh. His innovative tactics had not only won back the lands the Welsh had snatched from Ralph the Timid, but had also nibbled slightly more territory away from them. Harold, ever the sportsman, decided to build a hunting lodge for himself at Portskewet, now in the shadow of the M4 Severn crossing.

So, by 1063, Harold had built quite a reputation for himself and was indispensable to Edward. All was going well. And then either by design or by accident Harold made the worst mistake of his life.

NORMANDY

Compared with many of the characters in this book, Harold's life is richly documented, but from 1064 his history is told not only in chronicles written by monks but by the first ever comic strip: the Bayeux Tapestry.

It's an extraordinary work, strictly speaking an embroidery rather than a tapestry. If you've only seen reproductions, you'll have no idea of its scale and intricacy. It's 70 metres long, and was originally meant to decorate the nave of the cathedral in Bayeux, in the west of Normandy. In spite of the faded colours it still paints a vibrant picture.

It was commissioned in the 1070s by Bishop Odo of Bayeux from unknown crafts-people working in Canterbury. It not only gives us the Norman version of the political story between 1064 and 1066, but also offers tantalizing personal details that flesh out Harold's story. For example, it records the fact that in 1064 he set out from his manor in Bosham on a trip to the Continent. We get an idea of his egalitarian nature as he gives his men a hand dragging the boat into the water, his bare legs seen through the shallows. He takes a retinue and his hawks, so he's obviously going for some time.

Why did he go? The question has tantalized historians for nearly a thousand years. The version told by Norman chroniclers writing after Harold's death and supported by the tapestry goes like this.

While the Godwins were in exile, William of Normandy visited Edward, who promised him the throne of England. Thirteen years later Edward sent Harold on a diplomatic mission to confirm William's position as his heir.

There are several reasons to doubt this interpretation. First, it's by no means certain that William visited England in 1051. Many sources don't mention it at all. At the time

3

HAROLD

Bayeux Cathedral. Only the crypt and bits of wall date back to the time when Harold swore his fatal oath.

Harold (the man with the hawk) sets sail for Normandy.

William was tied up in a vicious struggle to establish his own position within Normandy. A foreign trip would have been a distraction.

Second, even if Edward had wafted promises around in a Normanophile mood, it's clear that he didn't consider the question of succession settled. Harold himself was sent to Germany in 1056 to bring back Edward the atheling as the next king. And when this atheling died, his son Edgar became the chosen heir in his stead. Nevertheless, William certainly believed some sort of promise had been made to him. And that poses a second problem for the historians. If it was common knowledge that William had also been promised the throne, why did Harold visit Normandy? He would have known he was putting himself in a very difficult diplomatic position.

One answer is that the offer of the throne had been made to William not by King Edward, but by the Norman Archbishop of Canterbury, Robert de Jumièges, after he had been forced to flee back to his homeland. If he'd promised William the English crown either on the basis of idle talk from Edward or without authority, no one in England would have known about it.

Whatever the reason, it does seem clear that Harold had no idea what he was sailing into.

Robert de Jumièges also seems to be the unwitting root cause of Harold's journey. In 1052, the jilted Archbishop had left the country with Harold's nephew and his youngest

114

HAROLD

brother as hostages. Rather than an official visit, Harold's quest was personal. He was bravely going to Normandy to negotiate the release of his relatives.

Things went wrong almost from the start. Harold's prayers saw him safe to the other side of the Channel, but then his ship veered off course and he ended up north of Normandy in Ponthieu. The duke there took him prisoner, and was only persuaded to release him after threatening noises from his neighbour, William of Normandy.

Harold was out of the frying pan and straight into a blazing inferno. He arrived in Normandy with a debt of obligation to the fearsome empire-builder who was to be his nemesis. The second most important person in England found himself William's virtual prisoner. His mission to free his brother and nephew had swiftly turned into something far more complicated and sinister.

William had a reputation as a successful but ruthless leader. He wasn't really French at all. As a Norman he traced his forebears back to a Viking called Rollo, the head of a band of marauders who had settled in the Rouen area in AD 911. Immensely successful colonists, these Vikings gradually developed their own French dialect and carved out their own realm and culture while still maintaining a relationship with the pirates from Scandinavia. Their leaders became known as the Duces Northmannorum, the Dukes of the Northmen.

William himself had led a charmed life. His father and mother were probably teenagers when he was born, five years later than Harold in 1027. His father was Robert Duke of Normandy, his mother a tanner's daughter. Born out of wedlock, he was known throughout his early years as William the Bastard.

In 1035 his father died while returning from pilgrimage, leaving his son in the precarious position of being duke at the age of eight. He survived a childhood that included the assassination of his guardians, the murder of his steward in front of his eyes, and being rushed away in the dead of night to avoid another coup attempt. As a result the adult William was ruthless, brutal, cold-blooded, and utterly focused on the acquisition and retention of power.

By the time Harold arrived, William had finished the job of securing his duchy and was looking for new challenges. Harold's Norman 'host' was no doubt cordial – there was feasting and all due ceremony – but Harold had no means of return to his homeland, and none was offered. Unaware of William's ambitions, Harold must have wondered what he could do to obtain his release. Meanwhile he had to travel round Normandy with William's court to his strongholds in Rouen, Falaise and Caen.

The Bayeux Tapestry emphasizes the clash of the two cultures. Harold is portrayed as the typical Saxon warrior, with flowing blond hair and a thick moustache. The English haircut was a source of wonder to the Normans. They played roundheads to the Saxon cavaliers. Norman fashion required having the hair shaved at the back. Even in England some churchmen worried about the effeminacy of the fashion for long hair. The famously saintly

Caen was badly damaged in the Second World War, but the ducal palace survives. Like Waltham Abbey, the earlier ruins of the Norman fortress have been overtaken by more expansive later-medieval buildings, but you can still get a sense of the intimidating surroundings Harold found himself in. Caen is about twenty minutes from Bayeux. If you don't want to drive all the way from England via the Channel Tunnel, there's a ferry from Portsmouth that takes you right to Caen, leaving only the town's complicated traffic system to negotiate. (My tip: head for Centre Ville, park and walk.) While in Caen, make sure you also visit the Abbaye des Hommes where William is buried.

Harold swears his final oath. Although cartoonish in some respects, the Tapestry is accurate enough for us to identify one of the relics that was used in making the oath. Harold's left hand rests on something with a distinct bobble on top. It's clearly meant to be a famous religious treasure known as the 'Bull's Eye', so-called because it was crowned with a single great jewel.

You get to Bayeux by taking the motorway west from Caen heading in the direction of Cherbourg. Once in the town, you can't go wrong. There are signs everywhere pointing you to the *tapiserie*. When you've seen it at the museum of Reine Mathilde, the impressive cathedral is only a short walk away to the west. The tapestry makes it quite clear that it was here Harold perjured himself in support of William's claim to be the next king of England.

Bishop Wulfstan carried a little penknife with him in order to hack off the locks of offending warriors as they knelt to kiss his ring.

William invited his famous Saxon guest to accompany him on a lightning campaign against the Duke of Brittany who'd been causing trouble. Harold couldn't refuse, and it gave him the chance to see the Norman fighting machine in action. When the two leaders met at the Battle of Hastings, Harold would have been well prepared for what was to come.

In his turn, Harold impressed the Normans with his bravery and strength. One notable event is remembered in the chronicles and the Tapestry. The Normans were crossing the River Couesnon which flows into the sea near Mont St Michel on the border of Normandy and Brittany. Some of the knights started to founder in quicksand, and Harold rescued two men in full armour, dragging them to safety.

Back in Normandy, William made Harold a knight. This may seem like an honour, but it was a two-edged sword. It implied William's feudal superiority and entailed an oath of allegiance from Harold. What followed was even more disastrous. William brought his guest to the cathedral at Bayeux and demanded that he swear a sacred oath on holy relics to support his host's claim to the English throne.

Such a solemn oath was taken extremely seriously in the eleventh century. Breaking it could mean damnation. One of the criticisms of Harold in the chronicle commissioned by his sister is that he was 'too free with oaths'. Whether this refers to this incident or is a general character trait isn't made clear.

116

But Harold was in an impossible situation. It's likely that he had only discovered William's ambitions while in Normandy. The oath may have been sprung on him, or perhaps William started pestering him while they were on campaign. Whatever the circumstances, Harold would have known that he had a get-out clause. This was an oath taken under duress. He must have taken it with the eleventh-century equivalent of crossed fingers.

The Tapestry sometimes gives cheeky hints that the Canterbury Saxons who were actually stitching it were adding their own gloss on events. The juxtaposition of Harold swearing the oath and then being released subtly underlines the fact that the oath was sworn under duress. Harold had no choice. Only when he'd done what William wanted was he free to go.

MORE BROTHER TROUBLE

Once back home, Harold was left to ponder the implications of his Norman trip and to work out his future strategy. Up until his Normandy experience he'd been happy to go along with the young heir whom he'd dragged back from Hungary. But he must have begun to realize that, if Edward died sooner rather than later, a new under-age king would be very exposed when faced with the charismatic force of William the Bastard. One simple answer to the problem was for Harold himself to throw his hat in the ring.

If so, his ambitions had no chance to mature before his career was overtaken by an event that was to cause a seismic rupture within his family and contribute to his eventual downfall.

His brother, Tostig, was in trouble. After ten years running the wildest of the English earldoms, Viking-influenced Northumberland, he'd fallen victim to a coup. It's been claimed that the locals didn't like a southerner being in charge, but in reality Tostig had just as good credentials as his illustrious predecessor Siward, who'd defeated Macbeth. Tostig's mother, Gytha, was Danish, so he like Harold would have spoken Anglo-Danish as well as Anglo-Saxon. For ten years he'd fitted into the area with no problems.

Tostig had a reputation for being firm but fair. The chronicles speak approvingly of how he had been tough on crime and tough on the causes of crime, by mutilating offenders and trying to break the Viking tradition of the blood feud which encouraged men to take the law into their own hands when a relative had been killed.

Just before the rebellion, Tostig had got mired in local politics. He'd been responsible for three assassinations of local thanes, two of whom had come to his hall under a promise of safe passage. Even this injustice might have been overlooked if Tostig hadn't hit the Northumbrians where it hurt: in the purse. The problem was tax. In the eleventh century, as now, people thought they were paying too much of it.

Here's a strange historical connection: Harold and his brothers would have known Lady Godiva quite well. Her husband was Earl of Mercia at the same time that the brothers' father Godwin was Earl of Wessex and Harold was starting his career. Typically, we only remember the part of Godiva's story that deals with her taking off her clothes and being spied on by the original Peeping Tom. But her famous ride through Coventry was supposedly the selfless act of an idealistic young noblewoman to try to persuade her husband to reduce the tax burden on the oppressed locals.

Ironically the Northumbrians actually paid far less tax than the rest of the country. Tostig was trying to regularize their tax position on King Edward's behalf by bringing them into line with the people of Wessex and Mercia. But it meant almost doubling the amount they had to pay.

On 3 October thanes from Yorkshire, with about 200 men, stormed Tostig's stronghold in York. They killed two of his personal guard and broke into his treasury and armoury – a sure sign that their grievance was money. They slaughtered 200 more of Tostig's men outside the city walls the next day. This sparked off a general rebellion throughout the earldom. Tostig was outlawed, and the rebels asked for Morcar, the younger brother of the Earl of Mercia and, as it happens, Lady Godiva's grandson, to come and be earl instead.

The rebel bandwagon gained momentum. It trundled down into the Midlands, where Morcar was joined by his brother Edwin of Mercia with his troops. They devastated the area, reaching as far south as Oxford.

This was a serious threat to the stability of King Edward's realm. His instinct was to crush the rebellion and reinstate Tostig. He put his top man on the case. Harold was despatched to deal with the rebellion and report back at a summit in Oxford.

Harold was a consummate politician, but this was the most difficult negotiation of his career, the ultimate conflict between heart and head. It swiftly emerged that the Northumbrians wouldn't capitulate or have Tostig back without a fight. Harold, knowing that William of Normandy was looking for an opportunity to assert his claim, would have realized the potential cost of full-scale civil war in England. Reluctantly, he recommended accepting the rebel demands and depriving Tostig of his earldom.

Tostig was incensed, and accused Harold of deliberately fomenting the rebellion to get rid of him. It was such a serious accusation that Harold was forced to clear himself on solemn oath.

In truth, there could have been self-interest in Harold's decision. If he had started to think about taking the crown himself, Edwin and Morcar would be essential allies. At about this time Harold, whose Danish marriage with Edith 'Swan-neck' had been designed to be dissolved when politics demanded, got officially married in church to the sister of Edwin and Morcar. It was a sign that Harold was firming up his support among the English earls.

However, Harold had always been close to Tostig, and had fought against the Welsh with him. A deliberate plot seems unlikely. Losing Tostig as an ally was a disaster for Harold. What Tostig was probably expecting was the same kind of family loyalty to the detriment of career and country that Godwin had shown to Swegen. Harold was either too cold or too noble to put his country before his brother.

But Tostig was now Harold's arch-enemy. He went into exile in Flanders with a burning grudge against his elder brother. All the chronicles make clear that Harold's eventual downfall came about because of this rift with his brother.

HAROLD THE KING

Christmas 1065, and the court of King Edward was crowded: 28 December was to be the long-awaited consecration of the abbey church at Westminster. But Edward never saw his pet project come to fruition. After carrying out his ceremonial duties on Christmas Day, he was taken ill and confined to his bed. He missed the consecration. A crisis was looming and on hand were all the nobles Harold needed to lobby.

The death of a childless king was a cause for concern. The atheling Edgar was too young. Coming from Hungary, he could barely speak English and had no home-grown support. With William threatening across the Channel, and the necessity of dealing with the rival interests of powerful barons, a child king was patently unsuitable, however good his pedigree. Harold, with his reputation for military prowess and fair-minded political dealing, was the obvious candidate.

This must have been clear to the dying Edward, because on his deathbed he seems to have nominated Harold as his successor. The Bayeux Tapestry, as you'd expect from a Norman-sponsored document, is unspecific, but shows the dying Edward with his wife Edith at his feet weeping, pointing to Harold.

Edward died on 4 or 5 January. On the 6th, the Feast of the Epiphany, his new church at Westminster witnessed two important ceremonies: Edward was buried and the new King was crowned.

Harold is enthroned as Harold II of England.

Harold had been unanimously approved by the witan, the council of English nobles. Harold Godwinson, the child of a thane made good, had become Harold II of England. Against all expectations, including those of Harold himself, it was one of the greatest social rises in English history.

Harold had been on hand, and had taken his chance when it was offered, but he knew that William wouldn't accept the fait accompli easily. Having seen him at close quarters, he had some idea of how William might react when the news filtered through. But however bad the imagined reaction, it can't possibly have measured up to the reality.

For William it was like losing his winning lottery ticket. He was told the bad news while out hunting. The Norman chronicle of William de Jumièges describes how he took off for home without saying a word and then sat with his cloak over his head or stood leaning his forehead against a pillar. When the shock finally wore off, he called his nobles together for a council of war.

In England, Harold was getting on with the business of being king. He was to have the second-shortest reign of any English king, and apart from his military movements we have very little detail of his rule apart from the usual comments in the chronicles about how he instituted just laws.

But we do know that he issued his own coinage. England was still an immensely powerful country and forty-four mints around the country produced silver pennies on a pattern issued in London. They were the basic unit of currency. On one side there's a stylized image of the king. You can see his moustache, but there's also a trimmed beard which may have been a fictional symbol of his wisdom and maturity rather than a portrait. On the reverse there's one word, *Pax*, the Latin for 'peace'. As a policy statement or a wish for the future, it was sadly misplaced.

In April what we now know as Halley's Comet appeared in the night sky. To the people of the eleventh century it was an omen of doom. But you didn't need to be a clairvoyant to know there was trouble brewing.

About the same time, Tostig sailed out from exile in Flanders and raided along the south coast. It was an irritant rather than a major threat. Harold knew that the main problem was William. On both sides of the Channel an eleventh-century arms race started, a fury of boat building and troop movements.

Harold assembled a fleet and stationed it on the Isle of Wight, anticipating an attack coming across the Channel. He called up the fyrd, reservists from farms and estates across the country, and positioned them along the south coast scanning the seas towards Normandy. Then he sent spies to France to see what the Duke was up to. We know this because some of them were intercepted – perhaps it was their long Saxon hair that gave them away – and, the chronicles say, ominously, they were 'treated with disdain'. But enough news got back to give Harold reason to pat himself on the back for his precautions.

William's fleet was assembled at Dives sur Mer at the mouth of the River Dives in Normandy.

Today it's a small fishing harbour with a marina for pleasure yachts. The only sign of a connection to the conquest is a 'Guilleme le Conquerant' arcade of souvenir shops and restaurants in the village centre, and, engraved above the west door of the parish church, a list of the noblemen who joined William in his great venture.

But it was in Dives 950 years ago that William embarked on the staggering logistics of assembling a fleet of 700 warships and transports for an invasion of England. Even though some of the ships were ready-made and belonged to the nobles who joined William's enterprise, this was still a massive undertaking. Historians have calculated that it would have taken about 1,400 oak trees and 40,000 pines to put together a fleet this size – that's about 2,500 hectares of forest. For those who are a little foggy about what a hectare looks like, we're talking about a pretty big forest.

Constructing the ships would have employed an army of workers over 8,000 strong in forestry, transport and shipbuilding. All of them had to be paid, fed and watered. And that's before the armourers, victuallers, grooms, smiths and soldiers started to assemble. This was preparation for warfare on an almost industrial scale. Such was the scope of William's ambition.

But the venture was also hugely risky. The fact that we know it was eventually successful can blind us to the gamble William was taking. Despite the conventional wisdom that an invasion needs overwhelmingly superior forces, the Duke of Normandy was proposing to take on one of the best-equipped, best-organized and well-resourced forces in Christendom. Given the odds against his success, one historian has gone so far as to rename the duke 'William the lucky Bastard'.

When he revealed his plans to the nobles of Normandy they were less than enthusiastic. The only willing volunteers were landless knights who had nothing to lose and everything to gain from a successful foreign campaign. But William needed the support not only of the Norman nobility, but also of the knights of neighbouring Brittany, Flanders and France. What changed their minds was a papal banner that turned a mercenary adventure into a crusade.

Pope Alexander II was a reforming pope. His main concerns were stamping out simony (purchasing religious positions), and making Church appointments a matter for the Church and not the ruler. These were policies that Robert de Jumièges had tried to institute during his short tenure as Archbishop of Canterbury. As part of this reforming campaign, the Pope insisted that all bishops should make the journey to Rome to receive the *pallium* (the mark of office) in person before their position was made official.

Stigand, Robert's replacement as Archbishop of Canterbury, was everything that Alexander stood against. He'd been excommunicated. He held the sees of Winchester and Canterbury jointly and without papal authority, and he was the King's man. Even the

English were a bit queasy about his position. The Archbishop of York rather than Stigand had consecrated Harold's church at Waltham, and, in spite of the claims of the Norman writers, Harold was probably crowned by him as well.

When William presented his mission against England as a religious crusade to rid the country of these abuses, Pope Alexander II gave him a banner and granted him permission to wear one of the relics on which Harold had perjured himself.

Once William had papal authority, the waverers among his knights literally came on board. The forces were readied, armour loaded, and horses – three per knight – led on to the ships. But when the fleet launched at the beginning of September 1066, it met a northerly storm that prevented it from crossing. The boats limped into St Valéry at the mouth of the Somme, and waited.

At the same time, on the English side of the Channel, Harold's forces also waited. And waited. Then gave up. The normal fighting season was spring and summer. As August turned to September, it seemed to the volunteers of the fyrd who'd all been fed and watered at great expense, that the time of crisis was over. They only had an obligation to serve for two months, and the reserves had been changed over once already.

On 8 September the reservists were dismissed to get on with the harvest. The fleet was sent back to London and, because of the same storm suffered by William's boats, sustained losses on its way up the Channel. The squall must have given Harold some comfort, though. Once the autumn storms had begun, the risk of invasion was severely diminished.

The King rode inland to London to prepare for the celebration of the feast of the Holy Cross. It seemed that the great threat of 1066 was going to be an anticlimax. Then, just as his forces had been disbanded, news came from the north. A great fleet had been sighted off the north-east coast. The wind that was keeping William penned in St Valéry had brought a new threat scudding down the coast from Scotland.

Tostig was back for revenge with 300 ships and the fearsome King of Norway, Harald Hardrada.

STAMFORD BRIDGE

King Harold of England had been looking the wrong way. After his careful preparations against the Normans, it looked likely he could lose the crown to an angry brother and a bunch of Vikings.

Tostig hadn't made an impression when he'd attacked England on his own, so he'd joined his meagre force of twelve ships to the mighty Norwegian fleet. Harald Hardrada was a toughest-of-the-tough Viking. His exploits were recorded a couple of centuries later by the bard Snorri Sturluson. Hardrada was a similar figure to Earl Thorfinn the Mighty, a physically enormous warrior who'd made his fortune as a mercenary in

Opposite: The bridge today at Stamford Bridge.

122

3

HAROLD

Grange
Fm

Primrose
Hill Fm

Weir

PH

P

Viaduct

Stamford
Bridge

Bu... ...ld
Hall

1066

66

reby
...ouse

...ck

14

PH

Town
End

Common
Fm

Primrose

18

56

18

7

10

B
F

32

Constantinople. He brought with him a large contingent of perhaps 7,500 battle-hardened men. Despite the grudge borne by Tostig, it's clear who was the leading partner in the enterprise.

The Norwegians sailed up the River Ouse and landed at Riccall before setting out for nearby York. King Harold's response was decisive. He'd already stood down his force on the south coast, but nevertheless decided on a lightning strike against the Vikings. After all, it had worked against Gruffydd of Wales.

Heading north on horseback with his elite personal guard, he covered 25 miles a day. Messengers sent out in advance arranged for forces to join him en route. On his way he got more bad news. On 20 September Tostig and Hardrada had won a long, bloody battle against a force of Northumbrians led by the brothers Edwin and Morcar at Fulford, just south of York. Losses had been heavy on both sides. It was clear that Harold would now have to take on the invaders without the aid of local troops.

The Vikings moved on triumphantly to York. It was as though the doorway to England had swung wide open. If the people of York expected reprisals from Tostig for their rebellion the previous year, they were pleasantly surprised. Hardrada obviously wanted to win their support by treating them fairly. But to ensure co-operation, the victors took hostages and moved north-east out of the city to the area round Stamford Bridge. Here they could feed their troops from King Harold's own estate at Catton, while awaiting the delivery of 500 more hostages.

Take the road from Tadcaster to Stamford Bridge. Nowadays there's a ring road round York, but if you drive straight in and walk through the city, you'll see where Harold entered through the gate to the south-east, then marched straight through the area now occupied by The Shambles, before exiting by the gate leading to Osbaldswick. From there it's just eight miles to Stamford Bridge.

The English King's rapid deployment worked like a dream. He completed the 190 miles from London to Tadcaster on 24 September, his footsoldiers slogging along double time behind his mounted guard. At Tadcaster he paused to assemble his troops. Then the next day he was able to march straight through York as the grateful citizens flung open the gates, and on to Stamford Bridge. Harold knew this area and he knew exactly where to find the invaders.

Tostig and Hardrada suspected nothing. It was a fine day. Such was their confidence that many of the troops had left their armour behind on their ships. There were between four and five thousand men lolling around awaiting the arrival of the extra hostages. Instead they saw Harold and his army appearing out of a dust cloud. Snorri Sturluson says that as they moved closer, 'their glittering weapons sparkled like a field of broken ice'.

The Norwegians were cut off from their boats by the River Derwent, so they sent for reinforcements from Riccall and moved across to the other side of the river.

There's a tradition that the entire English advance was held up by one fearsome Viking – known as a berserker – who held the bridge single-handedly, killing forty men with his axe. He was eventually removed by a crafty English spearman who floated out into the stream and thrust upwards into the unprotected area beneath the Norseman's chain mail.

Then the English poured across the bridge, and battle proper was joined in the old warrior tradition: two shield walls hacking at each other until a breach was made.

Hardrada died early in the engagement from an arrow in the throat, but Tostig fought on bravely until he too was cut down. There are dark and cryptic references in the chronicles to the biblical story of Cain who killed his brother Abel, so it seems likely that it was Harold himself who struck the fatal blow that killed Tostig.

A late rally from the Viking reinforcements coming from the ship was fierce but short-lived. The Viking chronicler calls it Orri's Storm after the man who led the charge. But the Norsemen were lightly armoured for speed, and exhausted from the long forced march from the ships. It wasn't long before they were fleeing back to them, pursued by the English.

The Norwegian losses were severe. The survivors fitted into just twenty-four ships of an original fleet of 300; 2,000 or more men were cut down at Stamford Bridge and left to rot. Sixty years later the pile of bones was still a local landmark.

The English buried their dead. Tostig's mutilated body was identified by a wart between the shoulder blades, and the corpse was taken off to York Minster to be buried with full honours.

To retrace Harold's route north in a car is virtually impossible. Instead of the M1/A1, imagine a road little more than a cart track and a mobilization of several thousand troops carrying heavy armour and weaponry. It's a feat that entitles Harold to be considered the inventor of yomping and blitzkrieg rolled into one.

Stamford Bridge itself is a community totally dominated by that one battle in 1066. In Harold's day it wasn't much more than a wooden bridge. Now it's a large village mostly comprising modern housing estates with names chosen to remind residents of their illustrious past, like Saxons Way and Viking Drive. But even before the time of unimaginative town planners, the battle was remembered in local place names like Battle Flatts Farm. Even the public lavatories are decorated with a mural designed by local schoolchildren depicting the events of 1066.

As for the eponymous bridge, go carefully. It's made of ancient stone and is so busy with HGVs heading to and from York that a small metal footbridge has been constructed running parallel. If a large Yorkshireman comes towards you from the south side, it's just possible to imagine you're crossing towards an inflamed Viking armed with a battleaxe.

Stamford Bridge underlined Harold's strengths as a general. He'd won an extraordinary victory against one of the most renowned warriors of the age. Always the diplomat, he allowed the remnants of the Norwegians to leave in peace after they'd sworn never to come back. They were true to their word. Harald Hardrada's incursion was the last great Viking assault on Britain. In other circumstances it might have been a victory whose significance ranked with Agincourt, Trafalgar or the Battle of Britain.

But the wind that had veered round to push the pitiful remains of Hardrada's great fleet out of the Ouse and back to Norway was stirring other sails: 300 miles to the south, William the Bastard ordered his fleet to hoist sail. It was a last-gasp attempt to wrest England from Harold the oath-breaker.

HASTINGS

William sailed from St Valéry on 27 September 1066 and landed next day at Pevensey. At first the Normans were wary of what hidden defences and ambushes might lie behind its walls. They didn't know that the English weren't castle people, and William was pleasantly surprised to find the fortress deserted. In fact there was no opposition at all. He ordered a temporary defence to be thrown up inside the ruins of the old Roman fort, but decided that Pevensey was too vulnerable to be a permanent base. On 29 September, he ordered his men to march twelve miles along the coast to hillier ground near Hastings and they built a temporary castle there.

Also on the 29th tidings reached him of Harold's remarkable victory against Harald Hardrada. This was the first he'd heard of the northern campaign and it wasn't good news. The last thing William wanted was to meet a conquering English force full of confidence as he edged his way towards London. It was probably this that caused William to dig in defensively at Hastings and wait for Harold near his ships.

Nevertheless he made his presence felt by raiding, looting and burning the surrounding farms and estates. The embroiderers from Canterbury who made the Bayeux Tapestry must have remembered the devastation vividly. They include a scene, for the first time in the history of Western art, of the effects of war on civilians. Two refugees, a woman and a child, flee from a blazing farm. They have no possessions with them. We can imagine the body of the landowner lying among the charred ruins.

At the same time as a messenger was telling William of Harold's success in the north, another messenger was giving Harold the news of William's landing at Pevensey.

Harold's determination and stamina were truly awesome. He wasted no time in setting off south again on the return journey of 190 miles. The volunteers from his tired northern forces were left behind and he took only the core of his professional housecarls. He must have sent ahead to rally more troops.

Pausing only to pray at the Holy Cross in his church at Waltham, he arrived in London on 8 or 9 October where his second army was assembling. It was here that he slipped up. William was holed up around Hastings with a force of no more than 10,000 men living off the land. Harold had the option of waiting in London until he had collected a massive and irresistible force of fyrd reservists from the abbeys and estates in the shires.

Why didn't he wait until he was invincible? We can only guess. Maybe he was buoyed with the success of his lightning strike against Harald Hardrada. Perhaps he wanted to try the same sort of surprise tactics on William.

Remember: Harold had already seen the Normans in operation during his enforced stay in Normandy. He knew that if the Duke broke out from the hills of East Sussex he'd be harder to remove. The Norman tactics would be to throw up defensive castles as they moved, so that they'd have a number of fall-back positions throughout Sussex and Kent from which to launch counter-attacks.

Maybe Harold calculated that if he moved swiftly to stall William's progress he could then call in his fleet to destroy the Norman ships, leaving him the easy task of wiping out a force with no means of retreat.

Whatever was going through his mind, Harold ordered his army to set out for Sussex straight away and called for more reservists to meet him near his estates at Whatlington, at a local landmark called 'the hoary apple tree' about a mile from the battle site. This tree was at a Saxon location called Senlac. Later French-speaking historians grimly translated

HAROLD

this as Sangue-Lac, the lake of blood, but it had no such connotations for Harold. Arriving on 13 October, he had achieved his first goal of cutting off William's route to the rest of the country.

But if he was aiming for surprise, he was disappointed. William's scouts were well-prepared and reported the English arrival. In response, William ordered his men to stand-to in armour all night in case Harold launched a surprise attack. In contrast to Harold, William knew that the die was cast. He couldn't afford to wait. The English forces would only get stronger, the weather worse, and his troops weaker. He had to act decisively.

Consequently it was Harold who was taken off guard. At about 5.30 on the morning of 14 October, William ordered his armoured troops forward on Harold's position. The English, resting after a three-day march from London (and far more than that in the case of those who'd done the return journey from York), had to prepare for battle in haste.

Which brings us to the Battle of... Battle!

Its residents should sue Hastings Town Council. For 900 years a town six miles away has insisted on giving its name to the most momentous event (possibly the only momentous event) in Battle's history.

Battle's economy has been funded by the Battle of Hastings for nearly a thousand years. In the eleventh century, spilt blood had to be paid for with a religious gesture, so after his victory William financed the building of Battle Abbey as a guilt offering. He asked for it to be located on the very spot where the battle took place. When the monks took the money and started laying the foundations on a more favourable site a few hundred yards away, William ordered the stones to be pulled down and re-erected exactly where he'd wanted them. So while doubt hangs over the topography of many battles in this book, a tour of Battle Abbey provides an absolutely clear picture of the layout of the Battle of Hastings and the course of the day's events.

Within the grounds of the abbey are a host of different architectural styles and periods, including the Victorian buildings of Battle Preparatory School. The ruins (it was also a victim of the Dissolution) are run by English Heritage. They cover four centuries of the medieval period. Sadly, the only stonework dating back to the eleventh century is hidden away ignominiously behind the school dustbins. But the essence of William's instructions still stands. Even today the fabric of the abbey acts as a guide to the fateful events of 14 October 1066.

Harold had chosen his ground well. A wall 150 metres long marks the exact line of his shield wall. The hill on which it sits has been levelled by about 4 metres to accommodate the building of the abbey. But even with the reduction in height, you can look south down the steep ridge to the valley where the Normans had to attack and see what a formidable defensive position the Saxons held.

They formed up in their traditional manner, Harold and his knights riding to the

Opposite: The stone marking Battle Abbey's high altar and the very spot where Harold fell in battle.

For Battle, take the A21 from either London or Hastings and look out for the A2100 which detours off it both north and south. Once you enter the town, follow signs to the abbey and park in the Pay and Display under the abbey walls.

battle, then dismounting and taking their place in the wall, so they could fight on foot like true warriors. Harold's shield wall would have extended for at least another 250 metres along the line of today's stone wall and would have been four, five or six men thick. In the middle were the professional guard with their fearsome war axes. They protected Harold, who stood behind them with his standard portraying a standing man laced with pure gold. Towards the fringes of the line were the reservists, more lightly armoured but still a significant deterrent of shields, spears and throwing axes (sometimes just stones strapped to a stick) to rain down on anyone struggling up the slope towards them.

William adopted the new style of warfare with a mixture of forces: infantry, cavalry and archers. This mix would in the end prove vital, but for a long time the conflict could have gone either way. As we've seen with Macbeth, an eleventh-century battle would normally last a couple of hours at most. In contrast, the Battle of Hastings was an epic, a grim war of attrition that dragged on all day. Harold knew that if he could hang on until dusk then he would have won. Reinforcements were drifting in all the time and he could look forward to regrouping the next morning and attacking William's depleted forces with fresh troops. William had to win that day, or all was lost.

To understand the task that faced him, walk round the battlefield to the bottom of the hill and imagine the energy needed to charge up the slope onto a living porcupine of spears.

The story of the battle is detailed in various chronicles. One tells how the first blow of the battle was struck by an entertainer, a Norman juggler caller Taillifer. He rode out in front of the English lines, taunting the enemy by throwing his sword high into the air. When an ill-disciplined Saxon rushed forward to attack, Taillifer lopped his head off and carried it victoriously back, causing the Normans to surge forward with pride.

At nine o'clock the battle opened with the blast of trumpets. As the Normans advanced up the hill they heard the din of Saxons screaming and beating their shields with their weapons. And in the middle was Harold with his battle cry 'Holy Cross', a reference to the miraculous crucifix that he trusted to bring him through the day.

William's cavalry rode in and threw their spears into the packed ranks of Saxons, while the archers and the infantry advanced together, firing and throwing their spears to try and get close. They all fell on to Harold's shield wall like waves against a jetty. The Saxons didn't budge. It was the Normans who broke first – a sudden panic starting among the men from Brittany on William's left flank that spread through the whole army. Word was that William had been killed. A retreat started, and it threatened to become a rout.

If Harold had followed up this sudden reverse with a concerted charge, he might have won the battle at this point. But either he was content to wait, or he'd been distracted by the deaths of his two brothers Gyrth and Leofwine in the centre of the line. Or he was too cautious.

Instead the Norman panic weakened Harold's own forces. Part of his right flank, probably the less disciplined reservists, couldn't resist temptation. Without waiting for orders, a section charged after the Normans.

In the mêlée of battle, William's horse had been killed, but a knight gave him another. Realizing that the panic was a crisis of confidence, William raised his helmet so that his troops could see he was alive. He then rallied them to a counter attack. The pocket of pursuing Saxons was cut off. They formed a separate defensive circle to the right of Harold's main forces, where they were slowly cut to ribbons.

And then there's a gap in the accounts. For six or seven hours the battle continued. There must have been some regrouping as Harold pulled his line together. It seems that William, having seen what a genuine retreat could do, used a tactic of feigned retreats to separate more Saxons from the flanks of the shield wall.

As more men died and William chipped away at the fringes of Harold's line, the shield wall contracted within the bounds of the ridge. This allowed William's cavalry to make the top of the hill and charge on the level rather than up a steep incline. William's mixture of forces was beginning to get the upper hand over the old-style warriors. And yet night was closing in. All Harold had to do was hang on.

But it wasn't the cavalry that won the day. The key to the battle is given by the embroiderers of Canterbury. At this point in the story little archers start to appear in the bottom margin of the Bayeux Tapestry.

Harold (with the arrow) is framed by the 'o' and the 'l' of his name. The figure falling under the sword of the Norman horseman is also Harold. You'll have to take my word for this because you can only see it really close up in the flesh, but there's a line of little holes extending from this falling figure's eye where the arrow has been unstitched at some time in the last 900 years.

It was dusk. There were about thirty minutes to go until darkness and victory for Harold. In the dying light William ordered his archers to change tactics. Rather than firing direct, they started shooting up in the air, their arrows then dropping and disrupting the shield wall, making chinks in the line for the cavalry to exploit. It was now that Harold was fatally wounded by that famous arrow.

There's been some dispute about the figure in the Tapestry clutching the arrow in his eye. Is it Harold? One account simply talks about an assault by mounted knights who cut Harold down and chopped off his leg and head. That fits well with the image to the right of the man being felled by the arrow. It is of a mounted knight chopping at a Saxon's leg with his sword.

But the Tapestry is usually quite accurate about where it places embroidered names to identify leading characters. The word Harold straddles the figure clutching the arrow. It may be that this scene is the eleventh-century version of a film storyboard: first Harold is accidentally wounded in the eye and, as he falls, a crisis of confidence among the Saxons gives the Normans their vital breakthrough. As the shield wall finally disintegrates, Harold is cut to pieces. According to an early account of the battle he lost (and this is important) his right leg completely, as well as the lower half of his left leg, and his head.

There's an obvious objection to this theory: the falling figure doesn't appear to have an arrow in his eye. But amazingly, closer inspection of the linen of the tapestry reveals a straight line of tiny holes extending from the figure's helmet where the arrow has come unstitched over the centuries.

With Harold dead and his standard fallen, it was all over. The English scattered, chased by the Normans into the darkness, but occasionally turning and ambushing their pursuers in fierce rearguard actions.

This final act of the battle was fought on the flat area of land above the medieval monks' refectory. The high altar of the church was positioned over the spot where King Harold II fell: a fitting tribute to the last Anglo-Saxon king.

THE AFTERMATH

William had won by the skin of his teeth. England would never be the same again. William's landless knights moved in, obliterating the Saxon aristocracy. French became the standard language of the upper classes and English society was turned upside-down as power was transferred to the foreign invaders.

Tradition says that Harold's body was identified by his old love, Edith 'Swan-neck', who recognized the corpse by 'certain marks on the body': moles perhaps, or, some say, love bites. His mother Gytha, preparing for exile herself, offered the weight of her son's body in gold for its return. It was the last demonstration of the legendary wealth of the

Godwins. But William refused. The last thing he wanted was a cult of the Saxon dynasty building up round the rallying point of Harold's shrine.

An enigmatic source in the chronicles simply speaks of him being buried by the sea, with an ironic reference to him continuing to defend his shores from his seaside grave. Another chronicle some time later records the tradition that Harold eventually came to rest in Waltham Abbey. So there's been some dispute over where Harold's body lies.

His supposed tomb at Waltham changed location three times. The abbey grew throughout the Middle Ages, and the bones were disinterred from their traditional tomb and relocated. Their final resting place is marked today by a stone near the old location of the high altar, about 20 metres away from the existing east wall of the parish church.

The monks of Waltham were great Harold fans and ensured that his reputation was kept intact after his death. Harold's Wood at Romford and Harold's Park at Nazeing in Essex were built on abbey lands, and keep his memory alive. Perhaps the fervent wish of the foundation to keep its sponsor's flame burning extended to a pious fraud about the location of his corpse. Given William's initial reluctance to let Harold's own mother have his body, it seems unlikely that he would have let the last Saxon king be buried at the shrine that would give him maximum publicity.

Still, for centuries it seemed the most likely option apart from an unmarked grave by the sea. And then in the twentieth century, a chance discovery threw up an alternative suggestion. It takes us right back to the other end of Sussex to our first location, at Bosham.

Under the new regime William, now known as 'the Conqueror', had taken possession of the little town as his private estate. The people of Bosham have always known there was a royal tomb in the church, but this was a child's tomb under the chancel arch belonging to King Cnut's daughter who drowned in the nearby millstream that runs along the west side of the churchyard. Then in 1954, during routine building work, an adult's tomb was discovered next to it. It was unmarked but, by its position, could only have belonged to someone of royal status. It contained the partial remains of a mature adult male. There was no head, no right leg and only half of the left.

The discovery of the mysterious second tomb at Bosham.

The bones were analysed, numbered and reinterred, and nobody thought any more about it. That is until recently, when a local historian started to match the details of the skeleton with the exact accounts of King Harold's death.

We know that Harold couldn't be identified except by marks on his body. It seems certain then that he wasn't just wounded in the eye, but decapitated and mutilated as the chronicles suggest. The Bayeux

Picture postcard Bosham as it is today at low tide. Difficult to imagine that this was once a port as important as Southampton.

Tapestry, based on contemporary accounts, shows a knight attacking his left leg, and the histories speak of his right leg being chopped off and 'carried right away'. The description exactly matches the corpse in Bosham.

Moreover, the location in Bosham fits the story of Harold being buried anonymously by the sea. Given its view over the Solent, Bosham was an appropriate but safe burial place for Harold. William could control the comings and goings on his own estates and ensure that the grave didn't act as a focus for pilgrimage or political discontent.

A way of life died with Harold. He'd achieved great things as a diplomat and a soldier. He put an end to the Viking threat that had been plaguing England for 300 years. He nearly won the Battle of Hastings. Without that arrow he might have gone down in history as another Elizabeth I or Winston Churchill.

Instead, the drips of cultural change that his father had so opposed became a flood. The new generation of Normans wiped out the existing ruling class and imposed a new and radically different culture and language. Historians have taken one side or the other, imagining the pros and cons of a Saxon victory at Hastings. But the transformation wrought by the Norman invasion was so complete that it's purposeless to play 'what if?'. English language and English identity are so rooted in a vibrant mixture of Norman and Anglo-Saxon that what would have happened if Harold lived must for ever remain a mystery.

FURTHER INFORMATION

Probably the best starter book on Harold is by Ian W. Walker, *Harold: The Last Anglo-Saxon King* (Sutton Publishing, 1997)

From the same publisher there's Harold's story put in a slightly wider political and cultural context by N.J. Higham, *The Death of Anglo-Saxon England* (Sutton Publishing, 1997)

For another view on Harold's family try Frank Barlow, *The Godwins* (Pearson, 2002)

For the military history there's Matthew Bennett, *Campaigns of the Norman Conquest* (Osprey Publishing, 2001)

And for the Battle of Hastings itself there is a fascinating book of essays edited by Stephen Morillo, *The Battle of Hastings* (Boydell, 1999). Lots of information about troop movements, logistics and the like.

For weapons themselves there's Richard Underwood's book *Anglo-Saxon Weapons and Warfare* (Tempus, 1999)

If you visit the church at Bosham, please buy two little pamphlets by local historian John Pollock, published by Penny Royal Publications: *Harold: Rex* and *Bosham Ecclesia* tell the story of the hidden royal tomb.

If you really want to get into the Anglo-Saxon period, try the aptly named *The Anglo-Saxon Age: A very short introduction* (OUP, 2000) or, for the very keen, Frank Stenton's much weightier – in both senses – overview, *Anglo-Saxon England* (OUP, 1971).

For the total enthusiast the original source texts:

Michael Swanton (trans.), *The Anglo-Saxon Chronicles* (Phoenix Press, 2001)

Snorri Sturluson, *King Harald's Saga* (Penguin Classics, 1966)

Ordnance Survey map numbers 197 and 199 give you the beginning and end of Harold's life in Bosham and Hastings. You'll find Stamford Bridge on 105, and the Golden Valley is on 149.

If you're off to France you might also want a Michelin map of Normandy.

The Tapiserie at Bayeux is situated right in the heart of the town and is impossible to miss.

CHAPTER 4

WILLIAM WALLACE – 'BRAVEHEART'

If Macbeth's story gives us a guide to the Highlands, William Wallace provides a
tour of Central and Lowland Scotland, and the Borders.

Time has erased much of the past, and countless living, breathing personalities have completely disappeared apart from their names. But there are a few rare moments from long ago that remain as vivid as if they happened yesterday.

For instance, we know exactly what the weather was like in Scotland on the night of 19 March 1286. It was filthy: sheets of rain lashed down, the wind buffeted the trees and tore at their branches, the visibility was awful. The reason we know this is because the storm provoked a tragedy that was to change the face of Scotland. And without that meteorological accident we might never have heard of William Wallace.

By rights, Wallace should never have come to our attention. His should have been one of those names that swim unnoticed in the currents of history. He wasn't a peasant, but he was a very minor nobleman indeed, far removed from the great aristocratic caste that ruled Europe during the medieval period. Essentially he was a nobody from Renfrewshire, who only came to the fore because of what we now call the Wars of Scottish Independence.

Opposite: Engraving of
William Wallace from
an anonymous painting.

CVL:WALLAS·SCOTVS·HOSTIVML·TERRO

WALLACE

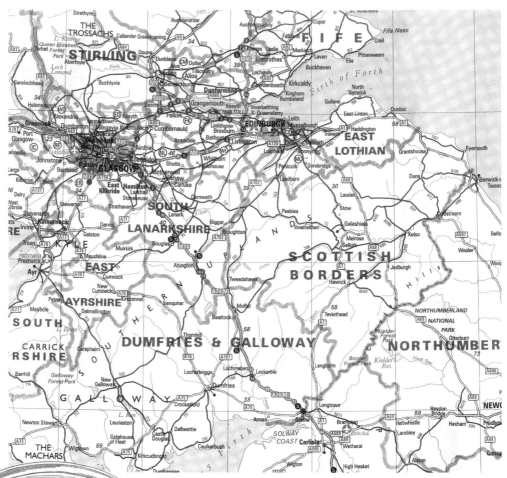

Central Scotland where Wallace's legend was lived out from the forests of Ayrshire and Lanarkshire in the South to Stirling and Falkirk in the North.

Like all our pictures, this must represent the epitome of heroism for the illustrator, but it's not that easy to see why.

For many years this lack of status counted against him, but to later generations it has given him added glamour as Scotland's national hero. And as a man of the people, it seems fitting that Wallace's life was lived in the main in Central Scotland, where most of the population are today. Beneath the housing estates, schools and factories of the area lies a trail of blood.

The best-known memorial to William Wallace is the movie *Braveheart*. It's a cracking film and contains nuggets of historical truth, not least in creating the spirit of Wallace, but it's not a failsafe guide. For a start, there's the title. Apologies for squashing the romance before we've even started, but Wallace was never actually called 'Braveheart' until the movie. That was a name reserved for that other posthumous hero of Scotland, Robert the Bruce. After his death Bruce's heart was preserved in a casket which was carried into battle at the front of the troops with the cry 'Forward Brave Heart'.

EARLY YEARS

Wallace's name tells us that his family, the Waleys, were originally from Wales. His ancestors were minor nobility in the retinue of Walter the Steward, from whom the Stuart dynasty would spring. Beyond that, concrete facts are pretty thin on the ground. Nobody ever thought that the young Wallace would ever be one of the great and the good, so they didn't make a point of recording his every move.

What knowledge we do have about his early life comes from the pages of *The Wallace*, a great narrative poem by a minstrel called Blind Harry. It's the source for the movie *Braveheart* and it's a rollicking rollercoaster of a story, though a dubious historic source. Harry gets things wrong. His work contains many obviously legendary elements and is about as impartial as Denis Law commentating on an England–Scotland game. So, unless other documents back him up, we have to take Harry with a pinch of salt and a strong dose of speculative common sense.

Blind Harry was writing in the middle of the fifteenth century, about 150 years after Wallace's death. He claims that his account is based on a Latin manuscript by John Blair, Wallace's private chaplain, although this has never been found. In parts it's obviously wildly inaccurate; for example, he invents a Battle of Biggar that never happened. It began to be criticized soon after it was written, particularly by a Scottish historian named John Major (no relation!), but this didn't stop *The Wallace* becoming for a while the most popular book in Scotland apart from the Bible.

Other earlier chronicles include John of Fordun and Andrew of Wyntoun's *Orygynale Cronykil*, which we've already come across in the Macbeth chapter, and equally partisan works from the English side such as the *Lanercost Chronicle* written by English monks who'd suffered at Wallace's hands. Given the lack of impartiality of all these sources, we just have to weigh the accounts against the balance of probability.

We think that Wallace was born some time around 1270, but even the name of his father is disputed. The earliest records leave a gap in the story, as though someone had gone off to check the facts and forgotten to come back and fill in the blanks. The tradition is that his father was Sir Malcolm Wallace, a second son, a minor knight with little land, and that Wallace was his second son and therefore without an inheritance of land. But then a few years ago a superb find turned up that turned this theory upside-down. It was a letter of Wallace's that came to light in Germany with its original seal. It showed that Wallace's father was called Alan and wasn't a knight at all.

Casts of the two sides of Wallace's seal. His family crest and information on the left and, on the right, the faint image of the bow and arrow that reveals his true vocation.

Opposite: At Elderslie with the help of a great two-handed broadsword and some blue facepaint I get into the spirit of Braveheart. (Move over Mel Gibson.)

Elderslie today is not on many people's must-see tourist attractions. It's a 'make-sure-your-car's-locked' town (that's a quote from a local resident!) off the A737 east of Paisley and Glasgow. Taking the main road through the town from Glasgow, you come across a small park on your left with a white stone monument dominating the road.

Wallace's home has also been the subject of much dispute. Harry says he comes from Ellerslie, which has traditionally been taken to mean Elderslie in Renfrewshire, although there are claims that he was brought up in a long-disappeared castle where Kilmarnock fire station now stands.

The memorial to Wallace at Elderslie marks the traditional site of the small palisaded settlement where he was brought up, and one of the plaques gives you an artist's impression of what the little community might have looked like. An archaeological dig in the 1990s uncovered a stone ditch marking the outline of a settlement, although of course there's no way of ultimately proving whether the young Wallace actually ran around here playing among the crofters and workers on his father's small estate.

We're told that Wallace was educated in Dundee, and later by monks at Paisley Abbey. Paisley is just down the road from Elderslie, and having seen the birthplace it's worth taking the main road back towards Glasgow and stopping off at the abbey. The church was founded in 1163 and the charter of foundation was witnessed by a Richard Wallace who may well have been one of William's ancestors. There is a now a stained-glass window to Wallace's memory in the church, showing him as a latter-day Samson.

As the second son of a very minor nobleman with no land, Wallace would have received the appropriate education for a boy of his status. He would have been taught Latin, French, and possibly a little Gaelic. He may well have been destined for the Church, the traditional dumping ground for impoverished sons of minor nobility, but his education would

JOHNSTON

4

WALLACE

Elderslie

also have included a thorough grounding in the martial arts, skills that stood him in good stead in later years when he became a warrior.

But the political upheaval that was to bring him to the fore was far away throughout his childhood. The Scotland Wallace was born into and grew up in was peaceful and prosperous. Above all it was an independent nation, ruled by King Alexander III.

Trade with other parts of Northern Europe was flourishing: Scotland exported timber, cattle hides and woollen products. Inverness was a famous centre for shipbuilding. We've every reason to believe that Scots were just as well-off as their English neighbours, with whom they maintained a polite and peaceful relationship. The custom revenue records show that the port of Berwick-upon-Tweed – then the largest and wealthiest Scottish town – produced by itself a sum equivalent to 25 per cent of England's entire customs revenues. (Which either proves the Scots were very wealthy or that the English were diddling the tax man.) And that doesn't take into account the fact that England's population was four times that of Scotland.

Economically, everything was going well, but by 1286 another problem was starting to threaten the country. Wallace was about sixteen when high politics and chance overtook both him and Scotland.

KINGHORN

Since the time when Malcolm had overcome Macbeth, kingship had passed from father to eldest son, but this system of primogeniture was about to prove disastrous. Alexander III had originally married an English princess, Margaret, daughter of Henry III of England and sister of the new King, Edward I. Before she died, she gave him a daughter and two sons, Alexander and David. Both princes had died by 1284 without producing heirs. Alexander III's daughter, who'd been married off to a Norwegian prince, had also died in childbirth. But she left a baby princess (also Margaret, but better known as the Maid of Norway) as the only descendant of Alexander's line. In an attempt to rectify this potentially weak position, Alexander remarried. His second wife was Joleta of Dreux, a French princess in her early twenties.

And so back to the stormy night of 19 March 1286.

It was late in the evening, after a council in Edinburgh Castle and a riotous dinner, that Alexander III made the snap decision to return home to his lovely young wife. Home was Kinghorn on the other side of the Firth of Forth from Edinburgh. Nowadays, even in a car with reasonable driving conditions the journey takes a good ninety minutes. In the thirteenth century it was a hard ride of several hours, and Alexander was much the worse for wear.

Opposite: Alexander III's memorial at Kinghorn.

Alexander's courtiers were dismayed. They pointed to the threatening storm and begged him to stop over. He was having none of it. Like many middle-aged men he refused

EDWARD I. KING of ENGLAND
LORD of IRELAND & DUKE of AQVITAINE

G. Vertue In & Sculpsit.

to admit weakness. He was in his mid-forties and fit as a flea. Also it seems he was no stranger to midnight dashes home to the royal marriage bed: after all, a king must do his duty. He set off from Edinburgh and made the rough ferry crossing across the Forth to Inverkeithing. There he was met by a nobleman called Alexander le Saucier who again implored him to break his journey. But Alexander carried on. Accompanied by three squires and two local guides, he set off along the coastal track to Kinghorn.

Then things went disastrously wrong. In the pitch black of the night and with the wind raging, the King became separated from his companions and lost his track. On the edge of the cliffs between Burntisland and Kinghorn, his horse must have reared or stumbled. He was found the next day at the foot of the cliffs, his neck broken, within a mile of his destination.

Six centuries later the Victorian Scots put up a monument to this accident on the main road to Kinghorn that runs along the top of the cliffs.

The monument overlooks the bleak holiday sands of Burntisland. Like many monuments, it's vaguely phallic in shape and the Victorians were blissfully ignorant of the irony on the inscription 'erected on the sex-centenary of his death'. Never has libido proved more costly to a country's future.

Looking out to sea, there's a smaller stone to the right of the monument with another inscription: it's one of the oldest poems in the Scots vernacular, a medieval comment on the wave of desolation that descended on Scotland at Alexander's death:

> Sen Alexander our King was deid
> That Scotland left in luve and lee,
> Away wes sonse of aill and breid
> Of wine and wax, of gamin and glee.
> The gold wes changit all in leid
> The frute failyeit on everilk tree.

As with Macbeth, here's another echo of that ancient Scottish belief that good kingship ties into the prosperity of the land; even the fruit on the trees withered in anticipation of what was to come after Alexander's death.

THE POLITICAL BACKGROUND: NORHAM

The childless Joleta returned to her family in France. Margaret, the Maid of Norway, was summoned back to Scotland to claim the throne and marry the five-year-old son of Edward I of England in an attempt to stabilize the kingdom. While prelates and nobles journeyed to and fro from Scotland drawing up documents and making arrangements for this impor-

WALLACE

If you cross the Forth from Edinburgh on the A90 road bridge, take the first junction after the bridge to Inverkeithing and follow the A921 along the coast. Just after Burntisland the road starts to rise up from sea level. The Kinghorn memorial is on your right. Cars zoom past at great speed today oblivious of the significance of the spot. There's a lay-by 30 metres down the road which is safest approached from the east, so you may have to go up the road a way and turn.

tant marital alliance, a ship loaded with goodies, including 28 pounds of gingerbread, was sent to collect the princess. It was returned by King Eirik of Norway who insisted on sending his daughter to Scotland on his own ship via his own territory of Orkney.

All the complex treaties and negotiations, not to mention the sumptuous arrangements for the festivities, came to nothing. The Maid of Norway fell ill on the sea voyage to Orkney and died shortly after her ship docked on 26 September 1290. Her body was sent back to her father in Norway. The dynasty that traced its roots back through Malcolm Canmore and Duncan to Malcolm II had ended. The Scottish throne was up for grabs.

One of the core beliefs of medieval Christendom was that kings are chosen by God. That was the theory. But it was clear that the Scottish succession needed some earthly intervention. There were several possible candidates, but two in particular represented immensely powerful and ruthless factions. John Balliol and Robert Bruce (an earlier relative of the man who was to restore Scottish independence in 1314) had their own private armies. Although a small committee of clerics and nobility without any direct interest in the race for the throne had been appointed as guardians, the country stood on the brink of civil war. They couldn't ask any of the aristocracy within Scotland to appoint the new king. That would imply that the arbitrator was superior to the crown. This was a job for a respected European royal. So they looked to their nearest neighbour for help: the international statesman to the south, Edward I. It was the wrong decision.

Edward I was certainly an impressive figure, but he was a dubious friend and an intimidating enemy. He was famed for his hair-trigger rages. Legend has it that he so cowed the Archbishop of York with one temper tantrum that the poor man simply slunk away and died. And to add to his emotional authority he was, like many of the Plantagenet line, imposingly tall. And this is no flattering exaggeration from an age where men were generally shorter than today. When a group of scholars opened his tomb in Westminster Abbey in 1774 they measured the corpse at six feet two. You can still see this tomb today. It bears a Latin inscription that tells you all you need to know about Edward's political ambitions during his lifetime: *Hic est Malleus Scottorum* – 'Here lies the Hammer of the Scots'.

Edward was ambitious and clever. He had a lawyer's mind and even when carrying out his trickiest plans would back them up with legal arguments. He had come to the throne in 1274, when William Wallace was still a child. He had lived through the turbulent uprisings against his father Henry III and was determined not to make the same mistakes. In order to command the respect of the English earls, he had embarked on a policy of expansion. By 1284 he had already brought Wales into the growing English empire. The appointment of Edward's son as the Prince of Wales, not to mention a line of newly built impregnable castles, ensured that the Welsh continued to respect the King's overlordship. In 1290 Edward had encouraged the English in their ambition to become a 'master race' by ethnically cleansing the country of the Jewish population. When the Scottish nobles asked

The ruins of Norham Castle are still imposing. The National Trust property is just outside the village, set on a steep hill overlooking the Tweed. Coming from the A698, it's on the right-hand side of the road before you enter the village. The property is seldom crowded, but it's still worthwhile getting there early to wander across the extensive ruins in total solitude. Looking north, the river and surrounding countryside create an air of pastoral calm and beauty. But passing through the gatehouse, across the moat, and on up to the massive stonework of the keep, it's easy to see what a power game Edward was playing.

Edward to help them out later in the same year, he must have seen the opportunity as heaven-sent. It was the chance to bring Scotland under his sway as well.

It took two years to choose the new Scottish king. During that time Edward, starting from a position of 'only wanting to help', undermined Scottish autonomy and carefully created a situation that had the seeds of failure already sown in it.

The process began in 1291 at Norham on Tweed.

Norham today is a tiny village off the A698 between Berwick and Coldstream. Now as then, it is just on the English side of the border, marked by the River Tweed. On the other side of the water is another little village, Upsettlington, which was called Holly-well-haugh in the thirteenth century. Seven hundred years ago Norham was far more important than it is now. It marked a significant crossing point of the Tweed. There was an abbey church and a castle, the imposing fortified residence of Anthony Bek, the belli-cose Bishop of Durham.

He had commanded the Scottish nobles to meet at Norham in the shadow of the castle. He had also summoned his feudal forces from the surrounding areas and had war-ships stationed at the mouth of the Tweed to create an atmosphere of intimidation and menace. Despite assurances and safe passes, many of the Scots decided to remain on the north bank and send a delegation. They swiftly learnt Edward's price for acting as adjudi-cator: the Scots would have to agree that Edward was overlord of Scotland.

The Scottish question, 'The Great Cause' as it came to be known, had roused Edward from the slump caused by the death of his wife Eleanor in 1290. In the months before the Norham parlay, he had been busy getting monks and scholars throughout the kingdom to research any historic claims that the English monarch might have to the overlordship of Scotland. Some of the stories that were brought forward as evidence seem plain silly to us: for instance, there was a legend that Aeneas of Troy expelled a race of giants from Britain and left the country to three sons, and that the one who ruled England ended up owning Scotland as well. This may be obviously untrue, but it was still submitted as part of Edward's case. Far harder for the Scots to deal with were the difficult historical precedents such as Malcolm Canmore's debts to Edward the Confessor, and William the Lion sub-mitting to Henry II as his feudal lord.

Nevertheless, when Edward opened negotiations by asking if anyone knew any reason why he *shouldn't* be acknowledged as overlord of Scotland, he received a polite but firm stonewall. 'Prove it,' came the diplomatic reply, causing a typical Edward explosion. The Scots then asked for an adjournment. Edward was content to wait. He had a trick up his sleeve. He knew that if the candidates didn't toe the line, he could hit them where it really hurt: in the wallet.

The great Scottish lords would have had a much more fluid understanding of their nationality than we have today. Although they might have seen themselves principally as

Scots, they were, after all, still part of the great ruling class of England, Scotland and Wales who traced their roots back to French and Norman ancestors. They were closer to Edward in blood and outlook than they were to the peasants who tilled their fields. North and south of the border the aristocracy spoke the same dialect of French. Those true-Scots names of the two main contenders for the throne, Bruce and Balliol, were really mangled French ancestral place names, Brix and Bailleul. And in keeping with their pan-European heritage, these great families had estates in France, Scotland and England. If they failed to follow Edward and refused to acknowledge his overlordship, these lands could be forfeit. It would be a heavy personal price to pay for principle.

On 2 June, Edward met the earls at Upsettlington. Balliol and Bruce, who had been part of Edward's army even before he was King when he was fighting the rebellion of Simon de Montfort, acknowledged the English king as their lord superior, as did six other claimants. Then followed a series of meetings there and at Norham between the 2nd and 11th. Events were starting to move to a climax.

> **11 June 1291:** Edward ordered all the castles in Scotland to be handed over to him, and Scottish officials to be replaced by English administrators. This was intended as a temporary measure to prevent civil war and was to cease two months after the king was appointed.
>
> **13 June–27 July:** All Scottish lords took an oath of obedience to Edward as superior and direct lord of the kingdom of Scotland.
>
> **3 August:** Edward created a court of 104 auditors to hear the cases of the candidates for the throne. After an initial meeting the court was adjourned until June 1292.
>
> **14 October–17 November 1292:** The court hearings culminated in Edward's judgement for John Balliol, which was announced at Berwick-upon-Tweed.
>
> **20 November:** John Balliol swore fealty to Edward at Norham.
>
> **30 November:** John Balliol was made King at Scone.

It was clear that Balliol was Edward's man. The promised return of the castles and administration happened more in name than in reality. Many of the English officials and their armed retinues remained in place. However, not for the last time, Edward had misjudged the people of Scotland. He believed that if you subdued the nobility, the ordinary folk would follow. He was wrong. Throughout the period of 'temporary' English control and Balliol's lame-duck kingship, spontaneous acts of dissent and rebellion spread through Scotland. The scene was set for the emergence of a fierce young Scot called William Wallace.

The traditional reason given for Wallace becoming embroiled in the maelstrom was a personal grudge. It's said that in an early clash with the occupying English, Wallace's own

father was killed. This has been supported by mention of a Sir Malcolm Wallace being killed in 1291 at a skirmish called the Battle of Loudoun. However, as we now know that Wallace's father was called Alan we have to doubt this interpretation. And the same seal that tells us his father's real name gives us clues to Wallace's career path.

On the reverse of the seal in the centre is the image of a bow. Far from being principally a broadswordsman (as seen in the Mel Gibson film), Wallace saw himself first and foremost as a bowman.

Archers were coming to the fore in Wallace's time. Welsh longbowmen had impressed Edward in his campaign in Wales with their skill and, once they were defeated, he made sure they were brought into his army. There's even a possibility that Wallace too may have been employed by the English army, which came up to Scotland in force in 1296. When soldiers employed by the English got out of hand they were tried in court, and there's a tantalizing reference in one such case to a William Wallace who, with his pal Matthew of York, had pinched some meat from a man in Perth. Is it coincidence or could this be a reference to the great freedom fighter? Perhaps. But I'd argue that if Wallace had fought as a bowman in Edward's army, he'd have been only too aware of the devastating potential of the weapon. As we'll see, he wasn't, and that was his Achilles heel.

It's more likely that the bow on the seal means that Wallace was a bit of a poacher. Instead of going into the Church, the landless nobleman took advantage of the general instability of the time, and went off to live as an outlaw in the forests of Selkirk, making a living as best he could. But somewhere along the line he switched from looking after himself to fighting for his country. And his conversion was due to the calculating cruelty of Edward I.

We're well aware today, because of Britain's uncertain position in Europe, that sovereignty can be an emotive but hard to define issue. The same was true in the thirteenth century of overlordship. John Balliol and the Scots nobles who swore fealty to Edward need not have thought they were selling out. The terms of the handover of power seemed to leave the Scottish King with full autonomy. Edward had pronounced Scotland an indivisible kingdom and not just another piece of territory like Northumberland. As Duke of Aquitaine, Edward himself had sworn loyalty to Philip the King of France as his overlord without compromising his English sovereignty. But with Scotland, Edward pushed his overlordship to the very limits.

His aim seemed to be to humiliate John Balliol wherever possible. Legal judgements made in the Scottish courts were referred to Westminster for appeal where Edward overturned the verdicts. When Balliol reinstated punishments Edward summoned him to London like a schoolboy to the headmaster's study. It was clear the relationship was reaching breaking point.

This happened in 1294 when Edward got into a row with his overlord, Philip of France, over some English sailors who'd been rioting in La Rochelle. Edward then went to

The Victorians slapped a railway straight through the site of Berwick Castle so the closest you can get to the place where John Balliol was proclaimed king or the townsfolk showed their bottoms to Edward is the railway yard. But on the far side of the railway and castle is a little park with a path winding down to the Tweed. You can still walk along the north bank and follow Edward's route into Berwick while admiring the ruins of the stone walls. Edward had these erected after sacking the town to defend it from reprisals. There are also traces of the medieval defences that he so easily overcame. If you come out of the town centre (past the later Elizabethan walls which show how the town has shrunk since its heyday) and turn right down Northumberland Avenue towards the sea, there's a grassy area on your right about 200 metres down the road. The long mound on the right between you and the houses beyond marks the line of the defences which in the thirteenth century would probably have been topped by a small palisade.

war with France and demanded that the King of Scots and various Scottish nobles should come and do feudal service and fight for him in Gascony. But feudalism had moved on by the thirteenth century. Fealty no longer meant provision of troops. Edward's demand was completely unjustified. Instead, the Scots offered themselves as allies to King Philip and came out against Edward. Edward responded by seizing John Balliol's English lands and moving north against the rebels.

BERWICK

It was 1296 when the first blows in a one-sided contest were landed by the Scots. A Scottish army led by John Comyn entered the border country in Cumbria and looted and burnt farmsteads, churches and monasteries along the border in Lanercost, Hexham and Corbridge. If the Scots thought such a demonstration would restore the status quo, they were mistaken. Edward was heading up the east coast with an army 8,000 strong. He was looking for an opportunity to teach the rebels, who had put themselves outside the King's Peace, a lesson. With Comyn's raiding party safely back over the border, it was the people of Scotland's economic hub, Berwick-upon-Tweed, who provided the perfect opportunity.

Five weeks earlier some English merchants had been murdered and their goods seized by the locals. Now Edward demanded restitution. To the east he blockaded the mouth of the Tweed with his fleet, while he approached Berwick from the west along the north bank. His offer of mercy in exchange for an oath of loyalty was met with a barrage of obscenities from the city burghers. It's likely this show of defiance included baring their bottoms to the English King – an insult similar to that offered by Mel Gibson and his men in the movie. There was a weird belief among the Scots that the English had tails, and showing their bottoms was a taunt to the deformed enemy.

Berwick had a castle but otherwise the defences of the town were pitifully weak. Edward simply bypassed the castle and charged into the town on his steed, Bayard, taking the defences at one leap. The castle garrison surrendered and was spared. Not so the town.

According to the strict rules of war at that time, the citizens of Berwick had put themselves beyond the law by rebelling against their lord. He was entitled to do anything to them in return. He did. The flag of the dragon was raised, the signal for wholesale slaughter. The cry of 'havoc' went up. It's from the French for 'plunder' and has come to mean chaos in English. Everywhere the soldiers killed, raped and looted. The only resistance came from a group of about thirty Flemish merchants who holed up in a building called the Red Hall and fired arrows. They killed Edward's cousin, and Edward personally ordered the building to be fired and the defenders burnt alive.

Estimates of the dead range from 7,000 (John of Fordun) to 60,000 (Matthew of Westminster). It's said that the Tweed ran red with blood and that Edward only stopped

4

WALLACE

the carnage after three days when he saw a woman being hacked to death by a soldier while in the very act of giving birth. A most terrible price had been paid. In an age when civilian slaughter and plunder were commonplace, Edward had set a new benchmark of savagery. Even the English chroniclers seem to realize that their man had gone beyond the pale.

Berwick never fully recovered from that blow. The massacre marked the first in a series of changes in its ownership over the next hundred years until finally it fell permanently under English jurisdiction (although to this day its football team plays in the Scottish league!). It's a backwater now compared to its status seven centuries ago. The thoroughness of its demolition by both English and Scots means there are few traces of Berwick pre-Edward.

Berwick was the base from which Edward launched a crushing humiliation of the Scots. Ignoring reprisal raids into England by a handful of Scottish nobles, Edward moved on and trounced the Scottish army at Dunbar. He sacked the abbey at Scone, removed the Stone of Destiny which he eventually took south to Westminster (see the chapter on Macbeth, pages 69–72), and stripped John Balliol of his kingship, literally. In a humiliating ritual he ripped the royal insignia from Balliol's tabard or topcoat, and ever after the deposed King was known as 'Toom Tabard' – Empty Coat. Balliol was taken off to England where he remained under house arrest until 1302. At Berwick Edward held a parliament where he presented the Scots with a document later known as the Ragman's Roll, a name designed to highlight its threadbare validity. The Scottish nobles were required to go through the rigmarole of signing up to it, giving written acknowledgement of their loyalty to Edward. Indeed, the word rigmarole itself is a corruption of 'Ragman's Roll', and celebrates the futile bureaucratic rituals the nobles were forced to take part in.

The story goes that on his way back over the border Edward turned to Earl Warenne, the man he was leaving in charge of the conquered country, and sneered his contempt for Scotland. *'Bon besoigne fait qy de merde se delivrer,'* he said, which means 'He who gets rid of shit does a good job'. By crushing the Scottish army and tying the nobles up in oaths and red tape, Edward thought he'd got rid of the problem of Scotland. He was wrong. A natural aristocrat, he hadn't even considered how the people of Scotland would react. But the bitterness provoked by Berwick and the English occupation caused spontaneous combustion.

Across the country, guerrilla acts of rebellion and riot kept the Scottish cause alive. And in the countryside of Ayrshire and Lanarkshire tales started circulating about an outlaw called William Wallace and his deeds of derring-do.

Blind Harry tells many tales from this early period. A typical story has Wallace fishing in a river, when suddenly five English soldiers turn up and demand his catch. Wallace says, 'You must be joking,' but offers them half anyway. Nevertheless, one of the English soldiers is so furious that a mere Jock should give him cheek that he draws his sword and lunges at

The cobbled area by the river round Sally Quay gives the best idea of how the medieval port of Berwick would have looked. If you find your way up through the main gate from the river and keep the cinema on your left you'll come to the corner of Sandgate and Bridge Street. This is the site of the Red Hall where the Flemish merchants were burnt to death.

Wallace. The outlaw immediately parries with his fishing pole, snatches the man's sword and lops his head off. Then he kills two more soldiers before the others escape.

Dedicated Wallace fans in later years located this incident of 'the bickering bush' at Irvine Water at Riccarton near Kilmarnock. But the story, like many in Blind Harry's account, is apocryphal. Nevertheless, Wallace was obviously active before we get an incident which is confirmed by other sources. The chronicles say that 'he raised his head' in May 1297. The four-month interval between that incident and his first major victory is too short for him to have established instant authority without having an existing reputation.

LANARK

This first corroborated incident was the murder of William Heselrig, Sheriff of Lanark, in Lanark Castle. But, according to tradition, it wasn't a political assassination but a crime of passion.

The story, which will be instantly recognizable to anyone who's watched the film, says that Wallace had fallen in love. He saw a maiden while at mass in St Kentigern's Church in Lanark and was instantly smitten. She was Marion Braidfoote from the nearby village of Lammington. The chronicles go on to tell how Wallace carried on a clandestine love affair and eventually married Marion. But the English appointee as Sheriff at Lanark, William Heselrig, also had his eye on Wallace's girl. He got his men to provoke Wallace into a skirmish. He was outnumbered but, before Heselrig's men could arrest him, Marion helped him escape into the hills. In revenge and 'full of lustful hate' as Harry puts it, Heselrig had Marion killed. Hearing of the slaughter, Wallace returned under cover of darkness to wreak his revenge.

The attack was swift and terrible. Wallace went straight to the Sheriff's quarters in the castle, surprising him in his bed. One blow of his enormous sword went straight through the Sheriff's skull down to his collarbone. Death would have been instantaneous, but a young follower made sure by stabbing the inert body three times. Then the Scottish raiders went on the rampage, killing the English at will, sparing only women and priests.

The first account of the attack on Heselrig and his men appeared in the 1350s when Sir Thomas de Grey, whose father had been one of the few survivors of Heselrig's garrison, wrote about his father's escape from Wallace's onslaught. But he didn't give any details about Wallace's motive. There's a possibility that the Marion story is a later invention and that the killing was a simple political or criminal act. The sheriff heard cases at his assizes. It's unlikely that the locals would have respected his authority. It could be that Wallace was being charged with other crimes and killed Heselrig to disrupt the legal process.

What is clear is that Wallace the outlaw had gradually changed into Wallace the scourge of the English, the fighter for independence. In an age where physical prowess

WALLACE

Opposite: The ruins of the church where Wallace first laid eyes on Marion Braidfoote.

The ruins of St Kentigern's Church still remain. They're in the middle of the municipal graveyard just out of Lanark city centre. Not so much remains of Lanark Castle. Lanark Thistle Bowling Club occupies the site. It can be reached by going down Lanark's high street and turning right at the little church which has a Wallace statue over the door and which is opposite the supposed site of the house Wallace shared with Marion. The bowling club is at the end of the lane. The entrance still echoes the shape of the castle gateway, and the plateau on which the innocent bowling green is set falls away to reveal the fortified position of Heselrig's stronghold.

was paramount he must have been a formidable fighter. He had a natural advantage. All the accounts of Wallace speak of him as a big man, perhaps six feet six or more. There's also a description of him having an arrow scar on his neck, but beyond that there's little physical description of him. What was obviously important was the sense of power Wallace conveyed. Not only was he good at fighting, but he had the charisma to attract and command others, even those whose social standing was higher than his. The people flocked to him. What lay behind this charisma was a single-mindedness, a devotion to a cause, that turned him into one of those extraordinary people in history who do remarkable things through the force of their own personality.

WILLIAM HOOD?

An archer who lives as an outlaw in the greenwood, a maid called Marion, an unpopular sheriff who gets his come-uppance: doesn't this ring a few bells? It's been claimed that Wallace was the model for Robin Hood. Flip on to the next chapter to see why the claims don't really stand up. It seems more likely that Blind Harry knew about Robin Hood and wasn't averse to pinching some elements from a southerner's story in order to spice up his tale of a Scottish hero.

While Wallace's campaign gained momentum in the south, his success was mirrored in the north by another guerrilla leader. Compared with the lad from Elderslie, Andrew Murray was a true aristocrat. His father, Sir Andrew, was a powerful nobleman and his uncle, Sir William, was nicknamed 'The Rich'. But, unlike some of the Scots nobility who switched sides when it was convenient, Andrew Murray was a troublemaking Highlander of the old school. Starting at about the same time as Wallace's attack on Heselrig, Murray carried out a brilliant campaign in the north-east of Scotland, clearing out the English from their strongholds in the Highlands. When Wallace joined forces with Murray the rebellion became a revolution. The English had to act.

Edward I was away fighting an unpopular war in France. He ordered a formidable army north under the command of Earl Warenne and Bishop Hugh Cressingham to sort out the rebels. Wallace and Murray were in Dundee when the news reached them. They immediately left the besieging of Dundee Castle to a subordinate and marched to head off the English at Stirling. They decided to take the English on at the crossing point. Its name was to echo through history.

STIRLING BRIDGE

Stirling Bridge was absolutely vital strategically. It controlled access to the Highlands. A thirteenth-century map by Matthew Paris graphically demonstrates its strategic importance. The Highlands are connected to the rest of the island only by the thin thread of the

bridge. If the English wanted to take back Scotland, they had no choice but to cross. The Scots were heavily outnumbered, but Stirling Bridge provided Murray and Wallace with the ideal location for a make-or-break battle.

The exact location of the battle was disputed until recently because nobody could find the remains of the original bridge. Then local archaeologists located some of its stone piers and, using the picture of it on the ancient town seal, worked out that it had crossed the River Forth diagonally just upstream from the existing fourteenth-century bridge.

Wallace and Murray had placed their lightly armed footsoldiers on the high ground to the north side of the river just to the east of where the university is today. The English with their heavy force of mounted knights and professional infantry were arrayed on the south of the river in the shadow of Stirling Castle.

Between the two armies lay the river itself and an area of boggy ground to the north where the Forth loops round at a right angle. This marshy area was crossed by a single causeway which followed the same course as the A907 does today from Stirling past the Wallace memorial and on to Alloa.

This boggy ground worried the English. Their classic battle formation was a broad line of horsemen who would charge shoulder-to-shoulder and deliver a crushing blow to the enemy. The marshy ground, though passable, would make a charge far less effective. In addition, the bridge was narrow with no rails. It would only take two riders abreast.

It was 11 September. The English made two false starts across the bridge and withdrew to allow time for last-minute negotiations. First they parleyed with representatives of the Scottish nobility then, as a last resort, two Dominican friars were sent under a flag of peace to try and bring the outnumbered rebels to their senses. They returned with a message from Wallace and Murray: 'We have not come for peace but to fight and avenge our country.' There was nothing more to be said.

Even then some counselled caution. Sir Richard Lundie asked to take a detachment of cavalry to a ford further upstream, creating a pincer movement and threatening the Scots' rear. But Hugh Cressingham, Edward's treasurer and a warlike prelate whom even English sources describe as fat and charmless, put his foot down. He accused the more cautious knights of wasting the King's money and told them to get over the bridge and mop up the rabble. And all this time the waters of the tidal Forth would have been rising, making the ground on the other side of the bridge even less suitable for mounted warfare.

Imagine those aerial shots of the start of the London Marathon with thousands of runners shuffling towards the start line. Now imagine the sight that greeted Wallace and Murray as they looked down and saw a similar number of armed Englishmen queuing up to cross the narrow wooden bridge. They couldn't have believed their luck; the English were shuffling into a trap.

For their part, the plumed knights must have thought that they would be given the

usual courtesy of lining up nicely in battle order. That was the etiquette of chivalry. But Wallace and Murray weren't like that. They didn't share the attitude of some of the knights who saw battle as a violent form of sport, a chance for excitement and honour. They were the thirteenth-century equivalent of street-fighters engaged in a last-ditch attempt to save their homeland. So they waited until just enough of the English had crossed the bridge: enough to fight and enough to kill. Then Wallace gave a single blast on his horn.

The nimble Scots flooded down the hillside and ran round either side of the chaotic mass of English cavalry and infantry. They cut off the bridge, preventing further soldiers from crossing, and blocking the retreat of those who'd already reached the killing ground. Then they set to work. It was less battle, more butchery. They slashed at the bellies and hamstrings of the horses, bringing them down in the mud. Then they dealt with the unseated riders: a spear through the visor or a knife under the throat armour. The English, deprived of mobility and space to operate, had no means of retaliation. Their costly armour was no protection as they foundered in the mire. The more lightly armoured soldiers who could swim fled back across the river.

We know of only one named English survivor. Sir Marmaduke Tweng from Yorkshire managed to hack a path through the solid mass of bodies on the bridge and make his way back to the English side. In contrast, the names of the fallen are plentiful.

We know for sure that Hugh Cressingham, the man who'd urged the English on to the slaughter, was one of the slain. Swapping clerical garb for chain mail, he'd made sure that he was in the first wave. When the Scots found the body of the hated English official he was stripped and skinned. It's said that Wallace himself took a long strip of skin and had it tanned and turned into a sword belt. Then pieces of Cressingham's dismembered body were sent round Scotland to celebrate the victory and to announce the start of a new regime. It would be headed by William Wallace alone. One of the few Scots casualties had been his partner Andrew Murray, who died from his wounds some time later in 1297.

Most of the battlefield today is covered by housing. You can get the best idea of the layout of the battle from the height of Stirling Castle. Look for the loop of the river lined with trees and the straight road crossing what was the boggy ground.

If you leave the centre of Stirling and follow the signs for the university, you'll cross the road bridge over the Forth. Parallel with this bridge upstream is the ancient stone bridge which was built to replace the one from Wallace's time. This connects two little parks.

It's worth taking time to walk across the span of the bridge and imagine the logistics of getting a thousand horses over something even narrower. Facing away from the city there lies before you a gigantic unofficial English graveyard. Up to 5,000 were killed, then stripped of weapons, metal, cloth, leather and anything valuable before being left to rot. William Wallace High School playing field is the largest area of grass left among the flats

Opposite: Matthew Paris's map is meant to be symbolically true rather than geographically accurate. A vast, fat England is at the centre of things and the great landmass of Scotland is reduced to a small top-knot (note the secure fence of Hadrian's Wall). Stirling Bridge, (marked 'pons') keeps the Highlands anchored to the rest of the country.

157

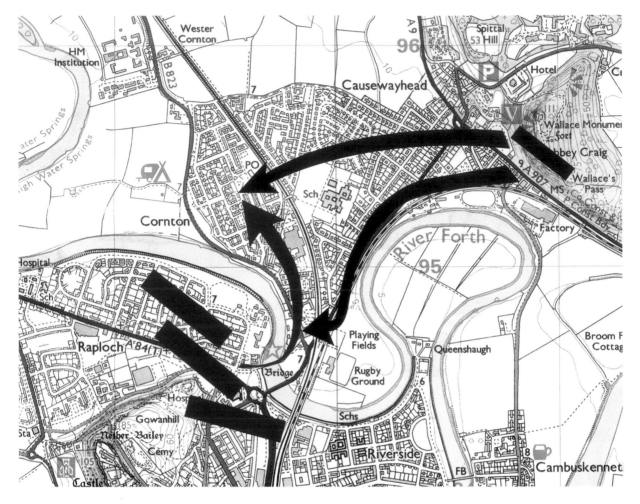

and houses. The ground has been drained since Wallace's time but there's something spooky about the fact that beneath the feet of today's battling young rugby players lie the last remains of such great carnage.

Stirling Bridge is far from being one of those forgotten battles of history. There's great pride in Stirling that 'it happened here'. The battle has helped to form Scottish pride, confidence and national identity. For the Scots, sharing an island with a southern neighbour who has far more manpower, technology and cash, Stirling Bridge is a beacon reminding them what can be achieved through sheer bloody-mindedness and canny planning. Wallace and Murray's victory was a masterstroke of military tactics, but it also gave Scotland hope. Their army had defeated overwhelming numbers of better-equipped soldiers. The fact that the vote for a devolved Scottish Parliament took place 700 years to the day after the battle has given it an added significance. Even before the tragic events in New York, the date 11 September was written deep in the Scottish psyche as the day Wallace defeated the English at Stirling Bridge.

ABBEY CRAIG

To mark the victory that was to be Wallace's greatest moment, the Victorians erected the Wallace Monument on top of Abbey Craig, the cliffs that rise above Cambuskenneth Abbey. It is the most tremendous statement of national pride, far more striking in its way than Nelson's column. Rising 67 metres above the already imposing height of Abbey Craig, you can see it from as far away as Falkirk. It looks like the great neo-gothic tower of a cathedral – only without the cathedral. And it is a centre of pilgrimage. When the foundation stone was laid in 1861, 80,000 people turned up to pay tribute. Now, since the film *Braveheart*, it has become an international attraction.

The entrance is at the bottom of a cliff, guarded by a modern chunky stone statue portraying Wallace as Mel Gibson. The bad news is that for all except the disabled and elderly, for whom there's a regular shuttle, access involves a steep stiff walk up the winding road to the top. Prepare for the sight of overweight American tourists strewn by the wayside mopping their brows and wondering how important their Scottish roots really are. Once at the top, the monument itself has another challenging spiral staircase ascent to see the various

The Wallace Monument on Abbey Craig.

exhibits. These include a fearsome display of ancient weaponry and the sword which, it's claimed, Wallace himself left in Dumbarton Castle.

The statue of Wallace in a niche on the corner of the monument is far better than the Gibson lookalike below. However, it flies in the face of history by portraying him as an elder statesman in his forties or fifties, whereas in real life he was only in his mid-twenties when he achieved his greatest success. The views of the surrounding countryside are spectacular both from the top and the base of the tower. Even for an Englishman, to stand there with the wind gusting, looking out over the hills, fields, the winding Forth, Stirling Castle, and the mountains blue in the distance, there's a vivid sense of what inspired Wallace. This was the homeland Wallace wanted to keep free.

There's no denying the importance of Stirling Bridge in the Scottish consciousness, but here's the cold water moment. Stirling Bridge was a symbolic and emotional triumph but politically it achieved nothing. There's even a good case for arguing that Wallace would have been better off losing the battle.

The English, though they may have appeared to be a single threatening entity, were deeply divided. In August 1297 Edward had sailed to Flanders with a small army intending to join up with his allies on the Continent and fight the French King Philip IV. But his allies were mostly defeated before he even arrived. His political opponents back in England were angered at the outrageous burden of taxation he had put on the country to support this foreign adventure. The country was on the verge of civil war. Secret alliances were being formed, stratagems laid and troops recruited. Then news came through of the disaster at Stirling. Scotland, which seemed to have been defeated so easily, had bitten back.

An upstart, a robber from outside the chivalrous classes, had caused the Earl Warrenne's army to flee in fear. The English chroniclers describe Wallace's rise as an attempt to turn a crow into a swan. Stirling Bridge smacked of overturning the social order as well as a political rebellion. It focused everyone back on their patriotic duty. Edward I swiftly reached a truce with the French, and the Continental war was over. He could begin the job of packing up the army and returning to England. His political enemies, who had opposed the Continental campaign while Scotland was in such a state of ferment, felt they'd been proved right. Wallace had united the English as well as the Scots. If he'd been less successful, England may well have imploded and Scotland might have been liberated by default.

If you leave Stirling by crossing the road bridge, you can see the Wallace monument in front of you. You are driving down the course of the narrow causeway. At the end there is a roundabout with the William Wallace pub in front of it. Carry on round a small dogleg. The monument is well signposted and, when you arrive, there's a large car park.

WALLACE'S CAMPAIGN IN ENGLAND

The shock to the English system wasn't finished with the defeat at Stirling Bridge. Wallace knew that Edward wouldn't take defeat lying down, so, once he'd mopped up the few remaining English still holding out in Scottish castles, he took the fight to the enemy. He

launched an invasion of the north of England. And in doing so, he confuses the clear and heroic image we've had of him so far.

After retaking the city of Berwick, Wallace's troops hit England in October 1297 and ravaged the border country of Northumberland and Cumbria. They avoided the heavily defended northern garrisons and instead went for soft targets: farms, abbeys and monasteries such as Hexham and Lanercost. It was a campaign of systematic plunder to boost Scottish reserves, but it also went much further. Wallace's stated aim was to remove any English-speaking people from the border country. In an age when national pride was beginning to coalesce into something we'd recognize today, its natural concomitant, ethnic hatred, was also emerging.

Of course, you can explain away the frustration of the Scots. There were years of wrongs to avenge, especially the atrocity at Berwick. The Scots chroniclers paint a picture of Wallace trying to moderate the excesses of his men, giving safe passage to monks and priests. But the English writers accuse Wallace personally and specifically of war crimes. His campaign of burning and pillaging was on a different scale to anything the English had experienced in recent years. Wallace was accused of a range of atrocities, some of them very odd indeed, like getting choirs of naked men and women to sing for him. They said he pushed monks into the river with their hands tied behind them so they would thrash about and drown while Wallace stood laughing on the bank. He's accused of burning schools with children inside, of slaughtering women, children and the old.

LANERCOST

Some of Wallace's sternest critics were the monks of Lanercost Abbey who'd suffered at his hands. They wrote the *Lanercost Chronicle*, which relates the story from the English point of view.

The abbey church and extensive ruins lie just by the River Irthing. It's an impressive National Heritage property with the advantage that there's a 'before and after' effect. The working church is built of the same red stone as the ruins outside; the only difference is that the church has a roof and glass. Tempting as it is to imagine the wave of destruction wreaked by Wallace and his hordes, the reality is that the abbey quickly recovered from Wallace's raid. The real vandal responsible for the wreckage of Lanercost was Henry VIII.

Wallace wasn't the only significant visitor. Edward I spent the last few months of his life here on his last campaign against the Scots, and there's an image of his wife on a corbel situated on the north-west of the intact building. There are also some touching indications of the life of a medieval monk still visible, like the board game etched into the stone of a window frame.

There's still an abbey at Lanercost, set in a field about three miles from the western end of Hadrian's Wall. Coming from either Carlisle or Newcastle, you'll be on the A69 (if you're approaching from the east you can also stop off at Hexham, another of Wallace's targets), then follow local signs at Brampton for Hadrian's Wall and Lanercost.

Lanercost doesn't paint a pretty picture of Wallace, but perhaps we shouldn't judge too harshly by the standards of our own time. As we've seen in previous chapters, controlling a nation required a frightening capacity for violence. In any case, the onset of a harsh winter put paid to the Scots' plundering and they retreated north. Now Wallace's task was to prepare for the return match with the English. To give Wallace authority, on his return he was knighted at Selkirk, possibly by Robert the Bruce. Then Sir William Wallace was made Guardian of Scotland. In the absence of the King and on his behalf, Wallace was now in supreme command.

It's one of the interesting things about Wallace that he never sought power for his own sake. He's one of those remarkable people who act for a cause, even when it's to their own detriment. In all his dealings he acknowledged King John Balliol as the true ruler of Scotland. He saw himself as merely a stopgap.

WALLACE THE GUARDIAN OF SCOTLAND

Wallace now set about re-establishing political and economic order. The one artefact we have which gives us an unequivocal link to him reveals something of his policy. It's the letter that's now in a museum in Lübeck in Germany whose seal has told us so much about his background. Wallace dictated it to a secretary before he invaded England and before his partner Murray died. It's from them both as commanders of the Scottish army to the mayors of Hamburg and Lübeck. The bulk of Scotland's trade had been with Holland, Germany and Scandinavia and Wallace assures the mayors that it's business as usual now that the English have been kicked out, and guarantees their merchants safe passage to all the ports of the kingdom of Scotland. It's likely that this is the sole survivor of a number of similar letters that went out to merchants across Northern Europe, in an attempt to revive Scotland's economy.

Wallace expected to be obeyed as he readied Scotland for Edward's backlash. Walter Bower's *Scotichronicon* describes how he had a gallows set up in every major town to 'encourage' backsliders. That this was not just a gesture is proved by his readiness to hang some men in Aberdeen who failed to turn up for military service. But it wasn't the ordinary people who gave him the most to worry about. His prime concern was the nobility with their shifting sense of loyalty.

Many nobles had given and broken their oaths of loyalty to Edward, and some had even fought for the English against Wallace. While Wallace was on a roll, they flocked to his side, but he must have known that for many, this was sheer expediency. The great earls must have been as shocked as the English chronicles to find an outlaw in charge of their country.

Wallace had already gone some way towards countering the influence of the nobles within the army. Instead of organizing the men in the traditional way according to their loyalty to a specific earl, he had instituted a ruthlessly egalitarian system of command.

Bower describes how he created a list of Scots between the ages of sixteen and sixty so that he could organize conscription. His system reveals that Wallace's education must have included the classics. The basic unit of the army was five men with one in charge of the other four, a Roman *quaterion*. For every two units, one man would command the other nine (a *decurion*), and doubled again there'd be one man in charge of the other nineteen. This carried on up to units of a thousand men (a *chiliarch*). Any disobedience at any level was punished by death. Above them all was Wallace, the general who could rely on a chain of command that was flexible and didn't depend on the existing social system. And having structured his army, he started to drill them in new techniques to counter the expected English manoeuvres.

He invented a battlefield tactic called the schiltrom. It was designed to maximize his resources. The basic weapons of the Scots were spears of varying sophistication, and the dirk, or knife. Swords were fantastically expensive and archers were in a minority. At its most basic a Scottish spear was a length of sharpened hardwood about 10 or 12 feet long. Wallace's schiltrom was essentially a hedgehog of spears: a circle of up to a thousand men (the *chiliarch*) in close formation with their weapons in a tight-packed mass impregnable to a charge from front and rear. The key to the formation was that the men should be able to move as one and not break ranks. Like the Romans' shield wall with their deadly swords stabbing to the side, the schiltrom was a living organism creating strength through organization. Wallace knew he couldn't rely on the English being fooled again.

FALKIRK 1298

Edward I meant business. Six months after the disaster at Stirling, he landed in Kent and made his way to York to take personal charge of the operation against the man the chroniclers call *ille latroi*, 'that robber'. An invasion was scheduled for June with a massive army. The English writer Hemingburgh tells us Edward mustered 4,000 heavy cavalry, 3,000 light horsemen and 80,000 mostly professional infantry including large numbers of Welsh archers. Even allowing for the usual exaggeration, this was clearly a major mobilization.

But such a large army needed feeding, and Edward's lines of supply were very long. Wallace decided to counter the invaders with a scorched earth policy. Towns and farms south of Edinburgh were fired and the population was shifted north of the Forth. If the English were going to eat, it wouldn't be Scottish food.

As the English moved north, scavenging for scraps of food in the devastated fields, they were harried by small detachments based in Scottish castles. Bishop Anthony Bek of Durham was dispatched to deal with these pockets of resistance. He had no siege machinery and sent an officer, Sir John Fitz-Marmaduke, back to Edward with a request for reinforcements. Edward's instruction leaves little doubt about his state of mind: 'You are a cruel man and I've often rebuked you for being too cruel, but now get going and use all your cruelty and I'll praise you instead. Don't let me see your face again until the castles are burnt.'

Strong words, but behind them was a growing air of desperation. Wallace's tactics were working. The enormous army lumbered forward, getting ever hungrier, but there was no sign of the enemy. Wallace kept retreating, waited until the enemy turned back through exhaustion, and then harried the stragglers. His strategy was backed up by raids on Edward's supply lines.

When the English reached Edinburgh their situation became desperate. Some supply ships had arrived at Leith but they only contained wine. This was unwisely rationed out and caused a massive drunken brawl between the Welsh and English footsoldiers. When chaplains tried to intervene to calm things down, eighteen English priests were killed. It took a cavalry charge on his own forces with the loss of eighty Welshmen for Edward to restore order. When the Welsh threatened to go over to the Scottish side Edward, ever the diplomat, snarled that he'd be just as happy to take on both the Welsh and the Scots. For Wallace, everything seemed to be going to plan.

Then, not for the first or last time, the English were given a break through the treachery of the Scottish nobility. The English camped just west of Edinburgh. On 21

The Wallace Stone – a memorial to the Battle of Falkirk, but also a more general Wallace Stone. In reprisal for Wallace's head being displayed on London Bridge, a stone was knocked off the bridge itself and brought here; a symbol that Scottish pride could not be quelled by killing one man.

July, just when they were beginning to lose hope, the Scottish Lords Dunbar and Angus rode into camp with the news that Wallace's army was only eighteen miles away at Falkirk. It was what Edward had been waiting for and he immediately ordered a forced march along the south bank of the Forth. By nightfall the English had reached Linlithgow.

During the night there was a panic. Edward's warhorse trampled the sleeping King, breaking two ribs. Edward was in his sixties but, for all his faults, he was a tough old bird. In his youth, he'd survived poisoning in the Holy Land, and he wasn't going to let a last-minute injury come between him and his quarry. In spite of the pain, he mounted his horse to let his men see that he was unharmed. He ordered his men to resume their march even though it was still dark. It was now Tuesday 22 July.

No one knows why Wallace abandoned his hit-and-run strategy in favour of a pitched confrontation. Perhaps he was caught on the hop by the forced march and didn't want to be trapped at a crossing of the Forth with his back to the river, but there was no reason to believe that the starving English forces could have overtaken the smaller Scottish army. Maybe he thought that the English were sufficiently weakened, that he had the ideal location and the tactics to beat them. We can only speculate.

As Edward continued his march towards Falkirk, his scouts reported a flash of metal on a hill overlooking the town. Tradition holds that it was Wallace spying on the English advance. By the time English horsemen arrived, the Scots had disappeared, but Edward following behind knew that the main Scottish army couldn't be far away. He ordered his army to halt and the mass of St Mary Magdalene was celebrated on a makeshift altar. As the service came to an end, the early morning mist cleared to reveal the Scots preparing for battle on a hill below them in Falkirk.

Except I can't tell you where to look because no one can agree where the Battle of Falkirk took place.

Pinpointing this battle site is another of those Olympic sports for academics like trying to locate the scene of Boudica's last stand. The only clues the chronicles give are to tell us that Wallace deployed his men on high ground overlooking an area of bog (both sides must have remembered Stirling), with a watercourse or stream crossing the field. There are at least five main contenders. Even the psychic spoon-bender Uri Geller has been called in recently to try and divine the original location!

We may not have the precise location but we do know the story of the battle. Wallace had arranged his men in four schiltrom formations along the hill. One writer says that the spears were reinforced with a row of sharpened stakes. Between each of the four hedgehogs was a line of archers and behind them, his limited cavalry forces comprising the Scots nobility. As he saw the English squaring up he shouted to his men, 'I have brought you to the ring, now dance the best you can.'

WALLACE

The place where Wallace is said to have spied on the English advance is the Wallace Stone in Redding near Falkirk. I won't attempt to give directions through the back streets of the Falkirk suburbs, but with a street map and/or a little local knowledge you should come to the highest point in the area. There's a monument enclosed by railings with several Wallace relics, though not the eponymous Wallace Stone on which Wallace is said to have stood. The view is spectacular. You can see as far as the Wallace Monument to the west and way over the Forth valley to the fiery pipes of the Grangemouth industrial complex to the north. Sweeping on round to the east, you can see Linlithgow where Edward had spent the previous night. Turning back round to the west, all of Falkirk is spread out in front of you, and down there lies the scene of the great confrontation of 22 July 1298.

If you want to get an idea of the layout of the battle uncluttered by twenty-first-century development, try going to the Mumrils site, one of the more rural possibilities, near the main Edinburgh to Falkirk road. It's just off junction 5 on the M9 on the left opposite Mumrils farm.

The English hadn't eaten for a whole day. Edward wanted the last of the rations to be broken out so that his men could fight on a full stomach, but his nobles persuaded him to 'get up and at 'em'. Against his better judgement, he sent the English troops in hungry. It wasn't popular. The Welsh infantry, still smarting from their overblown pub brawl, were ordered in first, but flatly refused to face the spears of the Scots before the English aristocrats had had a taste of iron. So the barons moved forwards on to the treacherous surface.

Wave after wave of English cavalrymen drove their destriers gingerly across the boggy ground, up the slope, and on to the waiting Scottish spears. The conditions sapped the energy of the charging horses and the schiltroms held firm. They were well trained and confident. Again Wallace's strategy for his outnumbered forces seemed to be working as he rode up and down the line exhorting his men to stand firm. But then two things happened that changed the course of the day and Wallace's future reputation.

First, the nobility who formed the cavalry upped and left, and then Edward sent in his secret weapon: his longbowmen. Archers were nothing new. We've seen how they were used by William against Harold. Wallace had a few archers himself. But this was the start of the English longbow used in a totally new way: massed archers working together sending volleys of arrows over distances of 200 metres or more and firing so swiftly that each archer could have three arrows in the air at the same time. By deploying the same weapon in this concerted way, it was like turning a musket into a machine-gun. That's how it surprised Wallace the archer. In the following century the English longbow was to win the battles of Crécy and Agincourt. It came to be so hated and feared that English bowmen caught by the French would have their middle fingers cut off before being released.

The mainly Lancastrian and Welsh bowmen were part of Edward's infantry. They moved forward to the front line and decimated the schiltroms from a distance. The classic military response to archers should have been a horseback charge to break them up, but Wallace no longer had his cavalry at his disposal. What followed was carnage. The long-bowmen kept up their deadly rate of fire into the deliberately massed ranks of Scots, many of whom relied on the hedgehog rather than armour for protection. The archers couldn't miss. Eventually, the schiltroms had to break and, as they did, the English cavalry charged in to slaughter the broken and retreating infantry.

But why did the Scottish nobles leave the battlefield? Were they paid off, or did they again want to strike a deal with Edward? It's tempting to see the whole thing in anachronistic class terms, but historians have defended the nobility on the basis that they had no option other than death or retreat. Wallace's 'cavalry' may have been only fifty or so horsemen. They saw that the battle was lost and preferred to live to fight another day. It has to be said that Wallace also survived the battle, deciding at some point to retreat rather than die on foot with the last man in the schiltroms.

On the other hand, Wallace was the Guardian and the General. Leaving the field without his orders betrays a professional disdain, a fundamental lack of commitment to the common cause and an absence of fellow feeling with the men trapped in the schiltroms.

Or was the defeat simply Wallace's fault? There's a school of thought that questions whether Wallace was a great military leader at all. They point to the fact that when he was with Andrew Murray he won Stirling, and when Murray was dead he lost Falkirk. But although the end was so devastating, the battle was fought on the right lines. The schiltroms held the cavalry, their training paid off. According to the accepted strategy of the time, Wallace did everything right. He was simply overtaken by an advance in military technology.

The casualty figures are put at 10,000 Scottish dead. Hardly any of those were buried. Two of the few marked graves are in Falkirk graveyard. The ancient church, the Fawwe kirk, gave its name to the town, and is steeped in history. The graves of Sir John Graham and Sir John Stewart are in the graveyard at the south-east end of the church. They were two of the handful of barons who didn't desert Wallace. In Blind Harry's poem it is Wallace himself who finds Graham's corpse on the battlefield and gives his tribute.

My dearest brother that I ever had
My only friend when I was hard bestead
My hope, my health, O man of honour great
My faithful aid and strength in every strait.

Graham's grave is surrounded by railings. As one grave-slab has been worn away by time, another has been placed on top so that now the grave is well over a metre high. Stewart's grave is more obscure. You'll find it on the other side of the path.

For Wallace, the defeat was not only political but personal. His men had been slaughtered, he had let Edward into Scotland again and he had lost his credibility. His one strength had been to organize and fight and now, after only nine months, he had been crushingly defeated. Not long after Falkirk he either resigned or was quietly removed from the guardianship. In a return to business as usual, his place was taken jointly by two of the most powerful earls. They were John Comyn, from the most dominant family in Scotland, and the Earl of Carrick, the soon-to-be-immortal Robert Bruce. As yet there was none of Wallace's selfless love of country about either of these two. Their relationship was the sort of wary stalemate that the original election of John Balliol had been designed to avoid. Eventually Bruce was to murder Comyn in cold blood to seize power.

Edward hadn't emerged unscathed from the Falkirk campaign either. He found the energy to drag his army on and sack Stirling and Fife, but then he turned round and headed for home. His troops were still starving and were plagued by disease. As they headed back through the Lowlands they were harried by remnants of the once united Scottish army. It was clear to Edward that Scotland was going to be a tougher nut to crack than he had anticipated during his blitzkrieg of 1296. The Battle of Falkirk marked the beginning of a long war of attrition, with Edward returning year after year to chip away at Scottish resistance, to take back another castle, to hang a few more rebels and win back from the nobility that fealty he felt they had betrayed.

THE CAMPAIGN ABROAD

A lesser man than Wallace might also have gone back home to lick his wounds and quietly retire. He'd given the national cause his best shot. But he was more stubborn and committed than that. He came bouncing back off the ropes because he never gave up on the cause he believed in. Blind Harry attributes this to a lesson Wallace learnt as a teenager from his uncle, a priest at Dunipace in Stirlingshire. He took as his personal motto a Latin tag that runs:

> *Dico tibi verum, libertas optima rerum*
> *Nunquam servili sub nexu vivito, fili.*
> *(My son, I tell you truly, freedom is the greatest gift,*
> *So never live under the yoke of slavery.)*

Academics seem to agree that, for all its inaccuracies, the movie *Braveheart* manages to convey the truth of William Wallace in this unswerving commitment. But for those whose only knowledge of the man comes from the film, it may come as a surprise to learn that whereas his period in power was only nine months, he was to plough on in one way or another for seven more years before his final betrayal.

It was clear that a military solution was out of the question for the moment. Some of the nobles continued to lead sporadic resistance (which perhaps justifies their decision to fight another day) but it had nothing of the momentum of the earlier uprising of Murray and Wallace. And so, in his wilderness years, Wallace the tough giant of an outlaw transformed himself into Wallace the diplomat.

When he was finally captured, he was found to have incriminating documents (now lost) including safe conducts from the King of Norway and Philip of France. Our knowledge of Wallace during the period from 1298 to 1303 is fairly sketchy but it seems that he went abroad to canvass support for the Scottish cause from France and the Pope. This was the thirteenth-century equivalent of an appeal to the United Nations.

But it was not an official trip. John Comyn at least was in the dark about Wallace's departure. There's evidence from 1299 of a row between the two new Guardians of Scotland, Comyn and Bruce, over whether they should confiscate Sir William's property as punishment for leaving the country without permission. Wallace was obviously going freelance.

4

WALLACE

The Australian with the dodgy Scottish accent who gave Wallace his new name of Braveheart.

Perhaps it was at least partly out of self-preservation. A period of travel on the Continent was also a means of keeping out of harm's way. After Stirling and Falkirk Wallace was a marked man. He wasn't important enough to do what the nobles did: ask forgiveness and pledge a new oath. To Edward, he was a common criminal to be hunted down and killed.

Despite Harry's dramatic stories of encounters with pirates, the facts of this diplomatic mission are mostly informed guesswork, but we do know he was in France until the end of 1300. There are records of payments made on his behalf by the French Exchequer. During this time he may have visited the exiled Scottish King, John Balliol. By then Balliol had been put out to grass at his ancestral home of Bailleul. Wallace, ever loyal to the appointed ruler and without an eye to the main chance himself, would have been able to brief 'Toom Tabard' and ask for his advice. It's likely also that Wallace pleaded Scotland's cause with Philip of France. There's a letter written in November from Philip commending William Wallace, Knight, to the Pope, Boniface VIII.

The Church in the person of the Pope was a force to be reckoned with in the medieval world. Even the most hard-bitten secular ruler paid attention to someone who held the keys to the Kingdom of Heaven. Excommunication was a terrible thing. Boniface VIII was generally well disposed to the Scottish cause. Edward had imprisoned several eminent Scottish clerics who had supported rebellion in England and this was seen as an unwarranted attack on the Church. In 1299 Boniface had issued a papal bull commanding Edward to leave Scotland. It explained that Scotland had traditionally owed loyalty to the Holy See, not England, and it ordered Edward to release the imprisoned clerics and hand over the castles, abbeys and churches of Scotland. This bull was served on Edward in August 1300, possibly while Wallace was preparing for his trip to Rome. Edward heeded the warning and withdrew until 1301, giving himself time for his lawyers to prepare a reasoned rejection of the bull. This shows how valuable Wallace's political pressure must have been.

But the political tide was turning against Wallace. Philip IV, who'd written the letter of recommendation to his agents in Rome requesting that they plead the case of 'beloved William Wallace', was not as solid a support as Wallace might have hoped. The relations with England that had broken down in 1294 were being gradually restored. There's even a story that Philip IV captured Wallace on his way back through France from Rome and offered him to Edward, presumably as another peace offering. It seems incredible that Edward wouldn't have jumped at the offer. However, either Philip didn't deliver or Wallace escaped before he could be handed over.

SELKIRK

When he landed back in Scotland in 1303 (Harry tells us that he sailed up the Tay), Wallace returned to the life he knew best, making raids on the English from the safety of

At the entrance to Leglen Woods, there's a memorial linking the two patriots, Burns and Wallace, poet and warrior. Unless you are a huge Burns fan and want to do the walk from Lochlea to Leglen on foot, you get there by taking the A77 from Glasgow to Ayr and turning left at the junction with the B743. This will take you eventually to Tarbolton but you need to turn off right after about half a mile at Auchincruive. The woods themselves are a little difficult to find as you have to make a right turn at the Auchincruive branch of the Scottish Agricultural College, and follow a no-through road down through the campus to the entrance. The monument is just on the far side of a pretty stone bridge that spans the River Ayr.

the forests of Selkirk. But at first, this resumption of military activity also had official backing. Far from being punished for taking himself off to the Continent, he was briefly accepted back into the fold. There's a record of him fighting as a commander with the Scottish army alongside John Comyn and Sir Simon Fraser in raids as far south as the border with Cumbria.

But Sir William, although he'd tried his hand at diplomacy, was too intractable to be a good politician. As Edward piled on the pressure, the Scottish nobility saw the wisdom of making at least a temporary peace with him to give themselves a breathing space. Not Wallace. Like Arthur Scargill or Edward Heath in our own time, he became a loose political cannon. He simply couldn't see why the essential rightness of his cause should be compromised. His continued opposition became an embarrassment and then a threat to any hope of establishing a fragile peace. Many Scots must have wished that Wallace would just shut up. But he plugged on with a small bunch of fellow desperadoes travelling round his old haunts in constant fear of capture.

Edward was desperate to capture Wallace. He'd raided Selkirk in 1304 to try to find him. The Scottish nobles were desperate for peace. Edward made assistance in catching Wallace the proof and the price of their loyalty. If a Scottish noble wasn't putting his back into the hunt for the outlaw, he could not be admitted to the King's Peace. It must have been a terrifying time for Wallace, keeping one step ahead of the law and relying on the silence of a network of supporters within the great sweep of the Lowland forests.

Despite heavy cultivation and deforestation, there are many places where you can still get a sense of the forest of Selkirk. Perhaps the most romantic location is Leglen Woods, the haunt not only of Wallace, but of his greatest fan and promoter, the poet Rabbie Burns, who played a leading role in reviving interest in his hero in the nineteenth century. When he was a boy, Burns regularly made the ten-mile return pilgrimage to the woods from his family home at Lochlea Farm, imagining the exploits of his hero. Wallace was his cowboys and Indians. He later said that 'the story of Wallace poured a flood of Scottish prejudice into my veins, as will boil along until the floodgates are closed in eternal rest'. The one thing he wanted to do above all was to write a song, a song that would be worthy of Wallace. And he did so years later, composing 'Scots wha hae' (see below).

ROBROYSTON

There's one more Scottish site on our Wallace trail. Burns once wrote, 'We are bought and sold for English gold.' Robroyston is the place where he was betrayed to the English by his fellow Scots. Again there's a big stone Celtic cross to mark the event, but the more atmospheric location is across the road. Some abandoned farm buildings stand in roughly the same place as the farm where Wallace spent his last night of freedom.

*Robbie Burns.
Inspired by Wallace,
he was a major
standard-bearer in
the search for
Scottish identity.*

By August 1305, it was eight years since Wallace's single great success at Stirling, but he was still a thorn in Edward's side. He was a symbol of Scotland's intractability. The noose had been tightening round him for some time, but even though Edward had been demanding action from the nobles as proof of loyalty they had been either reluctant or spectacularly inept at catching him. In the end, the man Edward chose to close the trap on Wallace was Sir John Menteith. Sir John had the advantage of being close to the outlaw. Wallace was godfather to Menteith's two sons. It has been suggested that Menteith, an uncle of the Sir John Stewart who died at Falkirk, bore Wallace a grudge for the way his kinsman had been left to be cut down. Others say he did it for the money. Either way the betrayal was personal as well as political.

Menteith is a paradigm of the shifting allegiances of the Scottish nobles. He fought with John Balliol at Dunbar in 1296, then joined Edward on his campaign in Flanders. He switched sides again in 1298 and was declared the 'King's enemy' in 1301, but was one of the first to accept Edward's offers of peace in 1303. He was rewarded for swiftly falling back into line by being made Constable of Dumbarton Castle in 1304. More rewards were to come his way after he had turned Wallace in.

Robroyston is now on the very eastern fringes of Glasgow. The locals today are reputed to refer to it as 'Spam City'. a place of burgeoning housing estates where aspiring couples survive on processed meat to pay the mortgage.

In Wallace's day it was all countryside. There would have been nothing here but the remote farmhouse where he stayed. It was known as Bishopriggs, the fields owned by the Bishop of Glasgow. Wallace was supposedly hanging round the Glasgow area to meet Robert Bruce, but after his eighth day here (he must have survived by keeping constantly on the move) spies informed Menteith of his whereabouts.

On the night of 5 August Wallace was sleeping at a farmstead with his mistress. (Another source calls her a strumpet. The whole issue of Wallace's love life has been skated over by his Victorian supporters who would obviously have preferred a chaste national hero.) We're told Wallace was also accompanied by his most faithful comrade Kerly. Menteith had two conspirators: John Short, a spy who'd wheedled his way into Wallace's camp, and Rob Raa, after whom the place was eventually named ('Rob Raa's Toun'). They surrounded the farm with a detachment of soldiers. Kerly was disturbed by the noise and ran outside only to be cut down on the spot, but Wallace put up a fight. After a brief skirmish he was put in chains and led away for trial. Although the English maintained that Wallace was only a robber, they wanted his defeat and humiliation to be public.

There's one tradition that Wallace was first taken to Menteith's stronghold at Dumbarton Castle. There's a Wallace Tower there still and Wallace's sword was 'discovered' at Dumbarton – left, so the story goes, when Wallace was taken away south for trial.

To get to the spot where Wallace was finally captured, follow the M8 from Glasgow, then take junction 13 on to the M80 to Stirling, leaving at junction 2 (signposted B765 Bishopbriggs). Turn right at the first roundabout, heading on the B763 for Robroyston, then straight over the next round-about on to the B812 (Kirkintilloch/ Lenzie). This road continues right at a third roundabout. The disused farm buildings are on your left as you leave the roundabout and the monument to Wallace's capture is approximately 200 metres down on the right-hand side of the road. (Wallace's Well, where he is supposed to have had his last sip of water as a free man, is a little further on the same side of the road as the monument, opposite the first left turn off the B812.)

Opposite: Westminster Hall, the centre of English government since the time of William Rufus.

However, there's no evidence to back up this tradition. Dumbarton is west and slightly north of Robroyston, whereas the road to Carlisle was south and east. Why make the detour? The rest of Menteith's actions were swift and furtive. Wallace was taken as quickly as possible to the border, travelling only at night. The fear was that if word of his capture got out, there might be a rescue attempt. A stay in Dumbarton would have allowed just enough time for the word to spread.

He was handed over to the Englishman Sir John Segrave at the border, then began the bruising journey south.

LONDON

On 22 August the party arrived in London. It's said that he was brought before Edward himself, but that the King refused to look at him. Edward was stage-managing the event to get maximum PR, especially with those distant audiences in France and Rome, while keeping up the pretence that Wallace was too low to bother about. When he got to London Wallace wasn't even kept in the Tower, the normal prison for political prisoners, but was held overnight in a private house at the end of Fenchurch Street belonging to Alderman William de Leyre, an ex-Sheriff of London. Early next morning Wallace was led on a horse to Westminster to be subjected to the travesty of a show trial.

Westminster then as now was the highest court in the land. You had to have a special reason for going there. You still do. To see where Wallace was tried you need to get a House of Commons pass. You can apply for one by writing to your constituency MP to establish that you're not an international terrorist, and then paying a small sum for a guided tour. It's well worth the time and effort. If there's any place above all the others referred to in this book where you get a sense of living history, it's Westminster Hall.

The Hall is 900 years old. It's the most ancient part of Parliament and nestles in the middle of the later, Pugin-designed buildings. It's impressively daunting. Designed as one big, high rectangle, there are no pillars to block the view and for a time it was the largest freestanding building in Europe. The great wooden hammer-beam roof dates from after Wallace's day, but the building has very much the same intimidating presence it would have had when he was marched in for his official humiliation.

It's still a working building. The hall is now a busy thoroughfare for MPs. They arrive through the double doors at the end and make their way to their offices through doors on either side, or up the imposing staircase underneath a great stained-glass window at the end of the hall. Even the presence of stacked chairs and modern space heaters doesn't detract from the magic of the place. As you walk along the length of the hall, the ancient flagstones are studded with plaques that remind you how much British history these few square yards have seen, most of it bloody and terrible: Thomas More stood here for his

174

trial, Guy Fawkes there, King Charles just a few paces on. And then, as you mount the main staircase, at the top of the second flight of steps, there it is: the little sign that tells you that near this spot Sir William Wallace stood before the King's Bench.

The five judges had been specially selected by Edward. There was John de Segrave, the soldier who had escorted Wallace from Carlisle, Sir Peter Mallory, Sir John le Blunt, Ralph de Sandwich and John de Banquelle. The last day on earth of our shadowy hero has been vividly recorded by eyewitnesses, including the chronicler Matthew of Westminster. The amount of detail we have from those few hours has enabled us to shed light on Wallace's earlier career. Ironically Edward's attempt to rubbish Wallace publicly and ensure that his reputation was nullified has given us an accurate guide to his history and so helped keep his memory alive.

This wasn't a trial as we would understand it. By way of a black joke, Wallace had been given a victor's laurels to wear so, to some, the whole scene had an echo of the trial of Christ. The English didn't see it like that. They had a job to do. There was no examination of evidence, no defence, no opportunity for Wallace to speak. Instead Mallory read out the catalogue of crimes on the indictment and then handed over to John de Segrave to pass sentence. The charges included homicide – the murder of Heselrig – sedition, robbery, arson and treason. Wallace was accused of raising forces against Edward and, even when defeated, refusing to submit and come within the King's Peace.

Wallace stood silent throughout except to interrupt Mallory at one point. He shouted that the other charges may have been true, but he couldn't have committed treason against Edward. Unlike other Scottish nobles he'd never given a feudal oath of allegiance to anyone but King John Balliol. It made no difference. The sentence of treason had been decided before Wallace reached London. For his alleged crimes against person, Church and King, Wallace was condemned to be hanged, drawn and quartered.

SMITHFIELD

Sentence was carried out immediately. First came a humiliating procession to the place of execution. He was stripped and tied to a wooden hurdle. This was then dragged behind two horses. He was face-up, with his feet by the tails of the horses, while his head on the hurdle bumped along the cobbled streets. The crowds were out in force ready to administer their own rough justice to the Scottish bogeyman. He was pelted with filth. Those who could reach would have got in a blow with a stick.

He had to endure this for over an hour. We're used to thinking of Westminster as right in the middle of London, but seven centuries ago it was a separate power centre. Both palace and abbey were some distance from the city. Wallace's lengthy and roundabout route to the place of execution was a deliberate part of his punishment. He was dragged from Westminster to the Tower of London, then to Aldgate and through the middle of the City to The Elms, just

outside the city walls. This was Smoothfield, which we now know as Smithfield, the famous meat market. A stone's throw from here they butchered William Wallace.

The dazed Wallace was brought to the gibbet. He's said to have made his confession and requested that a priest keep a psalter open in front of him while the executioner did his job.

Modern judicial executions are brought to a swift end by breaking the neck with the knot of the noose, but medieval set-piece hangings were about slow strangulation. For less public affairs than this, a prisoner might arrange to have a few friends handy to administer the coup de grâce by pulling on his legs, but Wallace had to suffer the full indignity. Swinging by the neck, his limbs would have been jerking, his eyes starting in their sockets, his tongue bulging. He was naked, so the crowd had the added amusement of seeing the involuntary erection that hanging produces, and the loss of control of bowels and bladder.

Death by hanging could take twenty minutes. But the executioner had to cut the victim down on the point of death and revive him for the next grisly stage, the drawing.

Once Wallace had regained his senses, his genitals were cut off. This was an optional added torment. Then his belly was slit open, and his innards were pulled steaming into the light. A fire was blazing close at hand. Roughly cutting off the intestines within the abdominal cavity, the executioner threw Wallace's intestines into the flames. In all likelihood he would have died from shock by now, but, as his senses misted, he might have smelt the stench of his own burning mortality. Nevertheless the highlight for the crowd was yet to come.

The heart is a muscle. It keeps beating for up to half an hour after brain death, but the medieval crowd didn't know that. All they saw was the amazing spectacle of the executioner, covered in blood from arterial spurting, cutting the still-beating heart from the mutilated corpse and holding it aloft. Only then came the quartering. Wallace's head was cut off and the quartering completed by hacking through pelvis and spine to make four human joints of meat, each with a limb attached.

SCOTLAND

Wallace's head was stuck on a pole and displayed on London Bridge. The four parts of his dismembered body were taken by Sir John de Segrave and publicly displayed until they rotted away in Newcastle, Berwick, Perth and, the scene of his greatest triumph, Stirling.

And that should have been that. The nobody had died a political failure. He had achieved nothing. Edward's grip on Scotland was tighter than ever. But like many autocrats throughout the ages, the King had underestimated the power of a martyr to inspire others.

The relationship between Wallace the idealist and Robert the Bruce the pragmatic politician has always fascinated observers. During his lifetime we've seen the uneasy way that the nobility dealt with Wallace's uncompromising quest for freedom, but it's said that his death inspired Bruce to go for broke. Seven months after the execution he was crowned king.

The spot where the gibbet was set up and the crowd waited to watch Wallace die, is marked by a touching plaque on the north wall of St Bart's Hospital. It's to the south of Smithfield Market where the square of West Smithfield with its trees and circular car park meets Little Britain. If you stand with your back to the plaque facing towards Smithfield Market and turn to your right, you'll see the only building that would have been around at the time of Wallace's execution, the church of St Bartholomew the Great. It's a beautiful building that was used as a picturesque set for Four Weddings and a Funeral and Shakespeare in Love. The show on 23 August 1305 was another crowd-pleaser.

Edward I, the 'Hammer of Scots', survived Wallace by two years. He died in 1307 with his work uncompleted, on his way to yet another campaign against the Scots. His last six months were spent in the guest house at Lanercost Abbey. It's said that he requested that his bones be boiled away from his flesh and carried into battle until the Scots were defeated. In reality he was buried in that tomb in Westminster Abbey, and the fight was carried on by his less accomplished son, Edward II.

On 23 June 1314 Edward II was defeated by Robert the Bruce at the Battle of Bannockburn. Using the schiltrom formation invented by Wallace, Bruce mimicked his success by trapping the English professionals in boggy ground near Stirling. And, according to tradition, his victory owed more to Wallace than that. Before the battle, Bruce made a passionate plea invoking the spirit of Wallace to inspire his men to fight for the freedom of Scotland. It was this speech that Burns immortalized in verse.

> Scots, wha hae wi' Wallace bled,
> Scots, wham Bruce has aften led
> Welcome to your gory bed,
> Or to victory.
>
> Now's the day, and now's the hour;
> See the front o' battle lour;
> See approach proud Edward's power,
> Chains and slavery…
> Lay the proud usurpers low!
> Tyrants fall in every foe!
> Liberty's in every blow!
> Let us do, or die!

But Wallace has also been immortalized in the land of Scotland itself. If Bruce is the official Scottish liberator, Wallace has been the people's hero. As his legend grew, people started to associate him with places close to them. In the latest edition of Blind Harry, there are eighty-three Wallace place names listed. Sites like the Wallace Stone in Falkirk became shrines to freedom. Local miners still march there each year to celebrate their freedom from virtual slavery at the end of the eighteenth century. Physical links to Wallace such as the Lubeck letter may be scarce, but it's fitting that he is remembered most in the very land that he fought to liberate.

FURTHER INFORMATION

This chapter only touches on the surface of the sites associated with Wallace. For a complete guide try David R. Ross, *On the Trail of William Wallace* (Luath Press, 2000).

For the history there are two good biographies fairly readily available:
James McKay, *Braveheart: William Wallace* (Mainstream Publishing, 1995)
Andrew Fisher, *William Wallace* (Edinburgh, 1986)

In the interests of fairness I should point out Anthony and Paul Cooper's book *William Wallace: Robin Hood revealed* (BVM Publishing, 2000) – but I still don't agree with it!

Blind Harry has been re-translated with a new introduction by Elspeth King. The original was called *The Actes and Deidis of the Illustre and Vallyeant Campioun Schir William Wallace c1508*, but this is the version which first appeared in 1722 by William Hamilton of Gilbertfield and is called *Blind Harry's Wallace* (Luath Press, 1998).

Ordnance Survey maps 64 for his birth at Elderslie and betrayal at Robroyston, 57 for Stirling, 65 for Falkirk and 70 for Leglen Woods where Rabbie Burns used to walk.

If you go to no other site, do visit the National Wallace Memorial, Abbey Craig, Stirling. Telelphone: 01786 472140.

CHAPTER 5
ROBIN HOOD

Where should we begin a quest for the real Robin Hood? In Sherwood Forest, of course. But we'll travel much further afield, through the hidden treasures of Britain's industrial heartland, from the Trough of Bowland in Lancashire, past unexpected sites in West and South Yorkshire down to Stratford-upon-Avon. First of all, though, let's look at a tree.

The Major Oak is the most venerable of the trees in Sherwood Forest. If you're anywhere near Mansfield, go and see it. At one time this mighty forest covered over 100,000 acres spreading north in an expanding triangle from Nottingham's city walls. Now just one pocket of trees, a site of scientific interest, remains on the west side of the B6034 just outside Edwinstowe.

The six hundred-year-old Major Oak stands in its own clearing, its vast branches propped up by great metal crutches and braces. In days gone by, pleasure parties used to throng round its massive trunk. Today the tree is railed off in order to ensure that the assaults of modern life are kept to a minimum. But gazing through its branches, the imagination of even the most casual sightseer will be drawn into the past.

Because this, as all the tourist guides tell you, is Robin Hood Country. Legend tells us that the great outlaw used the Major Oak as a meeting place and, although logic says that it would have been no more than a gleam in an acorn's eye in the days of the Merry Men, romance is the stuff of the Robin legends.

Robin is the greatest hero in this book and also the most shadowy. For half a millennium children and adults alike have been brought up on tales of his courage and audacity. The story has mutated through umpteen versions told in stories, ballads, novels, radio, film and television. We've all grown up with our own Robin. For my generation it was Richard Greene, playing out his adventures on a Sunday afternoon on the newly launched ITV; for my parents it was Errol Flynn, for my children, Kevin Costner.

This chapter, more than any other, presented me with a personal mission. Whereas many people leave Robin behind with childhood, the potency of the myth continued to fascinate me. I even made my own contribution to the evolution of the legend. In the 1990s I wrote a children's television series called *Maid Marian and Her Merry Men*. Robin didn't come out of it too well. He was a wimpy underling. Marian was the brains and driving force of the operation, Little John transmuted into a midget called Little Ron, and Will Scarlet became a Rasta called Barrington. While researching the show, I realized for the first time the sheer weight of academic analysis that has been applied to the subject.

So when I began writing this book and was faced with a quest for the facts behind Robin Hood, I already had an idea of the daunting complexity of the task.

The other characters in this book are solid flesh-and-blood people. However distorted, lost, or besmirched by history, we can be confident that they have a tangible history somewhere just beyond our grasp. But Robin is an enigma. Who was the real Robin Hood? Did he ever really exist? I knew that to answer these questions I had to deal not only with the challenge of getting accurate information from history, but also with the knotty problems of textual analysis. Finding a real Robin Hood would be a detective story, fitting tiny pieces of evidence together to try and come up with an image.

I also knew that I was merely the latest in a long line of literary Miss Marples looking for the man dressed in Lincoln green. People have been trying to track him down for at least three centuries. There were going to be no easy answers.

Historians have split into two camps: those who believe there was a real Robin but argue over who he actually was, and those who think that the lack of certainty is merely a sign that Robin is a nothing more than a storybook character. If you look him up in the original edition of Chambers' *Biographical Dictionary*, Robin has the distinction of being the only entry defined as a fictitious person. Would trying to find the real Robin Hood be as fruitless a task as attempting to track down the real Cinderella or the historical Superman?

I didn't think so. True, Robin exists in stories, and these stories have evolved and transmogrified over the centuries according to the audience. But the Robin legends are so earthy and so grounded in historical context that I sensed there must be a historical figure behind them.

ROBIN HOOD, PRINCE OF THIEVES

In the story as it's generally known, Robin of Loxley is a dispossessed nobleman. Previously, as the Earl of Huntingdon, he is a loyal servant of King Richard the Lionheart, but when Richard goes off to fight in the Crusades he leaves his brother John in charge. Big mistake. John is a swine of the first water, a latter-day Caligula. He confiscates land to give to his cronies, he fleeces the ordinary folk with swingeing taxes and lines his own pockets.

Robin of Loxley falls victim to the new regime and is deprived of his estates. He seeks sanctuary in Sherwood Forest. There he gathers about him a band of like-minded outlaws, who are happy to participate in a campaign of targeted thievery. Together they rob the rich representatives of the unjust regime and, rather than profiting themselves, spread the proceeds round to the poor of the area.

There are certain key members of his Merry Men who are almost as legendary as he is. His right-hand man is a human giant, ironically named Little John. He joins the band after Robin unwisely challenges him to a stave fight on a narrow bridge and loses. Other members include Will Scarlet, Much the Miller's son, Alan a' Dale and a renegade monk, Friar Tuck. Looking for the real Robin will involve trying to find real versions of these vivid characters too.

It will also bring us face to face with his enemies, in particular the Sheriff of Nottingham, King John's henchman in the area. The Sheriff is never dignified with a name – his title says it all. He's the one who runs the unjust system. He has evil intentions towards Robin's girl Maid Marian, and the tension between these two men is the driving force behind the many tales of capture and rescue, and deeds of derring-do.

The other main feature of the story is, of course, the absolute mastery of the longbow demonstrated by Robin and his chums. Even though they're wanted by the law, they show up at archery competitions in disguise and amaze everyone with their skill, before narrowly escaping at the crucial moment.

When Richard Coeur de Lion eventually returns from the Holy Land, he visits Sherwood Forest. Recognizing Robin and his outlaw band as true and loyal servants, he forgives them their supposed crimes and restores Robin to his rightful position.

But Robin still has a problem. In addition to the Sheriff, he has a host of other enemies including Roger of Doncaster. This villain has an affair with the prioress at Kirklees Priory, who is Robin's cousin, and they plot to kill our hero. He becomes sick, goes to Kirklees for medicinal bleeding and they murder him there.

And that's where the story ends. Robin is left in his remote grave. The man who no political power could vanquish is brought low by a conniving relative.

Even writing down the story in this truncated form, it's clear that there isn't a single coherent narrative. The Robin Hood tales are like the edited highlights of the weekend's

football watched late at night. They stand out as a series of unforgettable, almost dream-like episodes, but whether they're all from the same match, it's hard to tell.

Before we start to look for clues to Robin's identity, we need to sort some of the wheat from the chaff. The version of the story we have today is a composite with more embell-ishments than Elton John's living room. Our first job is to try and work out which story is likely to lead us to the real Robin. And as with the other historical figures in this book, one rule holds true: the best source is the earliest. Only if we can track down the original ver-sion of the story can we hope to get an accurate picture of the man on whom the story is based. In other words, before we look for the facts, we must get to the original fiction.

A LOAD OF OLD BALLADS

To demonstrate how far the modern version of the story has changed from the original, we'll start at the end of the sixteenth century. This was the age of Shakespeare, although at the time our foremost playwright wasn't treated as the demi-god he is today. He was just

Opposite: Catch it while you can. Sherwood Forest always comprised heathland, meadows and other terrain besides woodland, but the forest as we imagine it from the Robin stories is now restricted to small areas. When they came to make Robin Hood Price of Thieves with Kevin Costner, Sherwood Forest was rejected as a location because it didn't look enough like an American producer's vision of Sherwood Forest.

another writer/producer trying to get more bums on seats than his rivals. And one of his principal competitors was a writer called Anthony Munday. In 1598 Munday stole a march on his rivals by producing a play based on the already popular Robin Hood stories.

Why bother sitting through four hours about a Danish prince who can't decide whether or not to kill himself, when you could be watching all the thrills and spills of a real British hero? *The Downfall of Robert, Earl of Huntington* was a smash hit. Then, like all enterprising theatrical producers throughout history, Munday followed up his masterpiece with more of the same, the equally popular *The Death of Robert, Earl of Huntington*. Even if his titles weren't the catchiest, Munday knew his audience, and they loved Robert and his Merry Men. (No, that isn't a misprint – Robin and Robert were interchangeable names at that time. But more of that later.)

The hero Anthony Munday gave his audience was markedly different from the traditional Robin. This was the first time that Robin Hood had been given the title Earl of Huntingdon. Munday was writing during the English Renaissance, an era of great national pride. The noble classes were becoming interested in their English heritage, and playwrights were exploiting this newfound fascination to the full. (None more so than Shakespeare with his canon of plays about the Kings of England.) Munday had skilfully taken an existing folk hero and given him an aristocratic background in order to make him appeal not just to the groundlings, but to the folk in the posh seats too.

Before Munday, our hero was just plain Robin Hood. His story was passed down from generation to generation of lowborn freemen in traditional rhymes and ballads. The earliest reference we have to these tales is from 1377 in the poem *Piers Plowman* by William Langland. In it one of the characters, Sloth, says:

I kan noght parfitly my Paternoster	I don't know the Lord's Prayer very
as the preest it syngeth	well like the priest sings it.
But I kan the rymes of Robyn Hood	But I do know the rhymes of Robin Hood
and Randolph Erl of Chestre.	and Randolph Earl of Chester
	[another popular figure].

So, if there was a historical Robin, he must have been around some time before *Piers Plowman* was written. Ideally, then, we're looking for stories, written in ballad or rhyming form, which are earlier than 1377.

There are many such ballads about Robin. 'Robin Hood and the Curtal Friar' tells of a fight between Robin and a travelling friar who beats him in a wrestling match; 'Robin Hood and Guy of Gisbourne' recounts the tale of a knight coming to hunt Robin down and meeting a grisly end; 'Robin Hoode, His Death' relates the story of our hero's betrayal by the prioress at Kirklees.

The only written versions we have, though, come from over a century later – 1475 onwards. But from the Chaucerian English used, it's pretty clear that these ballads originate from at least a hundred years earlier. The oldest is called *A Gest of Robin Hood* ('gest', pronounced 'jest', is an old word for a story). It's a long poem of 456 four-line verses divided into eight parts, and it clearly combines lots of different tales into one coherent work.

The *Gest* takes us as close as we can get to the original version of the story. But what does it tell us about the real Robin Hood?

THE ORIGINAL STORY

Lythe and listin, gentilmen,	Attend and listen, gentlemen.
That be of frebore blode;	That are of free-born blood,
I shall you tel of a gode yeman,	I'll tell you about a good yeoman,
His name was Robyn Hode.	His name was Robin Hood.
Robyn was a prude outlaw,	Robin was a proud outlaw,
Whyles he walked on grounde:	While he walked around:
So curteyse an outlawe as he was one	As courteous an outlaw as him
Was nevere non founde.	Was never to be found.
Robyn stode in Bernesdale,	Robin stood in Barnsdale,
And lenyd hym to a tre,	And leant against a tree,
And bi hym stode Litell Johnn,	And by him stood Little John,
A gode yeman was he.	A good yeoman was he.
And alsoo dyd gode Scarlok,	There was also good Scarlet,
And Much, the millers son:	And Much the Miller's son:
There was none ynch of his bodi	Every inch of him
But it was worth a grome.	Was worth another man.

The story opens in the greenwood, the outlaws' hideout in Barnsdale. Robin tells Little John, Will Scarlet and Much the Miller's son that he can't sit down to eat without company, and sends them out to bring him a 'dinner guest'.

'Take thy gode bowe in thy honde,'	'Take your good bow in your hand,'
sayde Robyn;	said Robin;
'Late Much wende with the:	'Let Much go with thee,
And so shal Willyam Scarlok,	And also William Scarlet
And no man abyde with me.	And no man stay with me.

'And walke up to the Saylis,	'And walk up to Sayles,
And so to Watlinge Strete,	And so to Watling Street,
And wayte after some unkuth gest,	And wait for some unknown guest,
Up chaunce ye may them mete.	That you may chance to meet.
'Be he erle, or ani baron,	'If he's an earl or baron,
Abbot, or ani knyght,	An abbot or a knight,
Bringhe hym to lodge to me;	Bring him to lodge with me
His dyner shall be dight.'	His dinner will be cooked all right.'
They wente up to the Saylis,	They went up to Sayles,
These yeman all thre;	These yeomen all three;
They loked est, they loke weest;	They looked east, and they looked west;
They myght no man see.	And no one could they see.
But as they loked in to Bernysdale,	But as they spied on Barnsdale,
Bi a derne strete,	By a secret way,
Than came a knyght ridinghe,	They saw a knight come riding,
Full sone they gan hym mete.	And him they did waylay.

The three henchmen apprehend a knight dressed in tatty clothes. Robin's reputation has already reached him.

'Who is thy maister?' sayde the knyght.	'Who is your master?' said the knight.
Johnn sayde, 'Robyn Hode.'	John said, 'Robin Hood.'
'He is gode yoman,' sayde the knyght,	'He is a good yeoman,' said the knight,
'Of hym I have herde moche gode.'	'Of him I've heard much good.'

They bring him back to camp where he's given a slap-up meal. But of course, there's no such thing as a free lunch and, after eating, Robin tells the knight that he's got to pay the bill.

The knight apologizes. His son has killed a man and in order to pay the hefty fine, the knight's been forced to sell all his goods. Now he's only got ten shillings in the world, and unless he pays £400 to the monks of St Mary's Abbey in York, he will lose all his lands.

Robin instructs Little John to empty the knight's saddlebags to check if he's lying. When it appears he isn't, Robin lends him the money to pay the monks back. This loan is pledged against the Virgin Mary, to whom Robin is devoted. He sends the knight off with a new horse, a new set of clothes and Little John as his servant.

Back in York, the monks at the Abbey of St Mary's are rubbing their hands with glee at the prospect of claiming the knight's property. The due date of the loan has almost come and gone. The knight arrives just in the nick of time and astonishes them by emptying out £400 on to the table. But how can he pay Robin back?

The answer is that he doesn't have to.

In a reprise of the first part of the story, Robin sends his men to bring another guest to dine. This time they reel in a monk from – yes, you've guessed it – St Mary's. This guest pleads poverty too, but, unlike the truthful knight, he's lying. He's carrying £800.

Robin takes the cash. The outlaws justify this theft by saying it's the work of the Virgin Mary who's paying back the loan pledged in her name. To reward Robin's generosity, she's obviously sent one of her men from her abbey of St Mary's with the original sum plus another £400.

In a lesser-known Robin story, the outlaw sends a piece of toast to a starving Maid Marian in Nottingham Castle.

ROBIN HOOD OF THE *GEST*

So what does this part of the poem tell us about Robin and his world? First, that he's no dispossessed nobleman. Robin is a 'good yeoman'. This doesn't mean he was a peasant. He belonged to one of the lower orders of freemen in the medieval system. Yeomen were still expected to uphold certain standards of honour. Several times in the ballads Robin's 'worthy' behaviour is contrasted with the rudeness of people who should know better. Even though the knight is his victim, Robin is courteous to him. In contrast to the monks of St Mary's who aren't living up to their ideals, Robin is portrayed as a devout Christian, trusting to the Virgin to pay back his act of charity.

Nevertheless, first and foremost he's a crook, an outlaw pure and simple. The device of forcing people to dine, and then presenting them with a bill for however much they've got on them, is merely a colourful form of highway robbery. It may be based on his victims' ability to pay and on their truthfulness, but it's still a long way from robbing from the rich to give to the poor. The only people making money out of this scam are Robin and his men.

The true villains and victims of the piece are the monks of St Mary's. In today's popular culture, *Father Ted* and *The Vicar of Dibley* are a source of gentle comedy, and there's a sense of affection in the lampooning. Not so at the time the ballads were popular. Clergy like our monks were pilloried as hate figures. The writer of the *Gest* wasn't alone in his savage attack. At almost exactly the same time, Chaucer was reserving his choicest barbs for the clerics in *The Canterbury Tales*.

If you visit St Mary's Monastery today, don't be fooled by the tranquil mood of the park, or lulled by the romantic shapes of the ruined arches and decayed stone. Think like a medieval peasant, struggling for a living in a hovel. As you enter York's city walls, you are entering one of the greatest political centres of the medieval world. And the power in this realm, both political and economic, is in the hands of the Church.

Go first to the world-renowned York minster to get a taste of the splendour of intact medieval church architecture. Now return a couple of hundred metres to the gardens. Walk the course of the ruins of St Mary's and try to imagine a stone structure of similar scale to the minster just down the road. Stone was as valuable then as it is now. The only other stone buildings in the area would have been the parish churches in between. Otherwise housing was poor, squat and ramshackle.

The monks who lived in St Mary's belonged to the Benedictine order. They'd taken a vow of poverty, which meant that none of them had any personal possessions. Nevertheless, their community was immensely rich. The abbey had been endowed over the years with lands to support the monks' work. Noblemen had donated money in exchange for prayers for their immortal souls. But acreage that had been intended to relieve the monks from the worry of keeping body and soul together had mounted up and was now

You can still visit the remains of St Mary's Monastery in York. Head for York city centre and follow the local signs for the minster. St Mary's is located in Museum Gardens on the north-west side of the city. There's parking just the other side of the gardens.

190

an end in itself. The revenues from the wool produced by the vast herds of sheep on the abbey estates were massive. Monks were sectioned off to outlying houses in order to control the estates that were being farmed. Such small offshoots were attractive to lax brothers who wanted a break from the strictures of the cloister. These daughter or satellite houses soon became notorious for their immorality.

The abbot and prior of St Mary's weren't only captains of rural industry, they were also hugely powerful political figures. As the most literate people in society, clerics held key financial and political positions within the administration of medieval England. In fact the only thing they seemed unable to do was follow the godly life which they exhorted others to pursue.

No wonder they became the butt of popular culture. The Robin Hood ballads were cowboy stories and *Spitting Image* rolled into one. When the monk from St Mary's falls into Robin's clutches and is conned of every last penny, the audience would have cheered. The

The Major Oak – propped up but still going strong.

victim was only being reduced to the poverty he was supposed to profess. In the ballads it's Robin who seems truly devout, not the Church officials.

A lot of recent portrayals have turned Robin into a sort of medieval revolutionary. But in the *Gest* he's nothing of the sort. Although he strikes out at figures of economic power, he's got no desire to upset the status quo. He wants to help the knight to re-establish the system of justice which has been corrupted by the politicos of the day, not to bring in a new order. This Robin is essentially conservative.

But the single most important fact that the *Gest* tells us about him is this. He's not from Sherwood Forest at all. Robin is a Yorkshireman! Suddenly the ancient Major Oak deep in the heart of Sherwood has become nothing more than an old tree devoid of any real meaning.

ROBIN OF YORKSHIRE

In the first stanzas of the poem Robin sends Little John, Will Scarlet and Much the Miller's son up to Sayles to see if they can spot any travellers coming down Watling Street towards Barnsdale. This is a very specific geographical instruction. Our Robin was working in the area of South Yorkshire between Pontefract and Doncaster. Don't be confused by the words 'Watling Street'. It's got nothing to do with Boudica's route up the A5. In the Middle Ages Watling Street was a generic term for all old Roman highways, in this case the Great North Road.

This area was notorious for highwaymen. In 1306 a number of Scottish clerics who had supported William Wallace's rebellion were brought south to London. When their party reached Pontefract, we have records of their guard being doubled in order to make it safely across the forested bandit country between Pontefract and Nottingham.

It may come as a surprise that Robin spoke more like Geoffrey Boycott than Errol Flynn, but 600 years ago everyone knew Robin was a Yorkshireman. In fact by 1429, 'Robin Hood in Barnsdale stood' was a legal formula used to denote a self-evident fact.

At the time of the ballad, Barnsdale covered a large area of forest which stretched more or less continuously down to Sherwood. But Barnsdale Bar was a specific ridge north of the Went Valley, and it still exists. So we can locate the exact position of that first fictional hijack.

In Robin's day the Great North Road wound down the steep hill of Barnsdale Bar and crossed the River Went at Wentbridge. Today the A1 parallels this old route but skips over the valley on an enormous concrete viaduct that dwarfs the village.

In the later Middle Ages Wentbridge became a favoured place to break a journey. (The village still boasts the oldest remaining pub on the old A1, The Blue Bell.) But in the time of the ballads it was simply a crossing place, so the knight was probably pushing on to stay in Doncaster.

To get the outlaws'-eye-view of Wentbridge, come down the A1 after visiting St Mary's, leave the road just after the viaduct (directions for Wentbridge and Kirk Smeaton) and turn back on yourself to come down into Wentbridge. To get into the village you have to turn right at the T-junction with the old A1. But just before you get there, stop at the field gate on your right about 30 metres before the junction.

Above Wentbridge you can recreate the view that the three outlaws would have had of the poor knight. Sayles is a plantation of trees on your right in the shadow of the A1 viaduct. If you look down into the valley at Wentbridge you can make out the tarmac of the old road climbing up the hill to the north beyond some white buildings. You'll see at once what a good vantage point it is and how intimately the people who composed the ballads must have known the area and the tradition about Robin.

Now drop down into the village to get an idea of how threatening the route must have been for a medieval traveller. Bear in mind that there would have been significantly fewer buildings here in those days. The shallow River Went doesn't take much crossing, but the steep valley would have been heavily wooded, claustrophobic and dangerous.

Follow the directions opposite, and beneath your feet you can still see signs of the stones of the old road. This part of it was bypassed in the eighteenth century after several coaches, galloping down the hill to create sufficient momentum for the climb up the opposite side, crashed down the bank to the left. In Robin's day the road would have been a little wider, and without quite as much undergrowth on either side, and the unwary traveller would have been clearly visible from the other side of the valley!

If you look in the index of a road atlas you'll find a host of Robin Hood place names. As the fame of the outlaw spread, people liked to associate places with his legend. But Skelbrooke boasts the first records of a place associated with the outlaw. There's a mention in a document of 1422 of a Robin Hood's Stone. This was then equated by historians with the Skelbrooke site on the Great North Road known as Robin Hood's Well.

For at least four centuries, Robin Hood's Well has been a tourist attraction. Travellers used to stop here and, at a cost of one penny, were sat on a chair and admitted to the symbolic brotherhood of his band. In the eighteenth century the site was so well known that the architect Vanbrugh designed a cover for the well, an arched stone shelter about 3 metres high. Throughout the rest of Georgian Britain, savage punishments were being administered for highway robbery, but here one of the top architects of the day was being commissioned to celebrate the most famous robber of all. Although of course by then, Robin had become a member of the gentry and so was forgiven for his misdemeanours.

This once celebrated neo-classical relic looks a bit sad today. It's been moved from its original site to accommodate the building of a dual carriageway. It now sits at the southern end of a lay-by and weigh-station, dwarfed by HGVs and bypassed literally and metaphorically by modern progress. If you do miss the bypass you'll catch a glimpse of the cover on your left as you whiz by. You can get back to it by detouring round the villages at your next turn left. There's no well-shaft, of course, because Robin Hood's Well is no longer in its original position, and the eighteenth-century craftsmanship has been reinforced by modern concrete and steel. But Vanbrugh's work, as distinctive as his magnificent renovation of Castle Howard fifty miles to the north, is well worth a visit.

If you head north over the Went, past the Wentbridge Hotel on your right, then continue for a couple of hundred metres, you'll round a gentle bend. On your right is a bus stop and, just beyond it, is a track on the right heading uphill parallel with the road. Follow it and park as the track peters out at the last house. There's a footpath straight ahead of you. You are now on a tiny section of the old Great North Road, the Watling Street of the *Gest*.

If you want further proof that the original Robin patrolled the forests of South Yorkshire, rejoin the A1 after Wentbridge and head south for 2 and a bit miles. Near Skelbrooke you'll come to a lay-by, and by the side of the road you'll find Robin Hood's Well.

The fact that the well is such an early Robin place name doesn't necessarily mean that the historical Robin used it, but it does seem to show that early stories about him were current in this area around Wentbridge. A likely scenario is that the tales were entertainments for the valets and court workers in nearby Pontefract Castle, appealing to their sense of local pride. If there was a real Robin it means we should be looking for him somewhere round this locality of Pontefract, Wakefield and Doncaster.

TURNING OUR BACKS ON SHERWOOD FOREST

So what of Sherwood? Are we about to abandon it? In truth, Robin's connection with Nottinghamshire is tenuous to say the least. Almost every other part of England seems to have a better claim to him. In Cumberland there's a Robin Hood's Buttes (an archery practice area) recorded some 200 years later than the *Gest*; there's a Robin Hood's Hill in Gloucestershire in the seventeenth century, and even a Robin Hood's Walk in Richmond Park in Surrey personally named by King Henry VIII. But there's no record of place names associated with him near Sherwood Forest until 1700.

In the Middle Ages, the Royal Forest of Sherwood stretched from Nottingham's city walls almost to Mansfield. Nowadays there seem to be echoes of the Robin Hood stories all over the old forest. We're told that Will Scarlet is buried in Blidworth, the village where Maid Marian also came from. Marian and Robin got married in Edwinstowe Church, Papplewick was home to Alan a' Dale and so on.

Unfortunately most of this mythology, like the Macbeth or Wallace industry in Scotland, is simply an extremely successful marketing exercise. Without wanting to impoverish the tourist honey pots of Nottinghamshire, it does seem the county's done pretty well over the years at Yorkshire's expense.

But it's not just the lack of historical references that makes Sherwood a doubtful location for our hero. It wouldn't have made any practical sense for Robin to have been based there.

Sherwood Forest wasn't just a lot of trees. It was a vast area of mixed terrain: woodland, heath and scrubland interspersed with hamlets, used exclusively for hunting and hawking by the royal family of the day. It had its own separate force of specialist foresters who were employed to look after the game and protect the land against poachers.

The foresters had at their disposal a range of draconian laws with fierce punishments of death and mutilation for anyone unlucky enough to be caught breaking the forest law. Malefactors were hanged and left to rot in the forest to act as a deterrent. There was a prohibition on even entering the forest with a bow and sharpened arrows. Robin could have made the occasional foray there, but it would have been far too risky for him to have used it as a permanent base.

Opposite: Robin Hood's Well (minus well).

One of the less touristy things to do in Sherwood is to go to Papplewick and visit the medieval church. The village was once the headquarters for the foresters in the southern half of Sherwood. The first thing you notice as you enter is the eccentric eighteenth-century gallery that fills half the church, but turn to your left and look on the floor beyond the font where there's an ancient forester's grave. The occupant is anonymous. The grave is marked simply by an engraving of a bow and arrow, and a hunting horn suspended on a medieval shoulder strap which has a name close to my heart, the baldrick.

But if the Sherwood connection is false and Robin was really a Yorkshireman, what of his arch-enemy? Why was he confronted by the Sheriff of Nottingham and not the Sheriff of Leeds or Pontefract? Finding the answer to this will help us to identify a historical Robin, but first, let's see what the original Robin ballads tell us about one of the great villains of history.

THE SHERIFF OF NOTTINGHAM

In the *Gest*, Robin and his men get involved in a feud with the evil Sheriff of Nottingham. It starts when Little John, who gets a job working for the Sheriff as a steward, ends up having a fight with the cook and leaves in a huff when his dinner isn't served on time. By way of revenge he leads his former boss into the clutches of Robin and the outlaws. Robin keeps the Sheriff captive overnight and threatens to conscript him into their ranks. The Sheriff is appalled at the idea. He tells Robin he'd rather be executed than live such a life.

'This is harder order,' sayde the sherief,	'This is a tougher regime,' said the sheriff,
'Than any ankir or frere;	'Than any anchorite or friar;
For all the golde in mery Englonde	For all the gold in merry England
I wolde nat longe dwell her.'	I couldn't live long here.'
'All this twelve monthes,' sayde Robyn,	'All this twelve months,' said Robin,
'Thou shalt dwell with me;	'You shall live with me:
I shall the teche, proude sherif,	I shall teach you, proud sheriff,
An outlawe for to be.'	An outlaw for to be.'
'Or I be here another nyght,'	'Before I'd stay here another night,'
sayde the sherif,	said the sheriff,
'Robyn, nowe pray I the,	'Robin, I beg you,
Smythe of mijn hede rather to-morowe,	I'd rather you strike off my head tomorrow,
And I forgyve it the.'	And I'll forgive you.'

They set the Sheriff free. In return he promises not to bother them, but immediately goes back on his word. He tries to trap the gang by setting up an archery competition with a prize of a silver arrow for the winner. The band are such renowned archers that the Sheriff knows one of them is bound to win it. They go in disguise and of course the winner is Robin.

Oaths were a serious business in the Middle Ages. You'll remember how distressed William of Normandy was when Harold breached his solemn undertaking. The Sheriff gave his word not to attack Robin but broke it, so a major feud was born. Any medieval audience would immediately have understood how shameful the Sheriff's actions were.

What follows is the perfect narrative for a Hollywood screenplay. The outlaws are ambushed before they can leave the contest. Despite Little John being wounded in the leg, they escape in the nick of time and seek sanctuary with Sir Richard by the Lee, the poor knight they originally hijacked and helped.

In he toke good Robyn,	In he took good Robin.
And all his company:	And all his company;
'Welcome be thou, Robyn Hode,	'Welcome are you, Robin Hood,
Welcome arte thou to me,	Welcome you are to me,
'And moche I thanke the of thy confort,	'And much I thank you for your comfort,
And of thy curteysye,	And for your courtesy,
And of thy grete kyndenesse,	And for your great kindness,
Under the grene wode tre.	Under the greenwood tree.
'I love no man in all this worlde	'I love no man in this world
So much as I do the;	As much as I do thee.
For all the proud sheryf of Notyngham,	Despite the proud Sheriff of Nottingham
Ryght here shalt thou be.	Right here you shall stay.
'Shyt the gates, and drawe the brydge,	'Shut the gates, and draw the bridge
And let no man come in,	And let no man come in,
And arme you well, and make you redy,	And arm yourselves, and prepare
And to the walles ye wynne.'	And make your way to the walls.'

Later the Sheriff gets his revenge by capturing the knight and keeping him prisoner. And who comes to the rescue? Of course! Our plucky hero snatches the knight from the dungeons of Nottingham. (Underneath the castle in Nottingham there are caves where Robin himself is said to have been held. The knight's imprisonment is the earliest version of this tradition.) When the Sheriff comes in pursuit of his prey, there is a final showdown.

Robyn bent a full goode bowe,	Robin bent his bow full stretch.
An arrowe he drowe at wyll;	And let fly an arrow;
He hit so the proude sherife	He hit the proud sheriff
Upon the grounde he lay full still.	Who lay motionless on the ground.
And or he myght up aryse,	And before he could get up again,
On his fete to stonde,	And stand on his feet,
He smote of the sherifs hede	Robin struck off the sheriff's head
With his bright bronde.	With his shining blade.

This last section proves a general point about the whole tone of the early ballads. They're a lot more violent than modern versions of the story. In another poem, when his enemy Guy of Gisborne comes to the forest to try to trap Robin, the outlaw not only beheads him but also impales Guy's head on his bowstaff and mutilates his face with an 'Irish knife'.

With the Sheriff gone, the King arrives to try to deal with the lawlessness in the northern counties. When he's informed that the outlaw Robin Hood is to blame, he goes to the forest at Barnsdale dressed as an abbot with a retinue of monks. He is duly captured by the band.

Robyn behelde our comly kynge	Robin looked our comely king
Wystly in the face,	Intently in the face,
So dyde Syr Rycharde at the Le,	So did Richard of the Lee,
And kneled downe in that place.	And they knelt down in that place.
And so dyde all the wylde outlawes,	And so did all the wild outlaws,
Whan they see them knele:	When they saw them kneel:
'My lorde the kynge of Englonde,	'My Lord, the King of England
Now I knowe you well.'	Now I recognize you.'

The outlaws immediately submit to their King. But there's another surprise here. The King isn't Richard the Lionheart.

THE COMELY KING

The monarch in the *Gest* is described as 'Edward our comely king'. This may come as a surprise to those who are used to the story being set in the reign of King Richard the Lionheart, but the ballad's quite specific. Robin Hood lived in the reign of a King Edward.

There have been eight King Edwards since the Norman Conquest. Of these, only the first three are contenders because the ballads in which 'Edward the comely king' are mentioned were in circulation in 1377, and Edward IV didn't come to the throne till 1461. So we're left with our old friend Edward I, his son Edward II, or his grandson Edward III. Edward I was crowned in 1274, Edward III died in 1350. Some time between those two dates we should find the real Robin.

And there's other evidence to support this dating. The early fourteenth century was one of the few times when the Sheriff of Nottingham was powerful enough to be responsible for affairs in Yorkshire. Henry de Faucembourg was the King's representative for both Nottingham and South Yorkshire. But the most glaringly obvious exhibit to back up this historical context is the thing Robin's most famous for: his longbow.

Everyone knows Robin was a brilliant archer. But, realistically, this would only have been of symbolic importance in the early fourteenth century and after. During the reign of Edward I, the longbow rose to become the fearsome weapon for which the English were hated and feared throughout Europe. We've already seen how it was used to such deadly effect on the unsuspecting Scots at Falkirk. Because of the devastating part it played there, as well as at Crécy and Agincourt, some historians assume that it was a new weapon. They speak of the longbow as a recently developed version of something called the shortbow.

This is nonsense. The longbow goes back to prehistory. Similar bows have been found in third- or fourth-century archaeological digs at Nydam in Denmark, and we know they were around throughout the Anglo-Saxon period. In addition. longbowmen are clearly visible in the Bayeux Tapestry.

Obviously, the longbow wasn't a new piece of technology that superseded the mythical shortbow. The longbow got its name to distinguish it from the newly invented crossbow. Why then should its use in the ballads back up the assertion that the 'comely king' was one of the first three Edwards?

The answer is that Edward I discovered how awesomely effective the deployment of the longbow could be when he ran up against the Welsh archers on his campaign to bring Wales into his British empire. Within a decade, he was incorporating Welsh archers into his own forces. Soon counties like Lancashire and Warwickshire were building up a reputation for producing crack bowmen. The longbow was by now an old weapon used in a new and devastating way. The massed ranks of English archers created a devastating hail like machine-gun fire.

One theory is that firing the longbow at targets became a competitive craze, like skateboarding or hula-hoops, and spread like wildfire through England. This would account for the massive rise in its popularity and the consequent number of skilled bowmen available for military service.

This craze was then solidified into a national institution by success on the field of battle and royal decree. It was made a legal requirement for every able-bodied English male up to the age of sixty-five to practise archery every Sunday at the buttes (these were soft banks that prevented arrows overshooting). Here sticks were set up as targets called wands. The best archers, like Robin and Little John, could split one of these stakes in two at thirty or forty metres.

The centralized nature of English politics and the country's relative social stability enabled the English to develop this most democratic of weapons in a way that was impossible on the Continent. In comparison with France, where the aristocratic cavalry were still the main strike force, England's crack troops came from the yeomanry and working classes. Villages vied with each other to produce the best longbowmen of the county. Before the fourteenth century a great archer would have been little more than a yokel, but by the time of the first three King Edwards he was the David Beckham of his day: the perfect cultural atmosphere to create a hero like Robin.

An understanding of how this technology was used, plus research on the skeletons of British longbowmen, gives us a clearer idea of what Robin and the Merry Men might have looked like. The longbow needed to be long in order to make use of the tensile strength of the wood. The six-foot bow was carefully made so that the springy sapwood of yew was on the outside, offering flexibility as the bow was bent, while the more solid heartwood was on the inside providing the force of compression. The pressure exerted when the linen string was drawn was up to 300 pounds. The archers in the English army developed abnormally large chest and arm muscles on their right side (the drawing arm). Our Robin would have been no Kevin Costner. He probably looked a bit lop-sided: broad and especially bulgy on the right.

Warwick Castle is open almost every day of the year and the good folk who run it make it very easy to find. There are signs off the M40 at junction 15. You simply head for Warwick town centre on the A445, or follow the tourist signs for the castle. As you come into Warwick the car parks for the castle are on the right.

To see an archer in action today with a traditional English longbow, go to Warwick Castle where there's a daily show featuring a bowman who splits a centimetre-wide stick at 30 metres.

THE LANCASTRIAN REVOLT

So which King Edward is most likely to have been our 'comely king'? Only one seems to have made a tour of the north country as described in the ballads. In 1323 Edward II made just such a trip in response to a political crisis that had been threatening his realm.

We have a pinpoint historical setting for the Robin Hood stories at Barnsdale. Edward's crisis is called the Lancastrian Revolt, and it started in Pontefract, now just fifteen minutes by car from Barnsdale.

The ruins of Pontefract Castle give some idea of the scale of the original building. Buy a postcard of Alexander Keirinx's picture of the medieval castle, painted in 1625–30 before it was destroyed, and the ruins will spring to life. (You can also see the original painting in Wakefield Museum.) Pick out the bits of castle wall now remaining and locate them in relation to the nearby churches that also appear in the painting. Now pace out the breadth of the fortress and imagine its height. In 1322 it belonged to Thomas Earl of Lancaster, the King's cousin and one of the most powerful lords in the land.

But why did the Earl of Lancaster own a massive castle in West Yorkshire? More than that, how come Pontefract was his headquarters? The answer is that Thomas was vastly powerful, with lands throughout the whole of the north of England. If you believe the Lancastrians' side of the story, the King imposed swingeing taxes on his peasants after a series of disastrous harvests. Thomas, a social-minded soul, protested and a rebellion ensued. Yorkshire folk though will tell you Thomas was simply making a disguised bid for the throne.

The aristocracy didn't like Edward II at all. In the early fourteenth century the ruling elite was deeply conservative. These aristocrats believed the ranks of society were ordained by God, with the king sitting at the top of the pyramid. Edward didn't measure up for a host of reasons. He wasn't a patch on his father as a war leader. By losing the Battle of Bannockburn to Robert the Bruce (1314), he managed to undo all the gains that Edward I had made in Scotland. This lack of military grit was compounded by the fact that he was

Pontefract Castle 1625–30 by Alexander Keirinx. In later years, the dungeons were actually used to store Pontefract cakes.

Pontefract Castle in Yorkshire was one of the most impressive military strongholds in medieval England. Leave the A1 at the Knottingley junction, just north of junction 33 of the M62, follow the A628 towards the centre of Pontefract, and you'll come across signs for it.

gay and had what, for the time, was a scandalously open relationship with Piers Gaveston. The nobility might have turned a blind eye to this but he inflamed the situation by acting in a weird and inappropriate fashion. A proper king kept his dignity, didn't raise a finger to do anything a servant could do, was aloof and imperious. But Edward loved the idea of manual labour. He relished tasks that were the preserve of the lowest orders in society, flouting the divinely ordained natural order by acting like a navvy digging ditches.

And at the very heart of the discontent, as with so many other political problems, was the economy. Through no fault of his own there was a succession of failed harvests throughout the teens of the fourteenth century. This led to mass starvation, loss of revenue, and, when taxes were still kept at the same level, deep social discontent. It would have been a situation that even a popular leader would have found hard to weather. But Edward was far from popular. So some of the nobles used the poverty of the people as a pious excuse to get rid of him.

So Thomas Earl of Lancaster made an alliance with Robert the Bruce, who'd thrashed Edward II at Bannockburn. He rallied his forces at Pontefract, and in March headed north to rendezvous with the Scots. But if Edward wasn't quite his father, he was still no slouch. He intercepted the Lancastrian rebels at Boroughbridge. With the same reliance on the longbowmen who'd decimated Wallace's forces, he made mincemeat of Thomas's troops.

After the rout Thomas was taken back to Pontefract Castle, tried before the King then led outside the walls to be beheaded. His followers were outlawed and fled. Many of them sought refuge in the wild forests to the south around Barnsdale, where they continued to act as Wallace-style guerrillas.

But a year later, Edward faced mounting discontent from other members of the nobility elsewhere in the country. He needed the support of the north. In an attempt to heal the wounds of the previous year he made a northern tour which ended in Nottingham, during which he granted an amnesty to the Lancastrian rebels.

The parallels with the Robin story in the *Gest* are plain enough. So were Robin Hood and his men Lancastrian rebels leading a campaign against officialdom from the forests of Barnsdale in 1322? It's at least plausible. It would certainly have given political credibility to a hero who would otherwise have been nothing more than a common criminal.

But do we know of any historical individual who matches this description?

Before we start looking at potential candidates, it's worth revisiting the question of what people called themselves in the medieval period. Robin wasn't a separate name at that time. Robin, Rob and Robert were virtually interchangeable. Our Robin Hood is just as likely to be a Robert.

And lo and behold, in the court rolls for the Manor of Wakefield in the reign of Edward II we find a tenant called Robert Hood living with his wife Matilda. He bought a piece of land at Bichill in Wakefield in 1316, but the records show that he has lost it again

by 1357, indicating that by that date he was an outlaw. In 1317 the rolls note that he was fined 3 shillings for failing to turn up for military service against the Scots. He obviously didn't want to forgo his forester's livelihood for a distant campaign. But when he was summoned to fight for Thomas Earl of Lancaster in 1322, there's no similar record of a fine to show he refused to fight again, so it looks like he went off to take part in the rebellion.

Unfortunately, as this information comes from court rolls and property records, there's no background character or detail, so we don't know what happened to Robert Hood of Wakefield after the rebellion. Or maybe we do.

In the *Gest* there's a coda to the tale.

In what should be a happy-ever-after ending, Edward the comely king not only forgives Robin, he also takes the reformed outlaw into his private court retinue as a valet, a personal bodyguard. But life at court is stifling for Robin the outdoor boy. After just over a year, he's sick at heart.

'Alas!' then sayd good Robyn,	'Alas!' then said good Robin,
'Alas and well a woo!	'Alas and well away!
Yf I dwele lenger with the kynge,	If I dwell longer with the king,
Sorowe wyll me sloo.'	Sorrow will me slay.'

He begs the King to let him go back to the greenwood, and returns home.

And there's a Robin Hood in the medieval court rolls who does something similar. *The Records of the Exchequer* register Robyn Hode as one of twenty-nine men earning 3d a day as a 'valetz de la chamber', in the service of King Edward from June 1323. Not only that, but in November the following year this Robyn is paid off with a gift of five shillings because 'he can no longer work'. Could this Robyn and Robert Hood of Wakefield be one and the same person? If they are, their story fits very neatly with the one told in the *Gest*.

It's tempting to believe that Robert was a rebel yeoman who gave rise to the Robin Hood stories in the *Gest of Robin Hood*, was then forgiven and given a place as a royal bodyguard before returning to his former life. We know that Robert was a forester and he might well have felt constricted by life in the royal court.

Robert lived in Bichill (pronounced Bick Hill) in Wakefield. If you want to get there today, take a bus from Pontefract to the shiny new Wakefield bus terminus. You're now in Bichill, where the real Robin Hood may have lived with his wife before rebelling in 1322. Wandering through the bus station is what this book is all about. There's all the hustle and bustle of people travelling to and from Heckmondwike, Ravensthorpe and Dewsbury, and the sense of tangible history lying underneath your feet while vibrant everyday life continues all around you.

Lee in Wyredale, home
of Sir Richard by the
Lee, is a beautiful
hamlet. The area just
north of Pendle Hill and
Clitheroe, known as the
Forest of Bowland, is
worth a trip in its own
right. You can reach the
forest from the north by
leaving the M6 at
junction 32 or from the
south off the A59
via Clitheroe and
Waddington. The local
roads are complicated.
I'd advise getting a
good large-scale
map of the area.

As an outlaw, Robert's property would have been confiscated by the state. But that didn't necessarily mean that he would have permanently lived rough from the time he fled the Battle of Boroughbridge. Living in the forests was only really possible in the spring and summer months. During the winter (which would have been much more severe than it is now), an outlaw would have hunkered down at home or with relatives, secure in the knowledge that the weather would also prevent the officers of the law from organizing any effective search.

But the Lancastrian rebellion also helps explain the relationship between the outlaws and Sir Richard by the Lee, one of the main sub-plots in the *Gest*. The knight is described as coming from Wyresdale, meaning Wyredale in the Forest of Bowland.

Lee is in northern Lancashire. There seems to be no natural connection between a knight hailing from Lee and the rebels of South Yorkshire. But there is if the tale is set in the time of Thomas Earl of Lancaster. His estate formed an unbroken line from Lancashire through Ilkley into Yorkshire and the Pontefract area. During the Lancastrian Revolt there would have been insurrection throughout all his lands. It would have been essential for there to be communication between allies from either side of the Pennines. The argument that the Robin stories were originally set during the Lancastrian Revolt becomes more and more plausible.

THE MERRY MEN

Sitting in Wakefield bus station, we can congratulate ourselves on having nailed an individual on whom the Robin Hood stories could have been based. But Robin, especially in the *Gest*, never acts alone. He can't be separated from his fellow outlaws, the trinity of co-conspirators: Little John, Much the Miller's son and Will Scarlet. Are there any historical figures from the same period that match them?

The obvious person to start with is Little John. He's a brilliant universal character, the superstrong henchman, loyal to the end, the big brother who will always be there to get us out of scrapes. His relationship with Robin has been echoed in every 'buddy movie' ever made. But in the early ballads John isn't just a foil for Robin. He's very much his own man and plays a leading role in the story. He is also amusingly willing to take liberties with Robin. When the outlaws discover that Sir Richard by the Lee is poverty-stricken, it's Little John who tells Robin that he shouldn't just give him cash, but fit him out with new clothes and a fresh mount. He even measures out some of Robin's rich material for him.

*Opposite: The bus
station at Bichill,
Wakefield, once home
to R. Hood Esq.*

And at every handfull that he met	And for every handful that he took
He leped footes three.	He jumped three feet.
'What devylles drapar,'	'What sort of devilish draper,'
sayid litell Muche,	said little Much,
'Thynkest thou for to be?'	'Do you think you are?'

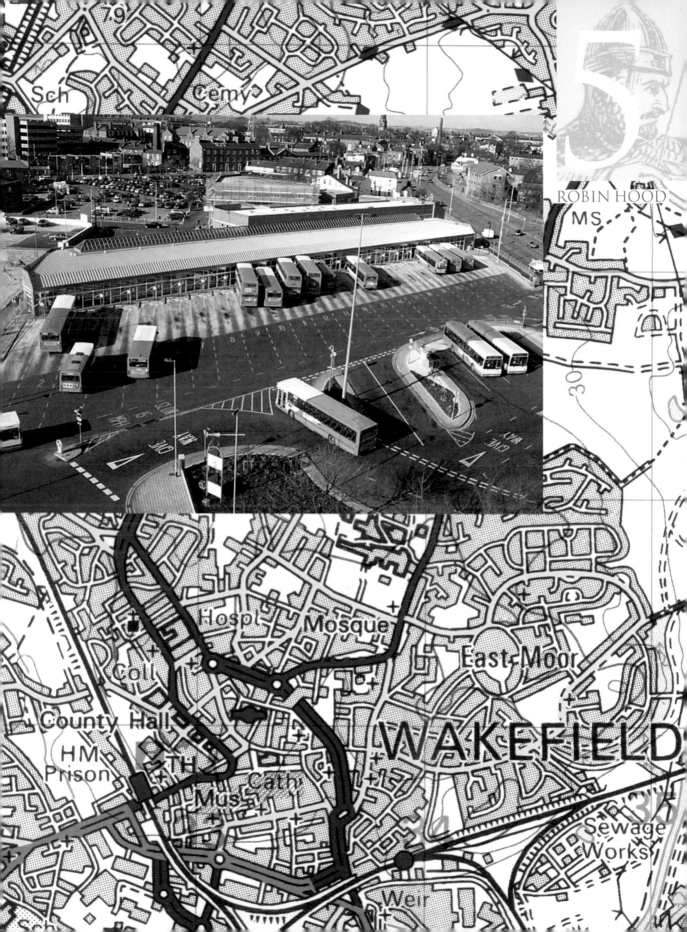

5

ROBIN HOOD
MS

WAKEFIELD

Scarlok stode full stil and loughe,	Scarlet stood stock still and laughed
And sayd, 'By God Almyght,	And said 'By God Almighty,
Johnn may gyve hym gode mesure,	John's happy to be generous
For it costeth hym but lyght.'	For it's costing him but lightly.'

So was there a real Little John?

Hathersage Church in Derbyshire is the place where he's traditionally buried. A grave was opened up in the eighteenth century, and an abnormally large thigh bone and a bow were found, which proved definitively that a big man with a bow had been buried there, although not necessarily that his name was Little John.

Unfortunately, according to the *Gest*, Little John didn't come from Hathersage. He hailed from Holderness, the area round Beverley near Hull. And Little John was just his nickname or alias. His real name was Reynald Greenleaf.

The leading contender for the real Little John is another criminal. In 1318 the house of a man called Simon of Wakefield was broken into and £138 stolen. The names of those charged with the crime include a 'John le Litel'. Five years later a Little John crops up again, this time in a case of poaching from the Archbishop of York's estate in Beverley. Again there's nothing to tie these two together except the name, but it's more than possible that they are one and the same person; a criminal called Little John operating in the Yorkshire area who then got involved with the rebel Robert of Wakefield.

Much the Miller proves less fruitful, and Alan a' Dale only starts appearing in the stories from the seventeenth century onwards. But there is a possible Will Scarlet from the Yorkshire area. In recent versions of the Robin stories, Will's been gaudily decked out in red to explain his name, but there was nothing sartorial about the original. In the ballads he's called Scathlock or Scarlock, which means 'lock-smasher'. Scarlet could have been the band's breaking and entering merchant.

But Scathlock was also a real surname. And we have a suspect by the name of William Scathlock from the very priory of St Mary's that appears in the *Gest*. He was a renegade monk who was thrown out of the abbey in 1287. This would have made him older than the other Merry Men – indeed, he would have been in his fifties or sixties by the time of Boroughbridge. But he's a possible contender none the less.

It's worth noting that all our Merry Men so far are, like Robin, yeomen. In other words, rather than a nobleman leading a bunch of yokels, this is a relationship of equals. Robin is curiously democratic. He rules by consent, and is touchingly fallible, as his frequent unsuccessful challenges to combat prove.

Sad to say, there was no Friar Tuck in the original ballads. In one of the early stories, 'Robin Hood and the Curtal Friar', Robin does pick a fight with a friar, but his name isn't

Tuck. As usual Robin loses, ending up on the floor in a wrestling bout. He then invites the doughty friar to join the outlaw band. It seems this story was the starting point for the later introduction of Friar Tuck.

Friar Tuck was certainly a known outlaw name soon after the completion of the ballads. There's a record of a friar of that name committing crimes in Sussex in the early fifteenth century. He was part of a gang who fleeced merchants, and turned out to be the chaplain of Lindfield near Haywards Heath. His real name was Robert Stafford. Presumably he used the alias Friar Tuck to protect his identity. Either the name was already well known because it was associated with Robin, or else it was a common criminal alias that was later incorporated into the Robin stories.

Now we come to the worst news of all. In the early ballads there's no mention of Maid Marian. In fact there's no love interest at all in the *Gest*. It's a tale about men being men: rough, tough and not at all soppy. Marian comes into the stories later. When Robin becomes a nobleman in Anthony Munday's play, he needs a lady. That's when Marian appears and she's stayed with her man ever since.

But even here there are strange parallels. Robert of Wakefield had a wife called Matilda. We don't know exactly what happened to her, but it seems likely that she too was outlawed and may have gone off to join her husband in the forest. In Anthony Munday's play Robin's wife is called Matilda. But when they become forest outlaws she changes her name to Marian. We don't know that Robert of Wakefield's wife assumed an alias when she fled Bichill but, given the number of outlaws who altered their names, it's at least possible.

There is, though, another explanation for the appearance of Maid Marian. Each Whitsun in the Middle Ages, the Christian feast and the coming of summer were celebrated. Mummers' plays and dances were integral to these revels and they included a stock cast of characters. One of these was Robin Hood. Another was a maid called Marian, usually played by a man. These two originally quite separate characters could well have become coupled in people's minds through their appearance in these simple knockabout plays. Their relationship would then gradually have became part and parcel of the Robin Hood stories. During the often rowdy festivities Robin and Marian were also responsible for collecting money for the poor, sometimes using strongarm tactics. From this tradition may well have sprung the notion that Robin robbed from the rich to give to the poor.

THE DEATH OF ROBIN HOOD

Marian may not appear in the *Gest* but there is one female character, and she is to be Robin's nemesis.

The story of Robin's last days is told in quite a sketchy fashion. He falls ill and is killed by a scheming prioress and her lover.

Than bespake good Robyn,	Then said good Robin,
In place where as he stode,	In the place where he stood,
'To morow I muste to Kyrkely,	'Tomorrow I must go to Kirklees,
Craftely to be leten blode.'	For a skilled bloodletting.'
Syr Roger of Donkestere,	Sir Roger of Doncaster
By the pryoresse he lay,	By the prioress he lay,
And there they betrayed good Robyn Hode,	And there they betrayed good Robin Hood,
Through theyr false playe.	Through their false play.
Cryst have mercy on his soule,	Christ who died upon the Cross
That dyded on the Rode!	Have mercy on his soul.
For he was a good outlawe,	He was a good outlaw
And dyde pore men moch god.	And did poor men much good.

Clearly the writer of the *Gest* assumes his readers are all ready familiar with this part of the story, but another early ballad, 'Robin Hoode, His Death', goes into it in more detail. The Prioress of Kirklees is kin to Robin. She has taken a lover and for some reason they plot Robin's murder. He goes to the priory for a therapeutic bloodletting, but the prioress draws enough blood to kill him, then leaves him to his fate. Little John arrives but is too late to save his old comrade. In later traditions, Robin takes his bow and fires one last arrow, after asking John to bury him where it lands.

The Three Nuns is an industrial-scale inn (pub grub, pub garden, children's play area, pool tables and so on) built on the site of a former hostel for visitors to the convent. It's named after the pre-Reformation shenanigans of three nuns who were frequent visitors to the hostel and were allegedly much keener on the vows of poverty and obedience than on the one that required chastity.

The *Gest* tells us that Robin died twenty-two years after returning to the forest (which, given the logic of the 1322 revolt, would be about 1346). His death provides one last fascinating parallel between our prime suspect, Robert Hood of Wakefield, and the world of the early ballads. Research has established with a fair degree of certainty that the prioress at Kirklees in the mid-fourteenth century was called Elizabeth de Staynton. And, extraordinarily, it seems she was related by marriage to Robert Hood. Elizabeth de Staynton was Matilda's stepsister!

There is, of course, no official record of Robert dying at Kirklees or being buried there. But Kirklees is only a short distance from Wakefield. As the evidence mounts, the whole story begins to have a compelling plausibility.

You can't just go tramping around the Kirklees Estate without permission. The owner,

Robin is reputed to have died at Kirklees Priory, which is owned by the Armytage Estate, and can be found between Mirfield and the M62 motorway in West Yorkshire. The entrance to the estate is an unmarked private road just down from the Three Nuns pub on the A644 Huddersfield– Leeds road.

Lady Armytage, does allow people in to visit Robin Hood's grave, but you have to write in advance and arrange a mutually convenient visit. And when you get there don't expect anything like St Mary's Abbey. The priory itself has virtually disappeared, abandoned during Henry VIII's dissolution of the monasteries. The building materials were presumably cannibalized for other structures in the area. But overlooking the lumps in the ground and the odd stone that are all that remain of the priory, is the derelict building where Robin is said to have been trapped by the prioress.

An exterior flight of stone steps leads you to a series of first-floor rooms. The one furthest from the main door is where our hero is supposed to have died. If you look out of the west facing window you can just see a line of trees on the ridge of a hill opposite. It's on this ridge that you can find Robin Hood's grave, a walled rectangle, topped with wrought-iron railings and deeply shadowed by yew trees. Unfortunately it's about 600

The site of Kirklees Priory seen from the building where Robin Hood is said to have breathed his last.

metres away, just over twice the maximum range for a longbowman in the peak of health. It seems to give the lie to the poetic fiction about Robin shooting an arrow and being buried where it landed. If he was on his last legs you'd expect his grave to be just outside the window!

But the grave exerts an extraordinary symbolic and emotional pull. If you've been looking for the historical version of a great hero and someone says, 'Here's his grave,' it's hard to ignore, even if your head tells you that you're being sold a wrong 'un.

Like the Vanbrugh cover for Robin Hood's Well, the grave has in fact been shifted more than once. Excavations carried out beneath this particular site have unsurprisingly discovered nothing but mud. There is an inscription in cod 'olde English' on one of the walls. But it's a nineteenth-century effort to try to establish the grave's credentials.

The original gravestone was first mentioned at Kirklees in an encyclopaedia of 1607. It was sketched in 1665 by a man called Nathaniel Johnston (see the sketch on page 214). Confusingly, alongside the name of Robin Hood is carved another, a William Goldburgh, whose identity is lost in the mists of history. Later this stone disappeared. A copy was made, but in the nineteenth century a belief sprang up that

chewing a piece of Robin's gravestone could cure toothache. In no time the replacement stone was chipped away by superstitious canal workers building the nearby Huddersfield and Calder Navigation Canal.

In many ways the story of the grave is symbolic of the quest for Robin himself. Looking for the truth is like being the Sheriff of Nottingham. Just when you think you've got Robin in your clutches, he slips through your fingers.

And that's true too of our Robert Hood of Wakefield. Just when we thought we'd nailed down the historical Robin to the period of the Lancastrian Revolt, new evidence emerges that challenges this assumption.

I said at the beginning that this quest wouldn't be an easy one!

ANOTHER ROBIN

There was a man from the little village of Fletching in Sussex, 200 miles from the forests of Barnsdale. His name was Gilbert Robinhood and he lived in 1296.

In the Middle Ages, you usually took your father's name, so a son of a Robin Hood might be called Robert or Robinson or Robertson or Hoodson or Hudson or even simply Hood. But the conjunction of two names in one surname is extremely rare. It seems to imply that the two names Robin and Hood already had a significance. This theory is backed up by more and earlier instances of this phenomenon which are coming to light. Robbehods or Robinhoods crop up in different parts of the country, and a surprising percentage of them have a criminal record. But the clincher is the case of William Le Fevre.

Le Fevre is an old French surname meaning 'Smith'. William was summoned to the court assizes in Reading in 1261 for taking part in a robbery. He failed to show up and was branded an outlaw. The monk acting as clerk of the court wrote the miscreant's name simply as William le Fevre. But the next year, 1262, we have a further reference to the very same case written by another anonymous scribe. In this record William's name is written as 'William Robbehod, Fugitivus' (Latin for outlaw). In other words, Robin Hood was a synonym for an outlaw at least fifty years before Robert Hood of Wakefield is first mentioned in any record!

So where does that leave us? Is all the Wakefield evidence useless after all? Not at all. Your time hasn't been wasted. Robert Hood of Wakefield is the likeliest contender for the Robin Hood figure described in the ballads, but clearly he isn't the earliest Robin Hood. Our tactic of seeking out the earliest published versions of the stories didn't allow for oral traditions that existed before the ballads were written. It now seems that the ballads were based on a real local hero, Robert Hood of Wakefield, who then had bolted on to him a tradition that was already in full flow. So, we mustn't discount the man from the bus station, but we also have to look for another, earlier candidate.

Opposite: The ruin of what is thought to be the guest house at Kirklees Priory. Robin is said to have died in a room on the first floor. From this angle, the window on the far right-hand side is where he would have fired his last arrow. Possibly.

You can still see the property owned by the outlaw Fulk Fitz Warine: Whittington Castle. It's one of those obscure out-of-the-way delights that you still run across in the British countryside. The picturesque ruins fronted by a half moat/ half village pond lie in the centre of Whittington in Shropshire near the crossroads of the A495 and the B5009. To get there, take the A5 from Shrewsbury (remember you'll be travelling the Roman highway taken by Suetonius as he hurried south to attack Boudica) and take the turning on to the B5009 to Whittington. From the north, travel south from Chester and turn on to the B5009 at Chirk.

And yet this is a curiously modern exercise. When the stories were composed, no one cared very much where the material came from. There was much less distinction in the Middle Ages between what we would call legends and factual history. So long as a tale had resonance and made a moral point it was accepted as true. Indeed, the same word was used for 'story' and 'history'. The point of retelling the past wasn't to discover an objective truth, but to give instruction for the present.

The story of Robin, even if there is a real person buried in there somewhere, borrows heavily from a host of other sources. There are parallels in the earliest Robin Hood stories with Hereward the Wake. Hereward fought a rearguard action against the Norman invaders in the Lincolnshire Fens and became a folk hero. He was a real person, but he's remembered in legends that couldn't possibly have happened in real life, many of which bear remarkable similarities to the stories of disguise, robbery and adventure in Sherwood.

In addition we've already seen that some people have claimed that William Wallace was the model for Robin Hood. He was a bowman, had his own Maid Marian and lived the same sort of outlaw life in the forests. There are a host of other similar heroes too, factual ones like Eustace the Monk, who ran a successful piracy operation from the Channel Islands until he was defeated by Henry III, and fictional ones like Adam Bell, Clim of the Clough and William of Cloudesdale (all Lancashire versions of the Yorkshire Robin) whose tales circulated up to the seventeenth century.

But the closest, and if we're looking to track down an earlier flesh and blood Robin, the most worrying, parallels are with the history of Fulk Fitz Warine.

Now long forgotten, Fitz Warine was once as well known a figure as Ronnie Biggs or the Kray twins. He was the outlaw of his time par excellence during the reign of King John, the brother and successor of Richard the Lionheart. Stories sprang up about him when he went on the run after a dispute over an inheritance.

In 1197 Fulk Fitz Warine's father died and Fulk expected to inherit Whittington Castle. But there was another claim to the barony from someone who had better contacts with King John. It could be that Fitz Warine killed this rival claimant, but all we know is that he lost his claim and in 1200 was outlawed. For three years he fought a campaign in the Welsh marches against the King before being pardoned in 1203. He fell out of favour again but, after John was forced to sign Magna Carta in 1215, he came back into the fold, living peacefully in Whittington Castle until his death in 1256.

The earliest surviving version of his story is from 1325–40, but it's believed that it was originally composed in the late thirteenth century, well before the Robin Hood ballads. It tells us that, like Robin, Fulk had a right-hand man called John (although in this case it was his brother) who entered the service of his master's enemy. Fulk's men took shelter from a local knight, Sir Lewis of Shrewsbury, and they accosted people and forced their victims to dine with them. Fulk captured King John in the forest and finally the two were reconciled.

So why should so much of Fulk's story end up in the tales of Robin Hood?

There are several possible explanations. The first is that there was no historical Robin Hood after all, and the Robert of Wakefield connection is a false one. The stories are fiction, a mishmash of legends from different sources, including Fulk. But why then does our fictional hero end up being called Robin Hood and not Fulk Fitz Warine? Why have the Robin stories survived in his name, while the story of Fulk has disappeared?

The second explanation is that there was a real person like Robin Hood of Wakefield who was made legendary by having a lot of other stories attached to him, including the ones about Fulk.

But there's another possibility. It could be that both sets of stories spring from another hidden character, an even earlier character called Robin whom we haven't found yet. And, lo and behold, there is another candidate from the reign of Richard the Lionheart. We seem to be turning full circle – getting further away from the Robin of the ballads and closer again to the story we were all brought up on.

BACK TO ROBIN OF LOXLEY

When Anthony Munday wrote his two blockbusting plays he was obviously tapping into some sort of pre-existing tradition. We know such sources existed because some of our Scottish historian friends, Andrew of Wyntoun, Walter Bower in his *Scotichronicon* and John Major, write about Robin Hood and Little John as historical figures. They don't give much detail and their tone is unflattering. They call Robin a murderer. Wyntoun and Bower set Robin in the thirteenth century, but John Major puts him in 1193–4 during the regency of Prince John, when Richard the Lionheart was away at the Crusades and subsequently imprisoned in Germany.

One of the names attached to Robin is Robin of Loxley. Because the early Robin ballads were set in the north of England, it's been assumed that this meant Loxley (or Locksley) in Yorkshire. But there's another Loxley – in Warwickshire, near Stratford-upon-Avon. It's a don't-blink-or-you'll-miss-it type of village, which perhaps explains why it hasn't been as prominent in the tradition as it might have been.

As you come down a hill there's a turning to the centre of the village on your left. By this time you've already missed the little church you're looking for! But the road is fast, winding and dangerous, so it's best to go into the village and then find your way back to the church and manor house on foot. As you do so, ponder on its connection with King Harold. You're treading ground that was once owned by ancestors of Bishop Odo of Bayeux, the half-brother of William the Conqueror who originally commissioned the Bayeux Tapestry for the city's cathedral.

It's most likely that you'll come to Loxley from the M40, in which case you take the A429 south from junction 15. As you skirt Wellesbourne turn right for Loxley at the third roundabout. The village is just a couple of miles down the road. If you're coming to it after a day out at Stratford, the easiest way is to take the B4086 to Wellesbourne, turn right and then right again at the next roundabout which brings you to the village.

Bishop Odo was an ecclesiastical aristocrat of his age, more interested in power, glory and status than the furthering of the Christian message. His conquests extended beyond his part in the invasion of England. He fathered several illegitimate children.

The indication of illegitimate descent in those days was to add a 'Fitz' to your family name. So Odo's English descendants were known as the Fitz Odo family. It was they who came to own the manor of Loxley. Until 1196 in the reign of Richard the Lionheart, the lord of the manor was Robert Fitz Odo (his surname rhymes with Skoda).

How does this candidate fit with the story? Well, by 1196 Robert was no longer a knight, but he wasn't dead. There's a record of a Robert Fitz Odo alive in nearby Harbury seven years later in 1203, although he seems to have been stripped of his title.

In a reversal of the usual tale in which Richard the Lionheart restores an outlaw's lands, it appears that this Robert or Robin was disinherited and declared an outlaw by Richard, and then restored by 'evil' King John when he came to the throne in 1199. The motive for King Richard's act of disinheritance seems to have been treason.

Richard the Lionheart had immense lands in France. We know that descendants of the Norman bishop, Odo, fought on the side of the French King, Philip Augustus, when he invaded Richard's territory of Normandy in 1193. If Robert Odo had sided with his relatives it would explain why Richard later turfed him out. King John, on the other hand, was

Right and opposite: The Loxley connection. Bearing in mind that the bottom bit of the gravestone is missing, do you think the design matches the 1665 sketch? I was genuinely in two minds.

on the French King's side. When John came to the throne, he would have restored the allies of his French lord to their former station.

Could this Robert Odo be the man that John Major is referring to in the 1400s as the original Robin Hood?

If you think it impossible that our great English hero would have sided with the French against Richard the Lionheart, carry on to the churchyard. Because here there's evidence that this theory of Fitz Odo as the prototype Robin Hood needs to be taken seriously.

Loxley Church is perched on a hillside overlooking a beautiful swathe of countryside towards Stratford to the west. It's important that you orientate yourself here because you have to find a particular gravestone in the graveyard. The main path into the churchyard comes from the south-west side of the church. You need to make your way round to the north side towards the church's west end. There, running parallel with the church, is a gravestone that bears an uncanny resemblance to the sketch of Robin Hood's grave by Nathaniel Johnston.

The inscription on the grave isn't dedicated to Robin Hood, though. It's to Constance, who belonged to the Cove Jones family, one-time inhabitants of Loxley Hall. But the stone itself is clearly much older than the inscription. The design and dimensions are similar to the seventeenth-century sketch (compare for yourself on pages 214 and 215).

We know that the original Kirklees gravestone disappeared, and that its replacement was broken up by superstitious canal workers. Why should it end up here? There are several possibilities.

Maybe it's just a coincidence. There are only a limited number of designs on gravestones. Finding two that look alike in different churchyards doesn't, at first glance, seem particularly significant. But the design on the original Robin Hood grave is quite distinctive.

Or perhaps this gravestone is a copy of the Nathaniel Johnston drawing – a tribute to Robin Hood by someone who wanted to tie their own Warwickshire Loxley into the legend.

Or just maybe this is the original stone itself, transported from Kirklees by people who believed that the true resting place of the original Robin Hood was here in the South Midlands.

It's a fascinating mystery, but the main objection to the last hypothesis seems to be one of common sense. Given the superstitious reaction of ordinary folk to the Kirklees grave site, the comparative neglect of Loxley is strange. If it was important enough to people from this area to transport a gravestone 120 miles south to Loxley, why would the shrine then be forgotten and defaced by removing the key name and replacing it with Constance (however dearly beloved Constance may have been)?

The gravestone is yet one more slippery detail about Robin. But the confusion over these pieces of stone doesn't remove the possibility that Robert Fitz Odo played his part in providing a catalyst for the start of the legend about a dissident outlaw called Robin Hood.

Indeed, Robert Fitz Odo is more than just another historical candidate. He's the most likely contender for the early tradition of Robin as a nobleman, which was then taken up by Anthony Munday and later universally accepted

Our patchwork of sources is at last coming together.

THE SPIRIT OF ROBIN

But what gave Robin the legendary status to outlast all his other contemporaries?

To answer this we must return to Sherwood Forest. Not to any of the traditional Robin sites in Edwinstowe or Blidworth or Papplewick, but to one of the hidden gems of the area: Southwell Minster. It's one of England's best-preserved but least-known cathedrals, a superb example of medieval architecture.

Southwell Minster.

Southwell Minster is well worth a visit. The easiest way to get there is on the A612 out of Nottingham, but it's more than likely you'll want to get to it from one of the towns in Sherwood. If so, take the A614 south as it runs through what was once the forest, turn east on to the A617 and then at Kirklington take a right turn and follow signs for Southwell. Once you're in the town, the minster's so big it's virtually impossible to miss.

There's much to see inside the church. Get a guidebook and explore at will, but for our purposes you need to make your way up the north aisle and follow directions to the Chapter House. The stonemasons here left a magnificent flourish behind them as a showcase of their work, in the octagonal chapter house where the cathedral authorities once sat in council.

It's phenomenally hard to carve lifelike leaves in a medium as solid and heavy as stone. The accepted medieval convention was to use a stylized shorthand: a stubby three-pointed representative symbol. But here the masons have covered every available corbel, niche and crevice with a forest of delicately wrought realism. There are oak shoots complete with acorns, beech and sycamore; ivy stems writhe and intertwine. And wound into this intricate design are strange faces peering through the foliage, some with roots and stems sprouting from their gaping mouths. These are known as foliate heads. They are, in this bastion of Christianity, representations of the ancient pagan nature spirit, the so-called Green Man.

Another name for this ancient puckish figure was Robin Goodfellow, otherwise known as 'Robin of the Wood' or 'Robin in the Hood'. And this Robin too has played his part in forming our image of Robin Hood. He's got nothing to do with outlawry, but he helps to account for the magic of the Robin stories, the peculiar timeless never-never land that the forest setting provides. There's an essential clash between the urban culture of the Sheriff based in Nottingham and the freebooting forest-dwellers. Robin's always framed by the forest. He makes forays into the town, he goes into the King's service, but he is drawn back to the greenwood. In the *Gest* he leaves his job as the King's bodyguard as though the life is being sucked out of him while he's away from his leafy home.

The spirit of this mischievous Robin was perpetuated in the Whitsun revels, with Robin creating chaos as he went around collecting money for the poor. It's this additional element that gave the Robin stories a universality lacking in the history-based legends of Fulk Fitz Warine and Robert Fitz Odo.

Certainly a Robin Hood with his origins in a pagan spirit of the greenwood appeals to our modern environmentally conscious age in a way that a bloodthirsty crook with a pious belief in the Virgin Mary doesn't. If these stone faces poking out from the frozen greenery of the chapter house are at last images of the original Robin, they're appropriately paradoxical: real representations of a made-up figure, solid yet insubstantial, mythic but cheekily human. After visiting all the sites and weighing up the evidence, it's these pagan mischief-makers hiding out under the very noses of the Christian authorities at Southwell who may well be the closest we can get to a Robin from the Middle Ages, and it's their spirit which, despite countless changes, is still central to the Robin legend today.

Part of Robin's appeal is that he's infinitely malleable. I wrote four series of *Maid Marian and Her Merry Men*, full of characters who took on a life of their own. Since it was transmitted there has been a spate of feminist treatments of the Robin stories, notably in

ROBIN HOOD

*The Green Man –
our real Robin?*

219

Kate Lonergan as Marian, Adam Morris as Robin and me as The Sheriff of Nottingham in the BBC children's series Maid Marian and Her Merry Men.

Opposite: Whatever academics may say, Robin has become the great mascot of Nottingham. This chunky statue stands in the shadow of Nottingham Castle.

the film *Princess of Thieves*. If we believe the experts, we can expect intergalactic and gay Robins to appear soon. And if there are, no doubt there will be concerned articles in the tabloids about the hijacking of a national institution. But our hero will survive without the help of journalists. One thing's certain. Robin will become the hero that the next generation needs and wants to hear about.

I've tried to treat Robin like the other characters in this book, to separate and distinguish between the fact and the fiction of his story. But in truth this isn't possible because Robin is both fact *and* fiction. His durability and continuing appeal relies on his universality and the fact that he isn't earthbound by one brief historical lifetime.

The *Gest* is clearly influenced by the events surrounding the Lancastrian Revolt, and we can be pretty confident that the flesh and blood Robert Hood of Wakefield was a major source for the Robin stories. We've also discovered other renegades and rebels whose names and stories became wound into the tradition, along with characters like William le Fevre who became 'Robin Hoods' by virtue (if that's the right word) of their criminality. For those who like their Robin aristocratic we have a candidate in Robert Odo, who provides a historical basis for Anthony Munday's character Robin, Earl of Huntingdon.

But these historical figures all needed the weight and grandeur of legend to make them great. They stole the clothes of Fulk Fitz Warine and others and borrowed the legendary gleam of Robin Goodfellow, the wraith of the forests. And because the resulting Robin was a mix of both the legendary and the historical, he was peculiarly satisfying and convincing to his audience: brave and kind, fair and tough, and just human enough to convince us that, in a better world, we, too, could be Robin Hood.

FURTHER INFORMATION

There's a welter of information about Robin, but very few general texts still in print. A brief search on the Internet, if you have access to it, reveals masses of fascinating bits and pieces. You can find everything from the complete text of the *Gest of Robin Hood* to a site claiming links between Robin's traditional grave and a weird sect of vampires. I'm just going to give you the address for the *Gest* (it's a fairly hefty document), and leave you to search and surf your way around for the rest: http://www.lib.rochester.edu/camelot/teams/gest.htm

J. C. Holt, *Robin Hood* (Thames and Hudson, 1989) is the most widely available book on the quest for the historical Robin.

Graham Phillips and Martin Keatman, *Robin Hood: The man behind the myth* (Michael O'Mara Books, 1995) is no longer in the shops, but is a good read from the library if you want to nail down a historical Robin.

Stephen Knight, *Robin Hood: A Complete Study of the English Outlaw* (Blackwell, 1994) takes a very different point of view. Knight doesn't think there ever was a flesh and blood Robin. But this is probably the best scholarly work on the subject, though hard to get hold of.

If you're from Nottingham you may feel I've sold the traditional Robin sites short. For a more comprehensive guide of all the places associated with Robin and his band, try these little books by a man who's so dedicated to the cause that he's lived rough in Sherwood for a week using only the tools of the Middle Ages:

Richard Rutherford-Moore, *On the Outlaw Trail in Nottingham and Sherwood Forest*, which is straight-down-the line for Nottingham and *Off on the Outlaw Trail Again* which deals with sites in Yorkshire and elsewhere. (Both by Capall Bann Publishing, 1998 and 2003.)

Ordnance Survey maps 120 and 129 give you all the 'traditional' Nottingham sites, but map 111 shows the Wentbridge area, map 105 does Pontefract and St Mary's York, map 102 covers the Forest of Bowland and map 151 takes you to the Warwickshire Loxley (and Warwick Castle).

ROBIN HOOD

PICTURE ACKNOWLEDGEMENTS

While every effort has been made to trace the copyright holders for illustrations featured in the book, the publishers will be glad to make proper acknowledgements in future editions in the event that any regrettable omissions have occurred at the time of going to press.

With thanks to the following for permission to reproduce their images:

Bayeux Tapestry Museum 114, 116, 119, 127, 131
BBC Picture Library 222
Bosham Church 133
The British Library 156
Colchester Museums 32
Collections/Angela Hampton 159
Corbis Images 169, 175
Dr John A Davies (Norfolk Museums and Archaeology Service) 25
Falkirk Museum 164
Fife Council Museums: Kirkcaldy Museum & Art Gallery 143
Friends of Southwell Cathedral 219
Glasgow City Council 140
Historic Scotland 62, 68, 72, 75, 91
Hulton Getty 144
Mary Evans Picture Library 5, 6, 9, 11, 13, 15, 17, 30, 53, 55, 95, 100, 137, 138 (Wallace),
    172, 181, 189
News International Syndication 50
Norfolk Museums and Archaeology Service 19
Perth & Kinross Council 89
Perthshire Tourist Board 78
Peter Froste 2003. All rights reserved DACS 34
Philips (copyright 2000) 54, 138 (map)
RCAHMS 152
Victoria and Albert Picture Library 80
Wakefield MDC Museums & Arts 201
Zoë Dominic 83

All other images reproduced courtesy of David Willcock
All Ordnance Survey maps © Crown copyright